BOMBER BOYS

ALSO BY MARIANNE VAN VELZEN

Call of the Outback

BOMBER BOYS

MARIANNE VAN VELZEN

ALLEN&UNWIN

SYDNEY·MELBOURNE·AUCKLAND·LONDON

First published in 2017

Allen & Unwin
83 Alexander Street
Crows Nest NSW 2065
Australia
Phone: (61 2) 8425 0100
Email: info@allenandunwin.com
Web: www.allenandunwin.com

Cataloguing-in-Publication details are available
from the National Library of Australia
www.trove.nla.gov.au

ISBN 978 1 76029 647 6

Map by Darian Causby
Set in 11.5/18 pt Sabon Pro by Bookhouse, Sydney
Printed and bound in Australia by Griffin Press

10 9 8 7 6 5 4 3 2 1

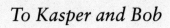

To Kasper and Bob

CONTENTS

AUTHOR'S NOTE

In April 2003, I went to Brisbane with a Dutch television producer to film the Anzac Day parade there. Our objectives were the Dutch pilots and crew members who had managed to flee the Dutch East Indies (or Netherlands East Indies, NEI) when Japan invaded the islands in World War II. They were part of the parade in Brisbane and marched under the flag of the No. 18 (NEI) RAAF Squadron.

It had all started some 60 years earlier, when the men fled the Dutch East Indies and headed for Australia. With the Indies in the hands of the enemy and the Netherlands overthrown by the Germans in Europe, the men who had escaped were now left stranded in Australia with no country to return to. These men, although keen to help battle the enemy, were too few in numbers to form a fully fledged squadron. The Dutch authorities, eager to have the men put to use, turned to Australia for help. Realising the awkward position of the Dutch exiles, the Australians agreed to supply ground personnel, mechanics and any crew members needed to form a squadron. The Dutch, in turn, would supply the pilots and pay for the aircraft and overhead costs. Just a few weeks later, on 4 April 1942, the two nations, working together, produced a peculiar mixed squadron: the No. 18 (NEI) RAAF.

On Anzac Day in 2003, I met with them, or rather what was left of them. Most men were already well into their eighties, some had toppled into their nineties, but many appeared remarkably fit and marched along as hardy as any twenty-year-old. After the parade, I was invited to join them in the Dutch Club in Brisbane. It was there that I realised what a strange and special friendship these men had. All around me Australians and Dutch sat shoulder to shoulder, animated friends reminiscing about their years together 'up north'. I soon found myself going into journalistic mode, jotting down the anecdotes they were sharing. They had such moving, gripping and strange stories to tell, so I interviewed some of them a few days later in their homes. After they shared their memories, I promised to write about it one day.

It took me thirteen years to finally write their story and get it published. The main problem with the storyline was the sequence of events and introducing a large number of individuals who would each tell their own story. I feared it would produce a book that was confusing and might become tedious. There was also another problem: three of these elderly men had explicitly told me they didn't want their names connected with some of the things they told me. One man explained to me, 'That was another place and another time. I have children and grandchildren now.' I started wondering about creating a main character, someone the reader could relate to, and letting him take us through that part of history, using true stories and following the actual timeline. The narrative soon demanded two characters. That's how Tom and Bob Derks came to life. They are fictional, moulded from the men I met in 2003. Tom and Bob relive those men's loves, their fights, their fears and their efforts to keep Australia's northern coastline safe.

Sadly, most of the men have now left us. This story is for them: the men who served in No. 18 (NEI) RAAF Squadron.

RANKS

The Dutch and the Australians had different names for different ranks and I have tried to be accurate for each man and his rank. Here is a list of equivalent Military Air Force ranks.

Dutch	Australian
Luitenant General	Air Marshal
General Majoor	Air Vice Marshal
Kolonel	Air Commodore
Overste	Group Captain
Majoor	Wing Commander
Kaptein	Squadron Leader
1e Luitenant	Flight Lieutenant
2e Luitenant	Flying Officer
Vaandrig	Pilot Officer
Onder Luitenant	Pilot Officer

Dutch	*Australian*
Adjudant	Warrant Officer
Sergeant Majoor	Flight Sergeant
Korporaal	Corporal

ABBREVIATIONS

KNIL	Royal Netherlands East Indies Army
KNILM	Royal Netherlands East Indies Airlines
NEI	Netherlands East Indies
NEFIS	Netherlands East Indies Forces Intelligence Service
DNG	Dutch New Guinea
ML-KNIL	Royal Netherlands East Indies Air Force
POW	Prisoner of war
RAAF	Royal Australian Air Force
WAAAF	Women's Auxiliary Australian Air Force

MEASUREMENTS

To avoid interrupting the flow of the narrative with anachronistic details, the place names used throughout the book are the names in use at the time—Batavia rather than Jakarta, for example. For the same reason, imperial units are used throughout. Here are their equivalents:

1 mile = 1.6 kilometres
1 foot = 30 centimetres
1 ton = approx. 1 tonne
1 pint = 500 ml

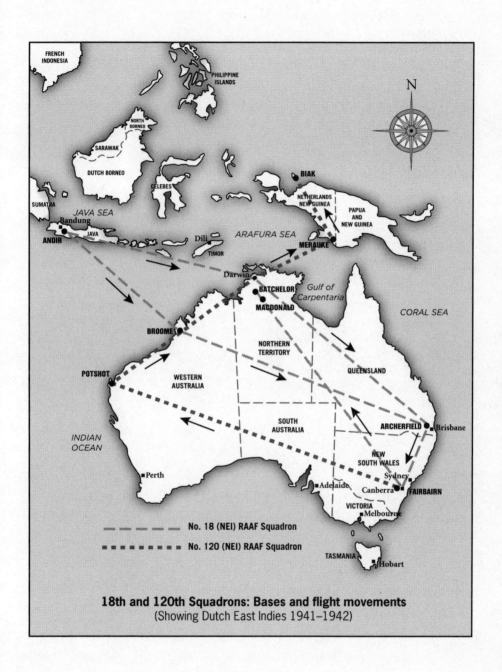

18th and 120th Squadrons: Bases and flight movements
(Showing Dutch East Indies 1941–1942)

1 JAVA, 1942

'We are shutting down. Goodbye, until better times. Long live our Queen . . .'

It was 9 March 1942 and Tom Derks knew he was in trouble when he heard the words spilling from a wireless. He looked inside the small hut from which the disturbing message had come and met the eyes of a Javanese woman with a small child on her lap. She looked away quickly; his uniform had told her he was in the military. Tom remained standing tentatively in the doorway, scanning the little room. When he finally located the radio, he stared for a moment in disbelief at its speaker, which now produced nothing but a cackle of static. The mother kept her eyes cast down, but the child flashed him a toothless grin.

When he asked the woman if the Japanese had actually landed, she finally looked up at him again, her eyes emotionless. A slight nod of her head told him it was true. She smiled as she touched her child's head with a caressing hand. The smile made Tom shudder. There was a strange smugness about it, almost like a sneer—it made him wonder if the woman was mocking him because she'd known something he hadn't. 'Christ,' he mumbled, stepping away from the doorway.

He needed to get out of there fast, and for the first time he cursed the fact that illness had prevented him from leaving Java with his unit days earlier. Because of the situation with the advancing Japanese, all leave had been cancelled, but as he was recovering, he was dismissed from duty for the week. He'd headed for the hills surrounding Bandung to visit his latest girlfriend, Sana, a sweet Javanese girl who worked in one of the hotels in the city.

Tom suspected his illness had something to do with the long hours of work and the lack of sleep. In the weeks after Pearl Harbor, his Netherlands East Indies transporter unit had been flying almost nonstop, dropping supplies for the Allied forces all over the islands. Dutch, British, American and Australian troops were fighting in a combined effort to stop the advancing enemy. Benzedrine had kept the exhausted pilots on their feet, but at some point Tom's body had refused to go on. Feeling ill, his fever rising, he'd visited a doctor, who thought he might have contracted dengue fever. The doctors at the hospital found no symptoms to back this up so they sent him on his way with a vial of pills and instructions to take it easy for a while.

His unit had left for Australia without him. Just short of two weeks earlier he'd waved them goodbye as they took to the skies. Fourteen pilots, with their mechanics and radio operators crammed into three Lodestars. They were heading for Brisbane's Archerfield Air Base, to collect a number of B-25

Mitchell bombers bought by the Dutch Government to help in the fight against the Japanese in the Dutch East Indies. *They should be back by now*, he thought, and hoped they were chasing the enemy off the island with those shiny new bombers. As he made his way through the jungle, he knew he needed to get back to them quickly.

He'd welcomed his illness and the leave from work but now he cursed himself. As he plodded downhill on foot through the jungle, he noticed the sky had turned that colour of wet cement so common to the tropics. The occasional rumbling he heard in the distance might be a thunderstorm, or could it be the sound of heavy artillery in the hills? He was confused.

It was strange to think he'd woken to a world that appeared so very peaceful. The green jungle hissed with life, birds screamed and chirped, and Sana had turned to him with her seductive little smile. Deciding he'd been in 'recovery' long enough, he'd kissed her goodbye that morning, intending to head back to his unit. When he'd tried to kickstart his motorbike the damn thing had refused to come to life. Some Javanese boys looked on in amusement as he tried to revive it, but all it did was sputter and cough. He couldn't help but wonder if they might have stolen the fuel from the tank while he was sleeping. He checked, but there appeared to be enough petrol left. After labouring for more than fifteen minutes, Tom gave up and dealt the bike a final frustrated kick. The boys offered to lend a hand and, after examining the bike, concluded it needed new spark plugs. They didn't have any but they could get some. Not today but tomorrow. Tom didn't want to wait, so the boys promised him they'd fix the bike and keep an eye on it for him. He gave them the last of his money, and hoped they'd keep their word.

Trudging down the dirt track from the hills, Tom had set out on foot to the main road to Bandung. The city was about ten miles away, and he knew that once he was on the road it wouldn't be hard to hitch a ride and he'd reach Bandung within the hour. But the message from the radio had thrown a spanner in the works and now he had no idea what to expect. Shutting down the radio station suggested the Japanese were already in Bandung. He didn't know where his unit was, and for all he knew they might have been captured.

It's a hard thing to kick yourself, but Tom almost managed. 'Stupid idiot,' he mumbled, realising he was stumbling along in a world that had changed overnight. Why hadn't he known what was happening? How could he have been so naïve? He felt like a blind man in more ways than one as he made his way along the narrow path through the thick jungle. Suddenly the path ceased, spitting him out onto the highway.

There is nothing as paralysing as doubt in a man's mind. As Tom Derks tried in vain to convince himself that it couldn't be true, that the Japanese could never have invaded the islands so quickly, the sound of what he now assumed to be artillery fire came from the direction of the city, picking up momentum and volume. Doubt settled in his mind like an uninvited guest, making him feel uncomfortable and cautious.

He needed to get to Bandung; he looked around, searching for something motorised that could take him to the airport. On the highway, people were scurrying past and the road was unusually busy. Coolies, their belongings stacked impossibly high on rickety bikes, pedalled past him, and men, women and children, all on foot, appeared to be in a great rush. He suddenly realised that almost everyone was heading in the opposite direction and that there were no whites, no Europeans among them. Stopping one of the men, he questioned him about the situation in Java's capital but the man just looked at him in disbelief for a moment and hurried on. Others he approached wandered away from him, as if he'd turned into the enemy overnight.

Tom observed the bustling swarm of islanders for a moment, contemplating the best course of action. If there were any Japanese coming out of the city he'd be hard to miss with his tall build, fair skin, blond hair and blue eyes, not to mention his uniform. *Damn it*, he thought, *I'm a walking target*. He stepped back into the foliage, hoping it was thick enough to conceal him.

It had rained for days and the jungle was wet and boggy. The mud clung to his boots like spongy dough, making it hard to move quickly; now it had started to rain again. His uniform was wet and would be soaked if the rain didn't stop. He paused again, weighing up his options as he peered through the foliage onto the road. *If everyone was moving away from the city, something or someone must be driving them out*, he reasoned.

The slopes of Bandung were wrapped in dense tropical rainforest but there was a cultivated strip where *sawahs*—rice paddies—created a mosaic of enclosed squares. Normally, clusters of women in colourful clothing would be working them, their straw hats warding off the rain or sun, their damp sarongs clinging to their agile bodies like tight wrappers. Standing motionless, looking up at the hills on the other side of the road, he noticed no women were working the fields. A few water buffalo waded lazily in the coffee-coloured water. Young naked boys rode them side-saddle, nudging the massive beasts forward with their sticks.

Did they know the enemy was kicking down the door? *They might not care*, Tom thought. From the moment he'd set foot on the island three years earlier, he'd never felt uncomfortable or threatened in the presence of the islanders, but he'd always been aware of his position as part of the privileged white minority.

Brash, confident and twenty years old, he'd been transferred from the Netherlands to the remote Dutch island of Java to complete his pilot training. A city boy who, together with his twin brother Bob, had dreamt of ways to escape the cold, wet and icy Dutch winters. His mother had died giving birth to the twins, and their father's sister had raised them. Over the years, she'd become a disillusioned and tired spinster, whose only purpose in life appeared to be trying to mould the boys into respectable men, and she set to her task with a hard hand and a sharp tongue. They were destined for a life as factory workers, and the prospect of the dull and monotonous work made the boys' need to escape ever more urgent. Opportunity came to them in the form of a newspaper advertisement inviting healthy young men to apply for pilot training and a posting to the Dutch East Indies. By now, a new leader in Germany was talking war and the creation of a great Aryan nation, and the boys didn't know what to think about the barking Führer.

The Dutch confidently shipped their soldiers off to the Pacific, expecting the Germans to respect their neutrality should a war develop. Tom and his twin Bob were in Java to complete their training a couple of months later. Their aunt was the only person to wave them off.

Bandung had been a fiesta. The boys loved both the city and its luxurious clubs. Uniformed, barefooted waiters hurried from one table to another, not making a sound as they walked on the polished marble floors serving steak and cocktails. European men dressed in dignified suits, and their wives always looked their best—it was a far cry from their lives in the Netherlands. After dark, the temperature in the cities was often stifling, so on weekends most of the Europeans fled to cottages in the mountains, where the evenings were pleasant and the nights cooled down enough to necessitate a blanket.

Tom embraced the warmth, never missing the Dutch winter cold. The melodic voice from the mosque found its way into his bedroom every morning as the muezzin announced the dawn of each new day. To him, it was the most wonderfully mysterious sound, although it of course made him aware that he lived and worked in a predominantly Muslim society. This didn't bother the Europeans born to the islands. The subject of loyalty, in the event of a Japanese invasion, was beyond question. The white people certainly didn't consider themselves the oppressors. Most of them had inherited some Javanese blood along the way, and quite a few had Javanese fathers or mothers. There were incidents, of course, from time to time, but on the surface of things, it appeared the Javanese people were content to live under white rule.

Tom had no idea if these modest but to him unfathomable people would turn to the Japanese now that the world had rotated, and greet them as fellow Asians and liberators. The Javanese smiled, bowed and lived their lives in humble silence, but that silence had a hint of eeriness about it. Those who felt it, knew it and recognised it.

Standing in the mud, Tom wondered if he might be better off taking his chances on the road with the islanders. He might stumble upon a Japanese convoy, he thought, but he also realised his options were very limited. Pulling his shoes from the clinging mud, he stepped onto the wet asphalt, deciding to join the people fleeing from Bandung towards Kalidjati. Like Bandung, the town of Kalidjati had an airfield. He'd have to be cautious, but by merging with the crowds he might be able to get to the airport there. In any event, taking to the road would enhance his chances of waving down a motorbike or car.

When he saw what looked like the outline of an army vehicle coming towards him, he sidestepped into the foliage again. As it came closer, Tom recognised the red, white and blue stripes, and realised it was Dutch. His heart skipped a beat. The vehicle was driving back to Bandung. If it was Dutch, as he assumed, he didn't care where it was going as long as it took him along. He waved his arms as he stepped from the roadside and the four-wheel drive slowed. Tom almost cried with joy.

It was only when the Dutch open army truck had almost stopped that Tom realised something was wrong. To his horror, he saw that the driver looked Japanese, and there were three olive-skinned passengers peering at him through the front window of the truck. The four men remained straight-faced as Tom's expression took on a look of shocked horror; he almost made the fatal mistake of making a run for it. It wouldn't have got him anywhere but dead, he realised as he raised his hands in a gesture of surrender. Surrendering would keep him alive for the time being, and he didn't much fancy a bullet in the back.

The uniform Tom was wearing—that of the ML-KNIL, the Royal Netherlands Dutch East Indies Airforce—suddenly made him feel painfully uncomfortable. He wished he'd dressed in civilian clothes, but he realised he could do nothing more than hope they wouldn't kill him on the spot. If the Japanese thought he might come in handy as a source of intelligence later, they might think twice about killing him. His uniform didn't have many stripes—he was a flight officer—but the Dutch uniforms nevertheless looked pretty impressive.

As one of the men got out of the jeep, Tom forced a faint but friendly smile, thinking it couldn't hurt the situation. The Japanese soldier was not amused; he yelled at him, slapped his face and roughly turned him around. After checking him for weapons, he tied Tom's hands behind his back, all the while yelling words that to Tom sounded strangely short but highly intimidating. He was shoved into the back of the vehicle next to another Japanese soldier, his captor squeezing in beside him. The car recommenced its journey and no one spoke. Tom found the silence just as intimidating as the yelling. With his body squeezed in between two enemy soldiers, the panic and terror so overwhelmed him that he almost threw up.

As they neared the outskirts of Lembang, a town just five miles from the capital, he watched as Javanese scurried around on the highway like lost ants. All sense of direction appeared to have vanished, and some were heading into the city while others hurried out. As the car unexpectedly swerved around a group of people and settled into a parking lot, he was jolted against one of his guards. He mumbled a half-hearted apology and smiled, but was pulled roughly from the car by the soldier who'd yelled at him earlier. Without warning, the tirade started again, and Tom lost his balance when the man pushed him forward. As he fell onto the concrete with his hands tied behind him, he scraped his face. In an effort to drag the Dutchman to his feet, the barking soldier grabbed a handful of Tom's hair and pulled upwards as hard as he could.

By the time Tom had finally managed to get to his feet, a significant portion of his hair had surrendered itself to Japanese hands, leaving his scalp feeling as if it were on fire. By now Tom had worked out that apologies and smiles were not appreciated by the Japanese, so he refrained from showing any facial expression.

Looking around, he recognised that they'd stopped in the parking lot of the iconic Isola Hotel, which overlooked Bandung from one of the higher slopes surrounding the city. It had been the venue for his brother's engagement party just a couple of months earlier, but now a push in the back made him stumble towards the entrance. Below, within the boundaries of Bandung,

Tom could make out the sound of mortar and shots. Someone was still holding the fort, he thought, so there might be a shred of hope left.

As he entered the hotel, he saw two men tied to chairs at the far end of the lobby near a window and noticed both were slumped. One looked badly beaten and hardly conscious, while the other, an American by the look of his uniform, simply stared in apathy as Tom was forced towards them. Grabbing a chair and placing it next to the other prisoners, a barking Japanese soldier forced Tom to sit down and then wound a rope around his chest. Pulling the rope tight, he tied its end to the back of the chair.

Slapping Tom's scratched face, the Jap yelled at him some more and thrust a gun under his nose to underline the point he was making. Tom nodded furiously, making it clear he got the picture. Yes, he was to stay put. Another slap. Yes, he understood. For no reason he could fathom, he was slapped one more time and then the four men left, their boots making confident, rhythmic clunking sounds on the marble floors.

Tom's face was hot where a Japanese hand had imprinted itself on his cheek like a stamp. He sat contemplating for a moment and then began to squirm in his bonds. He asked the American how long he'd been sitting there but the man, obviously terrified, shooshed him and resumed staring into the distance. Tom had no intention of passively staying put. The prospect of being battered and tortured by the Japanese, and ending with a bullet in his skull after they'd finished, wasn't the way he wanted to go. Being shot trying to escape suddenly had a morbid charm to it. It would end his life in a much quicker way, he decided, so he continued to wriggle, twist and struggle in his bonds. As he braced and relaxed his wrists, he felt the rope loosen and, to his surprise, it slowly began to slip.

'I think I can get my hands free in a minute. We could make a run for it,' he said, turning to the other men.

The beaten man did not even look up and the American told him he must be crazy. 'They'll shoot you like a dog,' he whispered as Tom pulled the rope from his chest and stood up from the chair, rubbing his freed hands.

'I'll untie you.'

The man looked up at him in horror. 'No. Leave me. I'll take my chances here with the Japs.'

Tom shrugged and stepped to the side of the open but shuttered window. He slowly opened the shutters and found himself gazing onto what looked like a deserted back garden. At the back of the garden a high wall prevented any escape, but he noticed that the wall was considerably lower at the side of the hotel. Low enough, he thought, for him to jump over. Conjuring up all his courage, he squeezed his tall frame through the window and heard the American swear. Tom ran towards the lower wall, but when he looked to the right he suddenly stopped in his tracks. He wasn't alone.

About twenty Javanese men, women and children stood silently at the rear of the hotel, their backs to him. They appeared to be reading a leaflet they'd been handed. Through a gap in the crowd, Tom saw a Japanese soldier sitting in one of the hotel's armchairs. Something that looked unmistakably like a huge machete rested on his lap. He was talking to the crowd in the same barking tones Tom had heard earlier. Sensing movement behind them, the people slowly turned to stare at Tom. For a moment, there were only stares, so Tom made a dash for the lower wall, hoping the crowd would partially block his escape from the Japanese with the machete. He jumped onto the wall, then stopped, arms flailing. The road loomed some ten feet below. Glancing back, he saw the soldier rising from his chair.

Tom jumped. There was little else he could do. When his feet hit the gravel, his knees buckled and he was sent rolling onto the concrete. Fumbling to his feet, he tore across the road and prayed the machete was the only weapon the soldier had. If the man had a gun, Tom would be dead before he could reach the other side.

Surprised that a bullet had not hit him and ignoring the shouting and commotion coming from behind, he took a left into a side street and ducked into what looked like a sewer. With no sense of where he'd end up, he ran, bent over, through the large concrete pipe. Praying that no one had followed him and that he wouldn't run into the enemy when he emerged at the other end. He could make out a light downhill in the distance, so he assumed he was headed for the city.

As his pace slowed, the pungent smell suddenly hit him—a mixture of shit, piss and other unimaginable debris—and trudging through the slosh, he retched. Collecting himself, he realised there were worse fates than having to brave the hotel's sewer.

As he ran, he thought about what he'd do once he reached the other end. He needed to get rid of his uniform, but he realised that would mean contact with the locals, and he had no idea who was with him or against him, nor whether he should take the risk. He'd hardly encountered any other whites, so most of them were probably hiding somewhere. The Japanese might not have seized the airport yet. Ever since they'd entered the outskirts of Bandung, Tom had heard the sound of mortars and gunfire, so he knew there were still soldiers putting up a fight. He'd head for Bandung's Andir Airport and try to find a plane—or even hijack one. He had to get back to his unit, to his brother, although he feared they might have been captured, or even killed. Pushing those thoughts away, he hurried through the concrete pipes. Getting to the airport was his only hope for the time being.

2 THE DISPATCH RIDER

On 15 February 1942, the day Singapore surrendered, a Japanese invasion fleet sailed towards Palembang oilfield in the south of Sumatra. After the Japanese bombed Pearl Harbor, they landed on Borneo, Sumatra and Celebes. The people who were able to flee tried to get to Java, which was regarded as a bastion that would stand firm against any attack from the enemy. Its capital, Batavia, had a natural bay and flatlands while Java's informal capital, Bandung, was sheltered by the surrounding high mountains.

At the very beginning of March 1942, the Japanese reached Kalidjati Airfield, capturing many Allied bombers and wiping out two British regiments stationed there. The cavalry vanguard of the KNIL made its way up to Kalidjati in an attempt to drive out the enemy. The Japanese, however, had seized many men and nearly all of their armoured cars and trucks. One of those confiscated armoured cars had stopped on the road as Tom Derks stepped from the foliage, and had fallen into the arms of the enemy.

When another Japanese division advanced from Merak towards Batavia, it became evident that Java would fall within days. Japanese artillery and bombers broke up most of the counterattacks by the KNIL and Allied forces. There was a final stand in the mountains surrounding Bandung but on 9 March the Dutch military commander, General Hein ter Poorten, declared Bandung 'an open city', and all Dutch and Allied military were ordered to surrender. Scattered groups had not heard General Ter Poorten's order and were still fighting. Resistance, although confused and sporadic, continued for a couple of days.

When Tom emerged from the sewer and heard the occasional crackle of firearms, he assumed the fighting had not stopped. Getting his bearings, he realised the airport was not terribly far from where he stood, although it would still take him an hour to get there on foot and with the light already fading it would soon be dark. Darkness wouldn't be a bad thing considering the circumstances, Tom thought. He knew his way around the city, having lived there for three years, an advantage he had over the Japanese. This and nightfall could enhance his chances of making it across the city alive.

A Javanese family brushed past him on the almost deserted street, most likely heading out of the city, out of the way of any crossfire. Tom grabbed the father's arm and asked if he could exchange the man's shirt and pants for his own uniform, but the man gestured no furiously with his head and hurried down the road. Poor bastards were heading straight into the arms of the enemy, Tom thought. When a small motorbike came towards him, he took a risk and stepped onto the road to wave down the driver. The motorcyclist, as cautious as Tom, only stopped his bike when he saw Tom's uniform. To Tom's own relief the man looked like a European and his uniform was Australian.

'They've bombed the bloody airport in Bandung,' he told Tom, still revving his bike. 'Not many Japs in the city yet, but I hear there are plenty surrounding it. The way things are going, it won't take them long to occupy the town. I'm getting out while I can.'

Tom explained that there was nothing the other way but the enemy. 'I just came from there.' Tom's accent was thick but he spoke English well.

The man looked at Tom and wrinkled his nose, 'God, you smell awful.'

'I've been crawling through a sewer for the past three hours.' He told the Australian that the Japanese were already in Lembang, just five miles down the road, so there was no use heading that way.

The man looked reluctantly back to where he'd come from. 'I'm a Don R,' he explained to Tom, who raised an eyebrow. 'A dispatch rider.' He had a message for his commanding officer, given to him by the Dutch high command, but there seemed no way to get it to him. 'My unit's stationed near Batavia, but that route is already cut off. So I'm hoping to get the message to my CO in some other way.'

By now Tom was desperate. 'Look,' he said, 'I'm a pilot. If we can get to Andir and find a plane we'll be able to get out of here.' Tom knew that if there was one aircraft only remotely operational, he'd be able to fly it. They had two options, he explained: to be caught, tortured and killed by the enemy if they decided to go to Kalidjati; or to die in a plane crash getting out of there. 'We might even make it out alive,' he suggested with a smile.

Weighing up his limited options, the Australian introduced himself to Tom as Norman Harris, then turned his motorbike around and said, 'Hop on.'

It was getting dark fast, and Tom pointed the way through Bandung's small alleyways and deserted back roads. Nearing the airport, Tom asked Norman to sidetrack into one of the lanes where luxurious European houses stood in tropical gardens. He needed to check up on someone, he explained. Norman gave a disapproving grunt and mumbled something about wasting time on a visit. Tom convinced him it was important.

Bandung's streets had become eerily deserted and silent as night fell, the only sound an occasional rumble. They turned into a wide lane marked by trees on both sides of the pavement and stopped in front of a large gated house. It was the residence of Emile la Grande, owner of one of the biggest jewellery shops in Bandung and father of Colette la Grande, the fiancée of Tom's twin brother, Bob.

His brother had met Colette six months earlier at a service-men's ball. She'd inherited a soft luminescent attractiveness from her Dutch mother and her French father's dark hair. After the party, Tom had confessed to his brother that he was truly jealous: the girl preferred Bob. After all, Tom mused, he was the tall good-looking and exciting one. Bob was considerably shorter, dark-haired and dark-eyed, and, so Tom thought, tainted with an incredibly boring and serious nature. Bob Derks and Colette la Grande were engaged just three months later.

Tom hoped his brother had already been able to get the family out of Bandung to Australia but thought he'd check just in case. As he walked up to the gates, he noticed they were open. That was strange, because the housekeeper usually shut them as soon as darkness fell and you'd have to ring to get in. Tom continued up the drive and approached the house; it appeared unusually deserted and the front door stood wide open. Occasional shadows appeared and disappeared as the moon passed through the clouds. He hesitated for a moment, then he stepped through the open doorway. He could hardly make out anything inside—it was pitch black. There was probably a blackout because of the attacks, he thought. Riding through the streets, they had noticed there were no lights on in any of the houses. Darkness engulfed most of the town.

He called out Colette's name, trying to sound confident, but the eerie silence in the house was unsettling. The piercing sound of his own voice alarmed him and he stood in silence for a moment, listening for any movement. When he stepped into the large sitting room, he noticed a broken vase on the floor and heard some kind of sound coming from the rear of the house, where the sleeping quarters were. Making his way towards the room where the noise had come from, he noticed a faint light filtering through the partly open door. 'Colette?' he called again. He gently pushed the door open, his tall wiry frame filling the gap.

He froze. Someone was sitting at the dressing table. Candle flames flickered, reflected in the mirror, scattering like butterflies in the wind. The figure suddenly turned and hissed at him. Paralysed by fright, both paused for a moment, but the person sitting at the mirror regained her bearings a fraction of a second before Tom. A heavy perfume bottle came flying through the air at his head, and would have hit him, too, had Tom not ducked on reflex. The bottle smashed against the corridor wall, clattering to the floor, the sweet smell immediately filling the hallway and seeping into the room.

'Farah?' Tom barely recognised the family's Javanese house-keeper. She looked different somehow but it was too dark to see properly.

'*Oh meneer! U moet vertrekken!*' The r's rolling from her lips turned the harsh Dutch into a soft and melodic dialect only people from the Dutch East Indies developed. She was urging him to leave but Tom wanted to know where the La Grandes had gone.

'Where are they?'

'*Vertrokken!*' Gone. It was only as he stepped closer to Farah that he saw what she'd done to her face. She had smeared herself with Colette's make-up but with only the candlelight to guide her had done a messy job. Smudgy reds lips protruded from her heavily powdered face, giving her the odd appearance of a kabuki actress who'd seen better days.

'What are you doing? What's going on here?'

'You go!' she said, 'They're coming. They'll take the best houses.' She waved her arm in the air expansively, to emphasise that the La Grande house would surely be one of the first houses confiscated by the advancing enemy. 'They left. Hours ago. Colette, mister and missus,' she added, pointing to the door.

Good. That was all he needed to know; they'd got away. Tom assumed his brother had managed to come back for them. '*Meneer* Bob?' he asked, but she'd turned her back on him and didn't answer him when he repeated the question.

Sitting boldly in front of the dressing table, with Colette's make-up spread out in front of her, the familiar and usually timid housekeeper filled Tom with a feeling of contempt and confusion. She turned again and looked at him defiantly. He half expected her to shoo him away, as she would a bothersome gecko. The way Farah looked at him made him painfully aware that life in this country was changing fast—it was no longer clear who was the master and who the servant. Farah did not cast her eyes down as Tom stared back at her. She held her ground almost defiantly, which was most uncommon for a Javanese woman. After he hesitantly turned his back on her to leave, though, she called out.

'*Meneer*!' Sir.

She stood up from the dressing table, and as she strode towards him slowly took something from her dress pocket. Tom thought for a silly second she might attack him with a knife, but instead Farah gently reached for his hand and placed something in his palm. It was Colette's pearl necklace, the one Bob had given her a few weeks after they'd met.

'Everyone, in a hurry. She forget. Give it to her.'

As Farah looked up at him, Tom noticed she'd been crying, the tears making tracks through the powder on her face. His anger suddenly turned to sympathy. They were all victims, he realised. The Javanese were just as uncertain about their future as any white person on the island. Who was to know who'd survive and who wouldn't?

'Take care, Farah,' he said softly, watching as she turned away and walked slowly back to the dressing table. She picked up a kohl pencil and resumed painting her face, drawing a line under each eye.

———

It took Tom and Norman Harris about fifteen minutes to reach Andir Airport. Norman killed the bike's motor and let out a soft whistle at the state of the airport and its runway. Both men were speechless. Impact craters pitted the runway and partially destroyed aeroplanes lay in a still-neat line. With their wheels retracted and propellers bent, they eerily resembled a row of shot buffalo. There were no humans to be seen; the place appeared deserted.

'What now?' Norman asked. Tom didn't answer but headed for the destroyed planes. He saw that most of them were old two-engine Lockheed Lodestars, planes he knew how to fly and had done part of his training in. Most of the planes had been located at Pameungpeuk on the south coast; Tom thought they might have been moved to Bandung at the last minute in an attempt to keep them from falling into Japanese hands. The mangled Lodestars were a sorry sight. Even if he managed to get one up and going, taking off from a runway full of potholes with no lights to steer the plane safely between the mountains was suicidal.

'I destroyed them,' said a voice behind them, and Tom and Norman jumped. 'I did it. I'm now in the process of breaking every bottle of whisky left in the officers' mess.' The slurred Dutch came from a pimply intoxicated boy—he didn't look a day over eighteen—with a smug smile on his face.

The boy introduced himself as, Max, the son of the airport defence officer. Before his father had gone home, he'd given his son permission to destroy the remaining aeroplanes, telling him to make sure they'd be no good to any enemy who found them. Max had demolished them with Dutch thoroughness. The boy explained, his chest puffing up with pride, how he'd first gone into the cockpits and set the landing gear of every Lodestar into the 'OP' position. The wheels on each plane had retracted, causing the aircraft to collapse onto their bellies. Max had then attacked the planes with the front loader of a tractor to finish off the job.

Tom asked if any B-25s had landed at Andir recently, but Max couldn't remember any.

'It's been busy,' he said, 'but mostly departing aircraft. If any planes came in, they'd leave a few hours later loaded with officials and valuables. They've all fled.'

When the boy saw the dismayed look on Tom's face, he added, 'Planes are still flying from Boeabatoe Road.' He brought an unsteady finger to his lips: 'Shhh. It's a secret. The Japs aren't allowed to know.'

With a proud grin, he zigzagged away from the two men, probably to finish the job of 'destroying' the alcohol stash.

'What was that all about?' asked Norman, who'd been unable to follow the conversation.

'The boy says there's a secret runway and aeroplanes are still flying from there. Boeabatoe Road. It's a new highway, still under construction. I know where it is. In the south of the city.'

Norman started the motorbike and without another word Tom hopped on the back. Fifteen minutes later, they arrived at the section of the Boeabatoe Road under construction. Men and women huddled at the side of the highway with anguished faces, craning their necks and pushing forward as an aircraft prepared for take-off. The few planes still in operation were the horde's only hope, but they knew their chances of securing a seat in one of them were probably futile.

Soldiers with guns kept the crowd at bay as the solitary aeroplane took off into the night. At the roadside soldiers dimmed the lights of the strategically placed hurricane lamps that served as improvised runway lights. Norman and Tom looked at each other in dismay. The plane was gone, manoeuvring through the mountain ranges as it gathered height. The chances of another plane arriving were becoming slimmer as each minute passed. They'd have to think of something else.

3 ATTACK ON BROOME

The Japanese had been steadily advancing, conquering one Pacific island after another, when Gus Winckel's transport unit left for Australia towards the end of February 1942. The planes took off from Andir Airport with fourteen additional pilots on board and clawed their way into the skies as Tom Derks waved them out. If all went well the pilots would return with nineteen brand-new Mitchell B-25s. The Dutch Government had ordered the planes months earlier, realising they'd be vital in the defence of the islands. The departing pilots expected the new aircraft to be waiting for them at Archerfield Air Base near Brisbane, but it soon became apparent that the delivery of the planes had been delayed because the Americans themselves, after the attack on Pearl Harbor, needed them in the South Pacific. They were promised new planes as soon as the Americans could deliver them but no one knew when that might be, so the Dutch pilots were forced to endure an anxious wait. Days went by with not one of the ordered planes arriving.

On 27 February, the Allied naval forces suffered a catastrophic defeat when the Imperial Japanese Navy destroyed most of their ships in the Battle of the Java Sea. The Strike Force commander, Dutch Rear Admiral Karel Doorman, had been killed, and the Japanese pushed on with overwhelming persistence. The Dutch unit waiting at Archerfield followed the news, their concern for loved ones back in the Indies steadily growing. Permission to take the two Lodestars to pick up their families was refused. No one wanted the planes and their crews falling into the hands of the enemy, they were told. Their orders were to stay put and wait until the situation became clearer. Soon the men began to beg for permission to return to the islands, but their requests were rejected repeatedly. Their frustration and anger mounted when they witnessed Dutch officers and officials landing at Archerfield with their families and even their pets.

Just a few days after the catastrophe on the Java Sea, Gus Winckel was ordered to take a plane load of weapons back to Bandung. Bob Derks and technician Charlie van Tuyn were to go with him and because this was a military transport, their specific orders were not to evacuate any women or children. They were to arrive at Andir, refuel and fly back to Australia with a group of important military officials. The orders specifically stated that these officials were the only people allowed to board the plane. Bob and Gus were denied permission to evacuate their own families.

After a relatively peaceful seven-hour flight, they landed on Andir. There had been a lot of enemy movement at sea but they had not encountered any action in the air. Charlie van Tuyn was pleasantly surprised to learn that his wife and small son had been able to board a civilian flight only hours before. Bob received no word about his fiancée; all he could do was hope she and her family had managed to get out. Gus still fretted about his son and wife, who was six months pregnant with their second child. He had no idea where they were and what they were going through. Together Bob and Gus planned to return to Bandung after this flight to find their loved ones. 'We've at least earned that right,' Bob said to his friend. When they flew back from Bandung on 2 March, their plane was packed with a group of highly placed officials and their families.

'I thought no civilians were allowed,' Bob spat as they saluted the higher-ranked officers.

'Evidently it all depends on the family and your rank,' Gus replied.

Because the enemy had targeted Darwin more than once, all Allied aircraft needing refuelling had been detoured to the relatively safe small pearling town of Broome. Winckel's final destination was Sydney, so he landed in Broome to refuel. When they approached the town, the weather was fine and bright, the sky almost cloudless, and as they touched down in the early morning hours of 3 March 1942, Gus sighed with relief. The return trip had been almost uneventful. Down below a Japanese ship had fired its machine-guns into the skies, the ack-ack spitting fuming ammunition in their direction, but they had been flying too high to be hit.

They taxied to the end of the runway in Broome, where their plane would have to wait its turn to be refuelled. The passengers, glad to leave the muggy plane, sat talking and laughing on the grass. They were not the only ones waiting. The small airport had become terribly busy in recent weeks, taking over most of Darwin's air traffic. It was not properly equipped to handle so many planes, but its people did what they could under the circumstances. A certain amount of patience was required from pilots and passengers, most of whom were only interested in arriving at their final destination as quickly as possible.

Similar hectic activity could be witnessed on Broome's Roebuck Bay, where nine Dutch Dorniers and Catalinas lay waiting for the tide to come in. The flying boats could not moor at the jetty to refuel because of the 30-foot tide difference. They were left with no other option than to sit further out on the bay and wait for a fuelling boat to come along. The flying boats were packed with refugees who had managed to escape from the islands. These men, women and children considered themselves lucky, knowing many had not been as fortunate. On the peacock-blue waters of Roebuck Bay, evacuees trickled out of the cabin of one of these planes and onto the wings. They had been locked up in the small hull of the aircraft for more than eight hours, where the air smelt of sweat and urine. Bathing in the early morning sun, they admired the Australian shore and felt optimistic for the first time in weeks.

As they waited to fuel, Bob sauntered off to the hangar in search of food and drink while Gus and Charlie inspected the one weapon with which the Lodestar was issued. Guns were not standard aboard the transport planes, but since the Japanese had become a serious threat, most transport aircrafts had been equipped with a machine-gun. Charlie was inside the plane, removing the gun from its frame, when an airport attendant came along to inform them it would take another 30 minutes for the fuel truck to get to them. He sighed audibly as he passed the gun to Gus through the pilot's window. At that very moment, the hair on the back of Gus's neck stood up: he heard the distinctive sound of planes flying in formation. He'd recognise it anywhere. Turning slowly, his hands still clutching the heavy machine-gun, he searched the cloudless sky.

Even above the noise of the American Liberator taking off on the runway, he could hear the drone. 'Is the RAAF flying today?' he asked one of the air crew while he studied the airspace over Broome, trying to pinpoint the sound. As the maintenance man's gaze moved to the heavens, Gus finally made out nine small specs on the horizon. Planes in formation were not a good sign unless they were your own, and these were coming in fast. When he recognised the red balls on the wings, he jolted. Nine Japanese Zeros were approaching. Banging the body of the Lodestar, Gus yelled, 'Charlie, get out of the plane!' and to the maintenance man, 'Sound the alarm! The Japs are coming!'

As his mechanic jumped out of the plane, Gus cried, 'Get the hell out of here and take those people with you!' Some of their passengers sitting on the grass were pointing at the 'pretty planes' coming in. A few large concrete pipes, probably meant for the airport's new sewerage system, lay scattered on the grass and Charlie realised they were the closest shelter. He ushered the reluctant passengers inside and hoped the pipes would be thick enough to withstand the enemy fire. If the Japs decided to throw bombs, he knew they wouldn't stand a chance.

The American Liberator, which had only just taken off, was struck by enemy fire as it tried to fly out over the bay. It crashed onto the water and sank almost immediately. At the same time, four Zeros veered off from the formation and headed for the flying boats on the bay while the remaining planes assaulted the runway, spitting bullets into the planes as they passed. Taking a stand behind a fallen tree trunk, Gus raised the machine-gun. A Zero approached his Lodestar and Gus clenched his weapon, resting the barrel on his left arm, the butt against his shoulder and his foot steady on the trunk.

A spray of bullets smashed into the ground around Gus as he stood his ground calmly, waiting for the right moment. Amazingly, he was unharmed. The moment the Japanese pilot flew his plane very low across the runway, Gus fired up the machine-gun, spitting bullets at the plane as it flew right into his line of fire. He saw the pilot—Osamu Kudo, they later learnt—smile as he passed, but the smile soon vanished when he realised his plane had been struck. Gus watched it sputter and hiccup its way onto the bay, burning from its tail end, then vanish from sight in the distance. It was all over in no more than ten minutes. The remaining Zeros discharged their extra fuel tanks over the town, saluted from their cockpits and were gone, leaving behind carnage in the bay and almost a hundred people dead.

It was only after the Zeros had left that Gus realised he'd burnt his left arm and hand holding the red-hot barrel of the gun.

Bob Derks came rushing out of the hangar. 'Christ!' he said as he approached the pilot. 'Gus, are you crazy or what?'

Winckel shrugged, clutching his painful left hand. 'They destroyed my Lodestar,' was all he said.

'Our flight commander definitely has some kind of death wish,' Charlie muttered as he emerged from the concrete pipes with the startled passengers.

The Lodestar was a mess. Gus counted hundreds of holes and stood sadly studying his shattered plane before Bob took him into the airport building to get his hand and arm bandaged. The ground crew fell silent as Gus made his way into the hangar with Bob at his side. They had all watched this crazy pilot holding a machine gun on the runway in full view of the approaching Zeros. Most didn't know if they should treat him as a hero or a fool.

'That was some show,' said an American pilot, grinning at Gus in admiration. 'What was the name again?'

'Winckel,' Gus said. 'Gus Winckel.'

'You are one crazy Dutchman, Gus Winckel.'

Gus flashed a pained smile at the American. 'I do get carried away at times.'

The pilot laughed and said, 'Sounds like an understatement.' He saluted and walked away, shaking his head.

A few hours later, another Lodestar found its way to Broome. Coming from Java, it had left Andir only a few hours after Gus had taken off. As the highest-ranking Dutch officer at the airport, Gus Winckel commandeered this aircraft, the only operational one left, to set up an evacuation scheme. He started flying wounded and stranded passengers to Port Hedland. The most seriously wounded were taken to hospital, while those with no or minor injuries could travel from there to Perth.

Roebuck Bay was a mess. The Japanese, assuming there were only military on board the flying boats, had managed to sink most of them. Many Dutch evacuees lost their lives in the flames that day. Some had sunk with their flying boats, trapped in the cabins, while others had been hit by bullets or simply drowned trying to reach the shore. The survivors now crowded together on Roebuck's jetty in search of a way out of Broome. Gus and his men flew as many of these stranded refugees to safety as they could.

Three days later, Gus flew a plane load of evacuees to Perth, leaving Charlie and Bob at Port Hedland. Not long before, Charlie's wife, Maria, and his eighteen-month-old son Johannes were reported missing. Mother and son had left on a DC-3 on 2 March and had been scheduled to arrive at Broome on the 3rd. The plane had never arrived.

'They might have seen there was something wrong and made a detour to another airport,' an airport official told Charlie when he asked if there was any word.

Gus had tried to reassure Charlie, but there was still no word on the missing aircraft. Charlie, understandably, wanted to stay in Port Hedland to await news, so Gus had told Bob to stay behind and keep an eye on him. Gus also ordered Bob to direct any incoming Dutch aircraft and their crews on to Archerfield in Brisbane, to await further orders.

Captain Sam de Mul greeted Gus when he landed in Perth, but the pleasantries lasted only a few minutes. To Gus's dismay and astonishment, he learnt that Sam had orders to send him back to Java. Immediately.

'Impossible!' Gus barked, 'Tell me they've made a mistake. You send me back now, you're signing my death certificate. I'll never make it back alive and you know it!'

Gus had been awake for more than 30 hours already, and all he wanted to do was sleep. 'I'll go tomorrow,' he suggested, 'after I've had a rest.'

Although he was eager to get his wife and son out of Java, he suspected he'd instead be sent out to pick up more officials. He knew the situation on Java would be almost hopeless by now, and that he'd need to be alert and awake to make it out alive. He needed sleep.

He held up his burnt arm. 'Find someone else,' he said.

'You have to do it,' Sam pressed. 'There's no one else with your abilities. There are some important people who have to get out of the place before it's too late. Sorry, Gus, orders from the military command.'

Gus gave him a look of contempt but Sam was unmoved. 'You know Java like the back of your hand, Gus.'

They all said Gus could fly through the Javanese mountains blindfolded. He'd been born and raised there, and no one could find their way in the dark like he could. Privately, Sam was against sending his best pilot out again, given the outcome was highly uncertain, but he could understand why his superiors had specifically asked for Winckel. Sam took off his cap, ran his hands through his hair and played his final trump card: 'Your wife and son will be waiting along with the officers in Java. If you go back you have permission to bring them back to Australia.'

Sam felt bad having to bribe a man he respected. He placed a hand on Gus's shoulder and watched as his pilot fought inwardly between logic and outrageous foolishness. His options were get his family to safety or die with them trying, or to stay in Australia and leave those he loved in the hands of the enemy. Tired as he was, the possibility of getting his wife and son out of Java was motivation enough to at least attempt going back. It was madness, but in the last few days the whole world seemed to have gone mad. He prepared to leave.

Reports of the enemy's advance on Bandung and the imminent capitulation of Batavia had reached Perth only that morning. Secretly, Sam de Mul gave his best pilot a five per cent chance of making it back safely. Gus's habit of flying beneath the clouds instead of above them, as others would to hide their aircraft from view, did not help his chances.

'I like to see the enemy before they see me,' was his explanation. He didn't want to be surprised by something he hadn't seen coming. They both realised that the slower Lodestar would be no match for the agile Zeros now ruling the heavens.

'Gus,' Sam said now, 'promise me you'll use the clouds for cover.'

Gus brushed Sam's hand from his shoulder and boarded the plane.

When he floated in from the skies, the crowd that had gathered on Boeabatoe Road let out a gasp. They had heard the sound of an engine just seconds before they saw the plane approaching, and wondered how the pilot had made it through the mountains in the dark. With trapped clouds obstructing any kind of view, finding your way through the massive mountain ridges without lights or a radio controller to guide you was nothing short of miraculous. There was still a radio controller doing his job at the airstrip though, and he skilfully guided the plane in. At the roadside, the soldiers sprang into action, lighting the hurricane lamps to turn the road into a runway. Just minutes later, the pilot expertly put his plane down.

Feeling rather elated at having achieved what some thought impossible, Gus walked across Boeabatoe Road, searching the crowd for his wife and son, picking up the pace when he spotted them standing among some soldiers. He knew he'd only done half the job; getting everyone back to safety would be a greater challenge. Standing to one side, a crowd waved and shouted at him, and for a moment Gus thought they'd come out to welcome him. But soon he saw their faces lit by the flickering storm lanterns and the dim moonlight, and realised they were grotesquely troubled. They had not come out to cheer him. They had come looking for a way out, eyeing him and his plane as only the desperately hopeless could. Their longing was almost palpable. A few men managed to break through but a group of soldiers pushed them back with their guns.

The crowd watched in anxious silence as passengers, packages and some kind of obscure cargo were all loaded onto the plane. When the aircraft doors closed, a distressed murmur rose from the people who realised they'd undoubtedly be left behind. They had been waiting for hours and now their last chance of escape was preparing for take-off without them. For a moment, it appeared the crowd would rush at the Lodestar, but the snapping sound of rifle safety catches being switched off was enough to stop the mob. Everyone knew the soldiers had orders to fire if need be. Engineers inspected the plane one more time before Gus climbed into the cockpit.

The sound of the motorbike approaching behind the crowd was drowned out by the Lodestar taking off. The plane's wheels lifted from the tarmac just as the bike slipped to an abrupt halt. Tom was almost launched from the back seat but regained his balance, jumped off and scrambled through the crowd, stopping at the edge of the road just in time to see the leaving plane gathering altitude. There was something vaguely familiar about the way the plane floated into the clouds without so much as a hiccup. Tom suspected the pilot was Gus Winckel and cursed himself. Had they arrived only fifteen minutes sooner, he might have got a passage out of this mess.

Tom held his breath as he watched the plane climb. The Japanese in Lembang must have heard it leaving. He could only hope that the enemy was engaged in other matters. He supposed his brother was on board and for a second had the childish urge to wave the departing plane goodbye. A few women started to weep as the aircraft slipped into the mountains like a shadow, disappearing from view.

When Norman Harris joined him on the edge of the asphalt, Tom could only shake his head in dismay. They'd have to find their own way out. The two men watched in silence, hoping the plane would make its way through the threatening mountain range safely. When the hum of its engines disappeared into the night, Tom turned to Norman. It was time to discuss escape tactics.

4 ESCAPE TO AUSTRALIA

After Gus flew off with his plane load of goods and passengers, Tom and Norman concluded that their only viable escape option was to return to Andir. Earlier that evening on Andir's runway, Tom had noticed that one Lockheed was still standing upright on its wheels. Its tail end was badly damaged, probably thanks to a run-in with the tractor operated by the zealous Max, but they might be able to repair it.

The airport was still eerily quiet when they arrived and the dispatch rider and Dutch pilot walked, almost on tiptoe, towards the mutilated planes. They both found it strange that the enemy had not yet taken over the airport buildings but they had no time to think too much about it. Getting out of there was a case of now or never. The Japanese were certainly on the airport's doorstep.

It had started to rain heavily, and as they approached the crouched Lockheeds, Tom's heart sank. Yes, one aircraft was still on its wheels, but the damage to its tail was much worse than he remembered. They were seriously running out of options, so he and Norman agreed to give it a try. They decided to remove the maimed tail from the standing Lockheed-12 and replace it with an undamaged one from another of the planes, but they'd need tools.

They hunted in the hangar without success, so they turned instead to searching the airport for Max. They finally found him lying under a desk in one of the buildings, catatonic. The room reeked of alcohol and the boy's snores were almost loud enough to pierce the walls. Max appeared to have lined up a row of whisky bottles on a shelf then shot them down one by one with the gun now lying on the table. They shook him several times but he didn't wake.

'This isn't going well,' Tom said as they stepped back out into the humid night. The rain at least had subsided for the moment.

Norman asked if Tom had any coins. All he got was a blank look. He explained that they could use them to unscrew the bolts. 'It will be a hell of a job but what other options do we have?'

Norman had grown up on a farm and was a handyman of sorts, good at fixing things. He thought replacing the tail end of a plane shouldn't be harder than repairing an old tractor, and he'd had a lot of experience at that.

The men rummaged in their pockets and set to work with a combination of Australian and Dutch coins. Examining the plane, they found out why it was still standing. Because the battery was missing, when the boy had switched the lever into the 'OP' position, the wheels had stayed in place due to lack of power.

Holding part of the tail while Tom loosened a screw, Norman appeared lost in thought. He still had an important note in his pocket he was supposed to deliver to his CO.

'When you ran into me I was just coming back from a visit to your Dutch General Ter Poorten. I was there to deliver a message from my commanding officer, Brigadier Blackburn.'

Arthur Blackburn, a Victoria Cross holder, had fought with the 10th Battalion at Gallipoli and was one of the first to land at Anzac Cove. He'd been driving his men on for the last three weeks. His reputation was legendary, even among the Dutch, and Tom whistled between his teeth. 'You're Blackforce?'

Norman nodded. He'd been dispatched to the brigade, he explained, when he returned from serving in the Middle East with an English regiment. Blackforce was composed of an assorted group of Australian and American troops. A machine-gun battalion, a pioneer battalion, a field company, members of the 131st US Field Artillery Regiment, 165 escapees from Singapore and a squadron of light tanks belonging to the Hussar regiment had formed the brigade. Like Norman, most of its 3000 men had just returned from the Middle East and were dispatched to Java to hold a solid defence line on the Tjiudjung and Tjianten rivers. Their orders were to protect Batavia and Bandung.

While the Japanese advanced, Norman had watched his CO's efforts turn from vigorous to fruitless, and had witnessed Batavia falling into enemy hands. As the situation became increasingly hopeless, the Dutch commanders, in an effort to prevent as many civilian casualties as possible by avoiding the Japanese bombing Bandung, had contemplated unconditional surrender. Arthur

Blackburn had sent his Don R to the commanding officer in Bandung, General Ter Poorten, the Commander-in-Chief of the Netherlands East Indies, to let him know that neither he nor General Sitwell, the commander of the British troops on Java, considered surrender an option. Blackburn acknowledged that he was duty bound to obey, should Ter Poorten order them to surrender, but he'd do so with reluctance.

General Ter Poorten had sent Norman on his way with a reply emphasising the order to surrender, but Norman had been unable to make it back through the enemy lines. When he set out for Batavia, the Japanese had already made it as far as Buitenzorg, and he was forced to turn back and head for Kalidjati. When he ran into Tom, he realised that the Japanese were everywhere. Norman feared that most of his company would be dead or captured by now, but he hoped some in his company might have escaped through the mountain range.

'You worried?' Tom asked, loosening another screw.

'Yes. It doesn't look very good for our lot.'

Tom wondered where his brother was. He hoped he was on the plane they'd seen leaving. The two men worked in silence, each contemplating the plight of the people they knew and loved. The rain had returned as drizzle, and in the dark they could see the mountains light up now and then. Mortars or lightning, who was to know?

They worked through the night and finally managed to join the undamaged tail end to the standing Lockheed. To keep the tail and the rear wheel straight they tied the two together with rope—it was all they had. When Norman filled the petrol tanks,

Tom realised they'd never be able to reach the Australian coast. The tanks would only give them four hours of flight time, but flying to Australia would take about seven or eight hours.

'Lots of spare petrol tanks on the airstrip,' Norman said. 'We could load two more tanks onto the fuselage and then lead a piece of hosing from there into the wing tank.'

Before Tom could answer, Norman climbed onto one of the collapsed Lockheeds and started to dismantle a wing tank. Adding two tanks would get them to Australia, but only just. As they fastened the tanks with bamboo and rope, they were faced with the problem of getting the petrol from the extra tank into the main one on the wing. Heading for one of the hangars, Norman said he'd be able to fix it.

When they were looking for tools, he'd come across a manual petrol pump and a long piece of hosing in a lonely corner in one of the hangars. He returned now with a look of triumph on his face. He bashed a hole in one of the Lockheed's windows, led the hose from the tank they had assembled on the fuselage to the one on the left wing, fastening it with good old duct tape. He twisted some copper wire around the end of the hose and pushed it into the opening of the tank, then stuck his fingers into the tank and opened the copper wings he'd made from the wire so the hose wouldn't come loose during the flight. The only disturbing thing, he told Tom, was that the lid on the wing tank couldn't be screwed back on and would have to stay open.

'Fuel might spill out and that would be a safety hazard, but then the whole project's pretty hazardous.'

Tom went back to the office to find Max. 'He might want to come with us,' he told Norman, who turned to the runway in the hope of repairing some of the damage. Using the tractor's front loader, he scooped up rubble and dropped it into the biggest holes. To flatten it he ran over the debris using the tractor tyres. Once finished, he inspected the runway. It would have to be enough. He'd done all he could.

Max was still lying under the desk but this time Tom managed to wake him. He was groggy, pale and complained of a head-ache, but seemed reasonably coherent. When Tom asked him to go with them the boy was adamant about staying: 'I was born and raised here and so was my father. We'll take our chances.'

The night and morning had disappeared as they worked on the aeroplane. Now, in the heat of the afternoon, Tom and Norman stood admiring their improvised handiwork.

'Good craftsmanship,' Tom gloated.

'Yes, but will it work?' Norman wondered aloud.

'Only one way to find out,' Tom said, climbing into the cockpit.

So that afternoon, while a crowd waited at Boeabatoe Road, hoping that through some miracle another plane would emerge from the skies to take them from Java, a jerry-built Lockheed-12 took off from Andir Airport just a few miles away. Tom twisted and dodged his plane around the worst of the potholes on the runway, until finally, hitting the edge of one of the larger craters, the Lockheed jumped clear, catapulting itself into the air.

They were off! As they gained altitude, Tom could almost smell freedom. He panicked for a moment when the lever that was supposed to retract the wheels failed. They were stuck, but under the circumstances, 'wheels out' wasn't a big issue. It was almost suicide to leave in daylight, but Tom had not wanted to wait until nightfall. He took a chance on the Japanese probably being too busy with matters on the ground to take heed of one solitary plane.

The air was muggy and humid, but although the sky was grey, it had stopped raining. The low clouds would hide them from the enemy but they also hid the mountains, and as Tom gathered altitude, he silently prayed they wouldn't run into the side of one. Both he and Norman held their breath, and neither spoke as their plane was gradually devoured by misty clouds.

Half an hour later, without a shot having been fired at them, they flew clear of the mountains. The veiled sky opened up above the sea, the sun blazing away the haze. Below them, the Indian Ocean twinkled in the sunlight like a sea of silver coins. The joyous sight did nothing to ease their anxiety. Somewhere down below them, Rear Admiral Chuichi Nagumo's fleet, equipped with aircraft carriers, was cruising that same sea. Nagumo was commander-in-chief of the First Air Fleet, Japan's main aircraft carrier force. Tom had heard that Nagumo was a strong advocate of combining sea and air power. If he spotted the plane, he'd send his fighter aircraft to destroy them. Their only reassurance was their knowledge that the Japs were not equipped with radar on their ships.

Strangely, the sky was empty and Tom prayed it would stay that way. After take-off he'd realised, a bit too late, that they hadn't brought a weapon along for the ride; there was no machine-gun to protect them if they ran into a Zero. So far, however, no enemy planes had attacked them and all around the view was picture-perfect. Small islands lazed in the sun and white surf nipped at their coasts, with dark blue sea and light blue skies as a backdrop. They knew it was all an illusion—there was a war going on out there in paradise. Tom flew on, keeping a look out for enemy aircraft or ships.

'Ay, Norman, which way to Australia?' Tom asked after they'd been in the air for a few hours.

'Ah, that way,' Norman replied, pointing south. 'Don't you have any coordinates?'

Rummaging in one of the cabinets, Tom extracted a school atlas from it, holding it up for Norman to see. 'This and you is all we have.'

Seven hours later, they'd still not encountered any trouble, and they started to relax as the sun nestled into the sea. There was also still no sign of land apart from small islands, and Tom began to wonder if they'd missed a mark and maybe gone off course. Had they drifted too far west or too far east? He had no idea. He looked to Norman for answers but the Australian only shrugged. Their petrol was beginning to run low and they couldn't afford to miss the Australian coastline. And then Tom noticed a line of foaming white surf below them, lit by a full moon. They had reached land. Flying over they saw nothing that indicated a town. In fact, they saw very little. Mostly it was pitch black.

That didn't mean they weren't close to a town, Norman said. He thought there must be a blackout situation. 'We must be near Broome or Port Hedland by now.'

They guessed their fuel must be almost non-existent. Tom dropped altitude, still steering south and further inland, peering anxiously into the dark for a strip of land or some kind of runway.

When the aircraft started to sputter, Norman hid his head in his hands. 'You're not going to tell me that after all we've been through I'm now going to end my life in a plane crash on home ground.'

'Not if I can help it.' Tom had been trained to land an aircraft 'dead stick'—without motor power—if he could find anything remotely flat to land on, even without fuel. At that moment a light from a building down below caught Tom's attention just as the plane's motor shut down completely. It was evident that he had now run out of options. It would have to do, he thought as he lost altitude. He pushed the lever that operated the aircraft wheels but they were still stuck in the down position. That wasn't good. A belly landing would definitely enhance their chances of surviving a crash on uneven ground, but they'd just have to take their chances.

'Here goes,' he said as Norman braced himself for impact. Watching the shrub pass in a ridiculous blur, Norman felt certain he'd die and muttered a prayer under his breath. They hit the ground hard, the engines roared and sputtered, and the wheels bounced and jolted over the rough terrain. It made their potholed take-off in Bandung seem quite a relaxed jaunt. On the plus side, their fuel tanks were empty, so if they crashed the plane would be unlikely to catch fire. It was a far-from-reassuring notion, though. They'd die regardless.

When the left wheel hit some kind of boulder, the plane tilted to the right, burrowing its wing into the ground. The right wing tore free from the body of the plane as the Lockheed overturned and skittled through the scrub for what seemed like an eternity. Finally, the plane came to a violent standstill and for a while they could hear nothing but the sound of its wheels spinning vigorously in the hushed night.

Norman wriggled out of one of the shattered windows, followed by Tom, who had a gash on his forehead and some shards of broken glass stuck to his fingers. Norman shook his groggy head to try to clear his vision, and for a silly moment he thought it was snowing. Noticing the blood, thick as oil, running down Tom's face, he asked if he was all right.

'My face and hands have seen better days. Other than that I'd say I actually feel better than I have for quite a while.'

'What do we do now?' Norman wondered aloud. 'Exchange relieved hugs?'

The answer came from the shadows. 'Where the hell did you two come from?' The voice was rough, but unmistakably female.

The figure that emerged from the darkness looked like it had just stepped out of a cheap American cowboy film. Dressed in trousers and a shirt, a hat perched on her head and a pistol in her hand, the woman could easily have been mistaken for a man. She stood there, pointing a gun at them with one hand and another gun hanging at her hip. It was all too much, Norman thought—their escape, the flight, the crash and now being held at gunpoint by flamin' Annie Oakley!

The two men fell to their knees in a fit of laughter. The sound tore through the star-sprinkled Australian night.

5 STAPLETON STATION, NT

Her name was Winnie Sargent; she packed two loaded guns and could ride a horse as well as any man. Her father was English-born Harry Sargent, who after travelling through North America and Canada had finally brought his family to Australia to settle at Stapleton Station, 70 miles north of Darwin. Over the years his wife, their six boys and seven of their eight girls had gradually drifted away until only Winnie and Harry himself remained to run the 786,000-acre cattle station.

In the quiet evening, father and daughter had heard the sound of an aircraft approaching. It wasn't a very unusual sound these days, with Allied aircraft heading for the Pacific on a daily basis, but after the first raids on Darwin and Broome just weeks earlier, Winnie and Harry had become more alert. One evening the week before, Winnie and their Aboriginal station hands had raced on horseback to wheel in cattle that had become frightened by the flaming trail of a Japanese bomber exploding close by in the pandanus swamp. Together, they had just succeeded in getting the mob of about 500 beasts to turn. The reality of war had landed on Stapleton Station's doorstep that night.

Just now, as the labouring roar of the aircraft engine came closer, Harry and Winnie had tensely sipped their hot tea and looked quietly up at the ceiling. The sound was fierce and approaching very fast. Harry spilt his tea when the deafening noise of a dangerously low-flying aircraft made its way over their homestead. Winnie jumped up and ran out onto the verandah, buckling on her guns. The Sargents had built their house on a hill, and in the moonlit evening she could just make out the aircraft racing across the scrub, its wheels bouncing in a desperate, helpless dance over bushes and dirt mounds.

Harry came out with a shotgun. 'Is it a Jap?'

Winnie shrugged. She peered into the darkness with nothing but the moon lighting the plane's path as it overturned in a field, breaking off a wing when it hit a boulder. Skittering along on its back, it eventually came to a standstill. As she raced to the stables, the station hands were scrambling out of their cabins. She led her horse out of the barn, then rode bareback in the direction of the downed aircraft, the alarmed station hands running down the slope in her wake.

She approached cautiously, unsure if the aircraft was Japanese. She knew what markings to look for and by now could recognise a Japanese Zero from a distance, but it had been too dark and it had all happened too fast. The broken-off wing lay propped up against the boulder, but there was no Rising Sun on it, so it must be Allied. She acknowledged the possibility that the pilots were badly hurt or dead, and braced herself for what she might find.

When Tom and Norman crept from the plane reasonably unharmed, she stared at them in surprise, her gun wavering in her hand. Their uncontrollable laughter annoyed her and she tersely inquired what they found so amusing. A teary Norman Harris told her what they had been through. He wiped his tears away and made sure she understood that they were certainly not laughing at her—her gun was still pointing in his direction. The station hands stood grouped together, alert and vigilant, ready to take action if need be.

Winnie took Tom and Norman back to the homestead, relieved one of them was an Australian. After tending to Tom's cuts she gave them tea and damper. They told Harry the story of how they had managed to escape Java together, but as the night wore on exhaustion took the place of adrenaline. Winnie offered the two fatigued men a bed for the night. They slept for almost fifteen hours.

Early the following afternoon, they emerged into the Stapleton dining room dressed in Harry's clothes, which Winnie had left for them when she took their uniforms to wash. It was a pleasant room, dominated by a sideboard decorated with specimens of gold, antimony, silver and copper. A set of buffalo horns adorned the space on the wall above it. A window looked out onto a grove of vivid green mango trees and pandanus palms gently swaying in the breeze.

Now Winnie came in with freshly made bread and butter and steaming hot tea. Harry walked in behind her, clearly ready for a chat.

'Thought you'd be hungry,' Winnie said, watching the men grope at the food on the plate almost before it touched the table.

They could see now that Winnie Sargent was about 40 years old. Besides being one of the best shooters and riders in the Territory, she also liked to read. She was not a beautiful woman; her features were sharp and her body stout and sturdy. Her best asset was undoubtedly her hair, now neatly tied back in a ponytail, which was as black as the fire irons. As her brothers and sisters left Stapleton one by one, Winnie had stayed, working with her father for years.

Harry was 70, white-haired, less sturdy than his daughter, but still fit enough to help out at the station. The two dug for minerals; split and trimmed wood; and mustered, killed and branded cattle. The station's main revenue was the cattle, but father and daughter had also searched the property for gold and silver.

'We even dug for gold sixteen feet down by the kitchen door,' Winnie told the men as they continued to wolf down the food. 'Not much gold around but we did find tin, silver, uranium and wolfram about,' she said, pointing to the specimens on the cabinet.

For a long time Winnie and Harry had not noticed much of the war, and even after the fall of Pearl Harbor life on the station continued to run along its usual course. 'We'd hear planes coming over every now and then. Americans with their

Kittyhawks patrolling the skies and sometimes, when we were out mustering, we'd see a line of tanks and army vehicles passing in the distance. When people from town came to visit or buy meat, we heard rumours about the Japs, how steadily they were advancing. We didn't really think they'd attack Australia . . . until they did.'

The Japanese had first come to Darwin on a cloudless day in the early morning hours only three weeks ago. A couple of false alarms in the days before had resulted in the evacuation of most of the women and children living in Darwin. They were transported to safer places down south. The day the Japanese came, the Royal Australian Air Force had no fighters based at Darwin. Only half an hour before the attack, the American Kittyhawks had returned from a mission in Timor and were parked on the runway with almost empty petrol tanks. The defence of Darwin in case of an air attack relied on ack-ack installations and the anti-aircraft guns on ships in Darwin's port.

Harry told them that Sergeant William McDonald had sounded the first alarm that morning, phoning a staff officer from his headquarters just north of the city.

'We've got Japanese planes,' he told the officer.

The officer said, 'Don't play games, Mac. How do you know they're Japanese?'

'They've got bloody red balls on 'em,' McDonald had replied.

'Well,' Harry said, 'just moments later they certainly identified themselves. And there were plenty of them against an almost defenceless target. It was like using a sledgehammer to crack an egg.'

Harry couldn't hide his disgust. 'In the nation's most extreme moment of danger there's no air defence from Broome to Townsville and every plane worth flying is no more than a heap of faulty metal.'

Harry was probably exaggerating, Norman thought. Most likely everyone, including the Americans, had been caught off guard, not really expecting an attack from the enemy on the Australian mainland. Norman and Tom were both shocked to hear that the Japanese were advancing so steadily; they had thought the enemy was yet to reach Australia. It now seemed they were much stronger than anyone had imagined.

'They hit Broome last week,' Harry said. 'They diverted some planes coming from the Pacific to Broome after Darwin was hit. Sitting ducks, they were. On the bay and at the airport. They say a lot of your Dutchies died in the raid.'

Tom realised that some of his unit, even his brother, might have been in Broome. Harry thought the war was being lost partly because of the Allies' weak air defence; Tom agreed and, as he wolfed down his food, he resolved to get back to his unit as soon as possible. They were all damn good pilots.

Everyone in Darwin—in the whole country for that matter— had been shocked by the ferocity of the Japanese attack on the town. 'Any kind of arrogant notion we had that this wouldn't happen, couldn't happen to us, was pretty well shattered after that,' Winnie said.

Just a couple of days after the attacks on Darwin and Broome, she told them, a Japanese plane had been chased over their house by a Kittyhawk before crashing in the nearby paperbark wetland.

Harry had ridden out there with a rifle, looking for the downed plane. He finally found it with a dead body inside—the pilot had been shot through the heart. He managed to salvage two bags full of soaked maps and papers, and drove into Darwin the next day to hand them over to Allied intelligence. He knew then that it wasn't over yet, and that the Japanese had much more in store for them.

Citizens and even soldiers panicked after the first attack on Darwin, fleeing into the outback. Some of them eventually ended up at Stapleton, where Winnie gave them a meal and sent them on their way. They left, but not before warning father and daughter that the sensible thing for them to do was to leave as well.

Harry laughed: 'We couldn't run from the Japs if we tried. Our feet are too firmly stuck in Stapleton territory.'

They'd never be able to uproot themselves, he said, so they watched as the fleeing guests turned to wisps between the anthills, and then they went back to work.

Winnie had started wearing her pistols after hearing stories about looting from the people passing through. Most people just wanted a meal, but some tried to steal the Stapleton horses and kill their cattle, so she armed herself. For the past three weeks, she'd slept with her clothes on, wearing her guns, listening for the sound of any disturbance among the animals.

'It was all just beginning to calm down a bit when you blokes suddenly fell from the sky.'

The food by now had disappeared and Tom and Norman sat sipping the last of the hot tea. Tom's need to find his unit was more urgent than ever. He expected they'd be equipped with decent planes by now—they'd all left in a state of euphoria at the prospect of fighting the enemy with wonderful new aircraft. It was the dream of every pilot in his squadron to fly a Mitchell bomber. Tom thought Darwin would probably have some kind of military authority in place, and there would certainly be armed forces there. Winnie and Harry were busy, but Winnie promised to drive them into Darwin the following day. The afternoon was already almost gone, so reporting to the military would have to wait until then.

While the Sargents rode out on their horses, Tom and Norman roamed the station. It was Tom's first encounter with the Australian landscape. It was a lot dustier and drier than Java, but he found its unique ruggedness strange and fascinatingly beautiful.

Stapleton stood on a slope, set some seven miles back from the road. In the distance lay a belt of dusty pandanus palms and flat plains that were home to thousands of termite colonies, which had dotted the flats with their 'cathedrals', creating miniature cities on the plains. Tom couldn't take his eyes from the mounds sticking up from the dry grass and turkey bush. Just below Stapleton's brown slope, a spring bubbled and water trickled into a creek full of bamboo. Tom sniffed the air and noticed it was scented with tropical henna and Japanese honeysuckle. Except for their injured and disfigured aircraft, lying in the paddock like an enormous overturned tortoise, the tranquil surroundings gave no hint of a war being in progress.

Wandering around the scattered cabins, they found their uniforms fluttering in the breeze on a clothesline between two paperbarks.

'Shabby trees, eh?' Tom said, pointing to the bark falling away from the trunks in ribbons.

'Australian, mate. You'll get used to them.'

A young Aboriginal girl emerged from behind a large sheet, surprising them. Tom stood mesmerised for a moment. Sunrays formed a halo behind her as the late-afternoon sun made its slow descent towards the horizon. With the setting sun in his eyes, Tom could not really see what the girl looked like, but the breeze pressed her dress tight around her stunning body. When he walked up to her, she flashed a shy smile at him and then almost instantly looked away to pick up another sheet, hiding herself behind it as she pegged it to the line.

Tom ducked around the sheet to take a closer look. The girl jumped back, giving him a frightened frown. 'Whoa,' he said putting up his hands, letting her know that he meant no harm. Her frown turned to a hesitant smile.

The girl was beautiful. Her skin was dark and shiny, and her dress playfully fluttered around her smooth curves. Her big round eyes glittered like wet basalt in the midday sun but their shape also betrayed some traces of oriental blood in her heritage. Tom asked if she'd washed their uniforms and she shyly nodded assent, looking away, focusing on some point in the distance.

'They be dry later. I'll bring 'em,' she said, still staring into the distance.

Tom's eyes involuntarily followed the girl's gaze to the spot she appeared to find so interesting. His eyes found nothing but small bushes and trees; as he shifted them back to the girl, their eyes locked for a moment. Quickly averting her gaze, she picked up her washing basket and hurried off, disappearing into the house through the back door. In spite of her dark skin, Tom could have sworn he saw her blush.

That evening at dinner, Tom asked Winnie about the girl at the clothesline.

'Ah, that'd be Grace,' she said with a smile. 'Beautiful, isn't she?'

Grace had come from the Beagle Bay mission up near Broome. Made a ward of the state when she was twelve, she'd been taken away from her parents. Her brother, George, worked at Stapleton as a station hand and had asked Winnie to take his younger sister in as a housemaid. The girl was miserable at the mission and she feared they might eventually send her to a family in Sydney or Melbourne. She didn't want to be sent to the city, George told them; he'd almost begged them to take her.

Winnie had gone to the mission with George and had quite easily gained custody of the fourteen-year-old child. That was five years ago. Grace had been with them ever since.

'Grace is a bit shy, but a pleasant girl and a hard worker,' Harry said. 'Does all sorts of odd jobs around the house.'

Winnie asked whether Norman or Tom had wives or girl-friends. Norman shook his head. Tom hesitated before answering, thinking of Sana, but she was far away and he'd only been seeing her for a month at most. *Who knows, I might never see her again*, he thought, so he shook his head.

When the men retired to their bedroom that night, they found their uniforms on their beds, clean, folded and ironed. Neatly draped on top of Tom's uniform was Colette's pearl necklace. In all the excitement, he'd forgotten about it; seeing it kindled his need to see his brother and get back to his unit. That night he fell asleep dreaming of aeroplanes, haloes and pearls.

As Tom slipped into his clean uniform the next morning, something fell from his shirt as he unfolded it—wattle blossom. He picked it up from the floor, inhaled its soft peppermint fragrance and smiled as he tucked the wattle into his shirt pocket and whispered her name. *Grace.*

6 THE BOMBING OF DARWIN

Winnie drove them to Darwin the next day. After a two-hour drive, they entered what had once been a tropical paradise of sorts. Winnie audibly sucked in her breath. She hadn't been to Darwin since the first attack on 19 February; the town she'd known was no more than a memory. Houses looked like they had been trodden on by some angry god, and in some instances the only thing left was a gaping crater. The streets were practically deserted and disconcertingly hushed. A young man came around a corner, hurriedly making his way up the street. There was no one else about, so they stopped to ask him directions. He told them he'd be glad to help if they'd give him a ride.

He introduced himself as John Bowden and said he was the telegraph operator in the new makeshift post office. The original post office, telegraph office and the postmaster's residence had suffered a direct hit during the raid three weeks earlier, he said, and were in ruins.

'All the staff at the post office were killed, including the postmaster and his family. The police barracks were struck and the police station almost destroyed. They had to dig through the rubble to find Constable McNab. He's being treated at the hospital.' The Australian General Hospital at Berrimah was still full of the wounded, John said, and the staff were doing what they could under the circumstances, but the wounds were serious and many people needed treatment.

Driving through the town, they saw numerous buildings that had either collapsed or were badly damaged. Streets where Chinese, Malays and Europeans normally bustled about were silent now. According to John, the city was in no way safe and other attacks would almost certainly follow. Those able to leave had gone and only soldiers had stayed to fight off the enemy.

'Some people still haven't been able to get out—they're staying in tents on the hospital grounds. Everyone who could walk headed for the bush after the attack, and the three of you should get out of here as soon as you can,' he advised them.

Darwin had been attacked twice by the Japanese on 19 February: once just before ten o'clock and again at midday. There had also been a couple of raids since.

'I think they'll be coming back,' John said. 'There are still naval ships and army planes coming into Darwin. As long as they think it will be worth their while, they'll keep coming.'

The harbour had suffered a terrible blow and it was rumoured that 21 ships were either sunk or badly damaged; it was still unknown how many sailors had lost their lives. Twenty-two wharfies had been killed.

'A friend of mine, Toby Giles, and his brother Cole were loading a ship when the raid started. Toby can only remember running along the wharf after spotting the planes when suddenly something blew him into the water. He's in hospital; lost his leg ... they never found a trace of Cole. Toby reckons a bomb must have landed almost on top of them.'

Harry had heard from the people fleeing Darwin that there hadn't been enough planes or artillery to defend the city. But John didn't think anything could have saved them that day. Anti-aircraft batteries stationed at Darwin Oval, Fannie Bay and other strategic locations around the town had done what they could, and ack-ack batteries had tried to defend the harbour. There hadn't been enough time to launch an air attack and only a few aircraft had been able to take off. The incoming enemy aircraft were mistaken for American Kittyhawks, which resulted in additional confusion.

'So when the Japs flew in, no one took much notice. We just thought it was more Yanks coming.' He didn't know if the defenders had managed to bring down any of the enemy aircraft: 'Some say one plane was shot down, but more optimistic rumours say there were four in all.'

Now he pointed to a building a little way up the road and told them they should be able to find someone with military authority there. Scattered army men were busy cleaning up the rubble on nearby properties. The temporary telegraph office was also up the road; John thanked them and warned them to take care, then hurried off. He entered a small building with

'Telegraph Station' scrawled across a wooden panel that appeared to have been hurriedly nailed above the front door.

Winnie dropped Tom and Norman off at the army building and they thanked her and waved as she drove off. She honked the horn, and was still waving through the window when she rattled around the corner.

Commander Andrew David Swan was a Scotsman—a fact immediately obvious from his soft brogue. He'd served in the British Army in India and on the Western Front, reaching the rank of sergeant. After completing his pilot training in Melbourne, he'd been sent to Darwin in 1941 as a senior administrator, then quickly worked his way up to commander in charge of the RAAF in Darwin.

After the first Japanese attack, Group Captain Sturt Griffith told Swan it might be wise to send all personnel inland as a precautionary safety measure. The town's essential services, water and electricity, had been badly damaged or destroyed by the attack, so Swan's message was passed on by word of mouth. Unfortunately, in the end, it became a Chinese whisper; many men misinterpreted the order as an instruction to abandon positions and leave town. Harry Sargent, who had found military men on his property just after the attack, had told Tom and Norman that all the troops had run off in a cowardly fashion.

'That was my fault and a misunderstanding, I'm afraid,' Swan told Tom and Norman.

Swan was not as surprised to see the two men at his headquarters that morning as they'd thought he might. In the past few weeks, quite a few stray soldiers had come in—not only Australians, but also a couple of Americans, Dutch and Englishmen. Some had managed to escape from the Dutch East Indies, Borneo or Sumatra, while others, separated from their units, had come to Swan seeking help. A couple of Dutch had even landed their planes nearby. Coming from the Dutch East Indies without any coordinates to rely on, they'd missed their designated landing spot, Broome, and, after running out of fuel, had been forced to ditch their planes on any flat piece of land they could find.

Swan listened intently as the two men told him their story. 'Well, they can't accuse the two of you of lacking imagination or guts,' he said.

He made a few phone calls, inquiring about Tom's unit and the possibility of using Norman as a dispatch rider, but useful information was scarce. 'These are trying times,' he said. 'It seems most of your lot are still in Brisbane,' he told Tom, 'so I'd recommend you transferring to Archerfield. You might as well go with him,' he advised Norman. 'There's not much you can do here, and Archerfield is a RAAF base. Maybe you can be useful up there.'

They thanked him and half an hour later were driven to the airport. From there a military plane, transporting people and goods, flew them to Archerfield.

Archerfield Air Base, to the south of Brisbane, was just a decade old. It had served as the city's main airport, but had then been upgraded as a military base for the RAAF at the beginning of the war. A new administration block with a control tower and hangars was built to accommodate the RAAF. Huts intended for army staff and pilots stood along the southern boundary.

Pilots and crews, optimistic and in good spirits, bustled by as Norman and Tom stood on the tarmac trying to get their bearings. Darwin had been a tragedy, but here at Archerfield the war seemed far away. Everything looked so neat and clean and efficient. Making their way across the runway to the administration block, the two men wondered if people here had any notion of the events that had taken place and were still unravelling up north.

A dark-haired man in a Dutch pilot's uniform appeared from behind a plane. Shading his eyes with his hands, he peered intently at the two. He let his arm slowly fall back to his side, then suddenly let out a shout and came running towards them.

'I knew you'd turn up sometime,' the man said in Dutch, slapping his brother on the back and hugging him tightly.

'You've shrunk,' Tom said to his smaller twin.

'Yes, well, I can shrink if I want. I'm older than you so I don't need to compensate.'

The two brothers were strikingly different in appearance. Tall, incredibly blond, with blue piercing eyes and handsome sharp features, Tom was the epitome of a northern European man. Bob, on the other hand, almost five inches shorter than his twin, was dark-haired and dark-eyed with a solid build. They were a quirk of nature—one of them cheeky with a hint of bravado, the other thoughtful and gentle. When he heard that this was the twin brother of which he'd heard so much, Norman was nonplussed. He could only stare at them in disbelief.

After shaking Bob's hand, Norman hurried off to report to the RAAF commanders at the base. Meanwhile, Tom and Bob headed to the Dutch quarters, where Gus Winckel and Charlie van Tuyn came out to greet him. There were backslaps all around as more men spilled out of their huts, crowding around him.

'It was you flying out of Bandung the other day, wasn't it?'

Gus nodded, surprised to hear that Tom had arrived at Boeabatoe Road just five minutes too late. It hadn't been an easy flight back; with his family and Major General Van Oyen on board, the load had been a very precious one. If General Ter Poorten was taken prisoner by the Japanese, Van Oyen would replace him as commander of the Dutch forces. He'd got them all safely back to Perth, where the general and his staff had disembarked without even taking the time to thank him. Gus had been furious.

'Ungrateful bastards,' he spat. He'd been almost tempted to throw them back inside, fly out to sea and drop them there. They laughed. All except Charlie, who looked absent-minded and troubled; he quickly excused himself.

'Don't mind Charlie—he's in a bad way.'

Bob told Tom what he'd witnessed in Broome, particularly at Roebuck Bay and the airport. He still experienced anguish at the memory of the dead people he'd seen—those unsuspecting refugees waiting on the flying boats, thinking they'd made it to safety but instead dying in a foreign bay.

'And then we received word about Charlie's wife and son,' Bob said.

Charlie knew that Maria van Tuyn and her baby son Johannes had left Java on the evening of 2 March on a DC-3 flown by Iwan Smirnoff, a Russian pilot who had escaped to the Netherlands after the Russian Revolution in 1917. Smirnoff had quite a reputation. Over the years he'd become one of KLM's leading pilots and set the record for flying one of the longest air routes in the world in just four days. On the evening of 2 March, Smirnoff's flight was a civilian one and he was authorised to take non-military along. Because the wife of one of the crew members had not come aboard, Maria and her baby, who were waiting, were given the spare seat so she could be reunited with her husband in Australia. Late that evening, Smirnoff took off, reaching the northern Australian coast just after the raid on Broome.

By then the Zeros had finished their attack and were heading west. They ran into Smirnoff's plane and fired at it, forcing the pilot to land on the beach at Carnot Bay, north of Broome, running it into the water to douse the flames. It was at this point that the plane had been reported missing, and Charlie and Bob had waited at Port Hedland, hoping for word. Rumours arose that a plane had been spotted on a beach near Beagle Bay mission and that there were survivors.

An Aboriginal man had spotted the downed plane and told the German missionary at Beagle Bay. The search party found Smirnoff alive on the beach with some of his surviving passengers and crew. Bob and Charlie received orders to pick up the DC-3 survivors, who had been transported to Broome, and take them to the hospital in Port Hedland. In Broome, Charlie learnt that Maria and Johannes had not survived the attack.

'He was heartbroken,' Bob told Tom, 'and now he just mopes around the base and can't really focus on anything.'

Tom had met Maria once on Java, just before she gave birth to Johannes. She'd looked so young and so very lively; it was hard to believe she was dead.

The story of the downed DC-3 took an unexpected turn. It seemed Smirnoff had been given a package just before take-off, with instructions to hand it to an official of the Commonwealth Bank in Sydney. For the Lodestar pilots it was not unusual to be transporting valuables—just before the Germans invaded the Netherlands, the Dutch Government had sent a fair share of its valuables to the Dutch East Indies, thinking they'd be safe there until the war ended. With the Japanese advancing fast, they did not want all their assets disappearing into enemy hands, so pilots travelling to Australia were often asked to transport gold, diamonds and other valuables. Smirnoff, however, had lost the package he'd been carrying.

Known as one of the ablest and most trustworthy pilots in the fleet, he'd been given a very valuable consignment of diamonds. During the Japanese attack, he was shot in the arms and legs, at least two members of his crew died, and a woman and child were seriously injured. With all this on his mind, Smirnoff simply forgot about the package.

Sometime later, he sent a man out into the water to retrieve it from the plane. He found the package, but then lost his balance in the waves, dropped it and had been unable to find it again. An Australian warrant officer by the name of Clinch, assigned to locate the missing diamonds, had at one stage suspected

Smirnoff of embezzling them. Smirnoff had reacted furiously to this accusation, and especially to the fact that everyone seemed more concerned about lost diamonds than lost lives.

On the flight to Port Hedland, Smirnoff had taken Charlie aside to tell him what had happened to his wife and child. Maria and Johannes had been shot during the attack and had died on the beach as a result.

'It gave him some comfort to hear first-hand what had happened to them,' Bob told Tom.

They sat in silence for a while and then Tom remembered the pearl necklace. He dug into his pocket and lifted it out, unable to stop a smile spreading across his face.

'Where did you get that?' Bob asked.

'From Farah. She said that Colette hadn't had time to take it when she left.'

'Left? Where did she go?'

'I thought she left with you . . .'

Tom's smile froze.

7 ARCHERFIELD AIR BASE, BRISBANE

Tom had convinced himself that Colette had been able to get off the island—that his brother had somehow managed to rescue her. Now he blamed himself for not probing Farah more precisely about Colette's whereabouts. Bob, realising his fiancée was probably still on Java, banged his head against a tent pole in anguish. Tom hung his head, ashamed for not having done more.

'It's not your fault,' Bob said, letting the pearls slip between his fingers like a rosary.

Tom thought they might still have got out somehow. 'We can ask around.' He knew that any pilot evacuating her would remember her—Colette made a stunning first impression.

Bob had the same thought, but the dismal look on his face turned into a worried frown. *What good is beauty in wartime?* he wondered. His fiancée's attractiveness might turn out to be a danger rather than an asset.

The next morning Tom presented himself at rollcall, his uniform clean and tidy thanks to Grace. His fiercely polished boots gave the impression they'd been dipped in oil. His heroic escape had been the talk of the evening and he felt every bit the part. He'd done his utmost that morning to look his best—not that it would do anything to impress his commanding officer. Willem Frans Boot all but hated Tom Derks. Boot had been an instructor at the Glenn Martin flying school at Malang on Java, and in the past Tom had frequently managed to suffer the wrath of his tutor. He was not the only one.

After fleeing to Australia, the men discovered that their dreaded instructor Boot had become their squadron leader. It was no secret that most of the men didn't like him. Some had even quietly wished he wouldn't make it out of Java. Although they acknowledged his skill as a pilot, they were very sceptical when it came to his abilities as a leader. The man was simply not a sociable kind of person, and he constantly misread the men's attitude towards him. He was aware, though, that his popularity among his men had hit rock bottom a long time ago.

He was insensitive to his fliers' needs and their anxieties regarding their families stranded in the Indies—he was unmarried himself, but that was no excuse. He appeared to have no idea how to implement orders and motivate his men. As a purist, he felt no need to 'spoil' his troops, so he got them out of bed in the early hours of the morning, instigating a rigid regimen of long hikes and physical training. His command in Melbourne had offered to board his men at Lennon's Hotel in Brisbane, but Boot refused, saying his men could live in tents. They were becoming ever more insubordinate as a result.

It was no secret that Boot disliked the brash blond half of the Derks twins and preferred the easier-going, darker-haired brother. Tom had promised himself and Bob he wouldn't be cheeky to the captain, and that he would not only look his best but also act accordingly. As Tom stood there at attention, though, Boot's haughty attitude immediately rubbed him up the wrong way.

'Well, I see that Tom Derks has joined us this morning, after tumbling from the skies,' the captain said, eyeing Tom with some disdain. He commented on the remarkable recovery Tom had made from his 'illness', adding that he hoped his pilot was feeling much better.

'Much better, sir!' Tom answered brightly. 'Although the doctor did mention that I was to take it easy for a while.' Which wasn't exactly a lie.

Boot, recognising Tom's reputation as a womaniser, inquired whether this doctor might be female.

Tom, hardly able to suppress his amusement, replied that the doctor had been 'very much a man', but the pilot's cockiness did not go unnoticed.

'Are you smirking, Lieutenant?'

Even though he knew he was making a grave mistake, Tom explained that what the commander was mistaking for a smirk was actually 'the unfortunate shape' of his face. Even Charlie van Tuyn could not suppress a smile, and most of the men sniggered. But Bob closed his eyes, waiting for the commander's wrath to descend on them all, mumbling 'idiot' between clenched teeth.

'Careful, Lieutenant, careful . . .' Boot warned, but this time he appeared willing to let it go. Realising that inflicting disciplinary measures on a man who had made a heroic escape from the Japanese wouldn't be a good idea, he did nonetheless make it very clear that Tom could expect his full attention in the weeks to come.

Being forced into inactivity while they waited at Archerfield these past weeks had destroyed the spirits of the Dutch. Their attitude towards their commander had turned from dislike to contempt, and in turn the commander's reaction to them had become hard and merciless. Most of them had spent time in detention, and they were often disciplined collectively for the misconduct of one. A large number of pilots and crew members had been unable to get their wives and children out of the Dutch East Indies; the dreadful realisation that their families would now be at the mercy of the Japanese fuelled the men's anger and frustration. The lack of equipment forced the men to lead a passive existence at the air base, and gave them time to contemplate the fate of their loved ones. They were on the verge of mutiny. The highest-ranked officer at the airfield, Major General Van Oyen, looked on with some concern as his men gradually started to spin out of control. Rebelliousness and excessive drinking began to occur more frequently.

Pilot Wil Burck more than once voiced his anger at not being permitted to fly back to Java for his wife and three small children. The only thing he'd been able to take with him when he left the island was his trumpet. Sitting outside his barrack in the evenings, he'd play melancholy tunes. He'd become especially angry when high-ranked officers greeted their families at the air base. After the surrender of Java, it dawned on most of them that it was too late to save anyone, but they still wanted to fly back. If they could only get permission, they could at least try to save someone or something. They were willing to die trying.

One morning Burck, devastated and furious, shouted that he was planning to hijack an aircraft. To underline his determination, he picked up his gun, saying he'd shoot his way to an aeroplane if need be. The men managed to take his gun away from him and he backed down, but everyone knew his anger had not abated. They couldn't blame him—most of them felt the same. Even Bob, normally a very reasonable and level-headed man, moped about the barracks and dreamt of ways to get back to Java.

To make things worse, the promised aircraft still hadn't arrived—no B-25s had been handed over and their superiors had no idea when they'd be delivered. By now, many combat planes—most of them P-40 Kittyhawk fighter planes—were landing at Archerfield, flown or shipped in from America. The Dutch crews were irritated because the Kittyhawks were standing idle on the airstrip and they failed to understand why. These planes could be valuable and important in the defence of Java. The Dutch pilots asked permission to fly them, but the RAAF bluntly refused because they'd need them in the near future to fight with the Brits defending British New Guinea.

The Dutch pilots and crews were forced to watch as every B-25 landing at Archerfield was shipped off to either Townsville or Port Moresby, earmarked by the Americans for the defence of Australia. They also had to hand over their own aircraft. They'd done this willingly at first, because there was the prospect of receiving a brand-new bomber in return, but now they were growing increasingly sorry. They'd become a squadron without planes, which left them feeling helpless and useless.

Spirits lifted when Captain Boot told his men that some of them would soon be heading to Jackson Airfield in Mississippi, where they'd learn how to fly the heavy bomber aeroplanes they'd been promised. Learning to fly B-25s and P-40s in the United States meant travelling away from the Dutch East Indies, but by now the bored men thought anything was better than waiting inactively at Archerfield.

Not everyone could go, however. As Boot finished calling out the names of the men who would be leaving, Tom, Bob, Gus and Wil Burck realised their names were among those that weren't on the list. Gus was pleased that Charlie van Tuyn had been listed to go—it might help him out of his lethargic state—but for the pilots and crews left behind, it felt like abandonment.

Just over a week later Norman Harris ran into Tom at the air base. Tom told him he was bored and that the endless waiting did not help lift his spirits. There were no planes for him to fly and every aircraft that came in went to the Yanks, the Brits or the Aussies. Even their own Lodestars had gone to the Allies.

Norman waved a leaflet. 'Looks like most of us will be moving to Canberra soon. We'll be quartered there as a new squadron. A Dutch–Australian squadron.'

Tom read the leaflet and discovered that in less than a week they'd be moving to Fairbairn Airfield in Canberra to form the

18th RAAF Squadron under the command of the No. 79 Wing in Darwin. The Dutch Army personnel who weren't leaving for Jackson would be attached to this squadron. The Dutch, not having enough air gunners and ground crew to form a complete squadron, had asked the Australians to supply the additional men needed. Norman had signed up as a dispatch rider; he and Tom would serve in the same squadron, although under a different command. The Dutch section of the squadron would be under the command of Boot—Tom groaned when he heard the man's name—but the Australians would answer to Squadron Leader Les Dawson, known as 'Smokey' to his men.

Smokey was an okay kind of bloke, Norman said. Strict but honest. The man had an air of authority about him, not because he was harsh but because it came naturally. He'd called Norman that morning, wanting to know what he did in civilian life and if he would have any problems being part of an Australian–Dutch squadron. Dawson was a 'blood and guts' type of man and Norman appreciated his straightforwardness. Norman thought he wouldn't be easy to deal with if he was rubbed up the wrong way, though. He was going to try to stay on the good side of him, just in case.

Tom read the leaflet again as they walked to his brother's tent. Canberra, Australia's capital . . . he had no idea what to expect. The streets were long and broad and lined with European trees, Norman told him. It was also cold, something Tom hated. After more copies of the leaflet had been handed out to the Dutch, the move to Canberra became the topic of the day. The Dutch version of the leaflet included a promise that at least five of the expected nineteen B-25s would be assembled, ready and waiting for them at Fairbairn. 'We'll see,' said a sceptical Gus Winckel. Another 50 Dutch Air Force men waiting in Melbourne were being added to the squadron.

Three bottles of whisky appeared from nowhere and Norman wondered if Tom had pinched them from Andir Airport the night they left. Perhaps Max had been unable to destroy the whole stash.

After they'd drained the third bottle, the men became rowdy and talked about stealing aircraft so they could fight the Japanese. From nowhere a plan emerged. Later Norman couldn't remember who came up with it. He couldn't understand what was said half the time anyway, because most of them would start to speak to him in English but in their tanked-up state they'd revert to Dutch after a few words. Wil Burck might have come up with the idea; he was the first to stop laughing.

The men knew that before they left for Canberra the last Lodestar and two DC-3s were to be handed over to the Americans, but it had been agreed that the Dutch would test-fly them to the American air base at Wagga Wagga.

'What if we turn it into a memorable test flight?' Wil asked. 'I'm not talking about stealing them.'

The others looked at him with apprehension, furrowing their brows. No one had a death wish, and they'd certainly be shot down if they took off in any plane without official approval. But their doubt soon turned to excitement when Wil proceeded to unfold his plan. If it succeeded, they'd make newspaper headlines;

it would put the Dutch and the upcoming 18th Squadron on the Australian map and give them a face.

'It will at least make sure people know we are here.' The plan was daring and would take all their skills as pilots to achieve.

Norman, unable to understand the Dutch plans, raised an eyebrow and threw a questioning glance at Tom. As the evening wore on, excited shouts turned into hushed and secretive whispers. When Tom explained what was about to take place, Norman shook his head in disbelief. After downing three bottles of whisky between them, none of the men was sober anymore. Norman had got to know Tom quite well during their escape from the East Indies. He believed the man was slightly reckless and brash, but not a complete idiot. He laughed and joked with his Dutch friends, but he didn't take their plan, fuelled as it was by alcohol, seriously. But as the effects of the alcohol wore off, he started to wonder if they'd really go through with it. He knew very little about the Dutch except that they did appear to be slightly unruly at times.

His mates in the RAAF had mixed feelings about the Dutch and had nicknamed them the 'Cowboys'. They were gutsy enough, no doubt about it. Gus Winckel's daring stunt when he'd stood on Broome's airstrip in full view of the advancing Zero fighter planes, firing a machine-gun from his hip, was legendary and had earned him the nickname 'Wild Bill'.

Who knew what else they were capable of, Norman wondered. For now Australia was their oyster, and they clearly felt they had to make a point.

8 FLYING UNDER THE BRIDGE

It was a hot clear day at Archerfield. Three aeroplanes standing on the runway were ready for their test flights. The men who would fly them lingered in the doorway of a hangar, smoking cigarettes in the shadows as they exchanged meaningful glances and secret smiles. Each plane took on a phantom-like appearance, flickering in and out of sight in the shimmering hot morning air.

Today was the day—if all went well, the pilots and their crews thought their stunt might just make tomorrow's headlines. The aircraft waiting for them in the scalding sun were two DC-3 KLM civilian airliners and one Lockheed Lodestar transport plane. Twelve men, ten Dutch and two Australians, Norman Harris and Bill Hutchinson, were to fly them to Wagga Wagga and, after handing them over to the Americans, report to Fairbairn Airfield in Canberra.

Before consigning the planes, each aircraft required a maintenance check and a trial flight to ensure they were totally operational. The men from Tom's unit had volunteered to fly the planes to Wagga, if only for something to do. Dirk Raab, one of the former civilian pilots from the KNILM, would be flying a DC-3 with his crew; he'd heard about the plan and wanted to take part.

The main incentive for the plan was to gain attention. It was also meant to be a rebellious act against Captain Boot to underline the men's disapproval of being forced to hand over their equipment. The general assumption was that Major General Van Oyen would not let the stunt pass without retribution, but even Dirk Raab agreed it would be worth it. Most of the Dutchmen agreed it was time to let Australia know they were there, and what better way to do it than in a display of airmanship?

The general feeling among the Dutch was that the focus of the Allied troops had shifted from trying to liberate and save the Dutch East Indies to saving New Guinea. As the Japanese invasion of the islands progressed, Dutch nationals at Archerfield, some of them born and raised in the East Indies, felt that the Australians and Americans were gradually losing interest in the Dutch regions in the Pacific. Being unable to do anything because of their lack of equipment and staff left them demoralised.

The Dutch suspected that most Australians had no idea they were in the country and they thought nobody really cared. The feeling that they were invisible spread through the ranks like mildew. That day Australia would discover that the Dutch were here. It would demonstrate they were damn good pilots, ready for action and more than willing to fly any plane available.

The Japanese had by now established a line of territory directly to the north of Australia, stretching from Rabaul in

New Guinea to Singapore. To stop any further advance, Allied troops were fighting on the ground in Papua and New Guinea, and those troops needed supplies, reinforcements, weaponry and as many planes as possible. There was no doubt that the Allies needed the planes the Dutch had brought with them to Australia; they'd heard that the Americans had paid the Dutch command handsomely for them. But these men would still much rather have been invited to join in the effort of chasing after the enemy. If the B-25s they had been promised were assigned to them in Canberra, they were confident they could send the Japanese running straight back to Tokyo—with the RAAF's 18th Squadron nipping at their bums.

In the past week, most of the Archerfield men had left for Fairbairn or for Jackson. Gus, Tom, Bob and a group of others had stayed behind to deliver the three aircraft to Wagga Wagga. Wil Burck and Norman Harris, who had been due at Fairbairn the week before, had straggled behind with excuses so that they could make the trip with their friends. Climbing into the waiting planes, they gave each other one last salute before they ducked into their cockpits.

Bob and Tom were pilot and copilot on the Lodestar, and Gus Winckel was flying one of the DC-3s with Guus Hagers and Bill Hutchinson as copilot and engineer. Dirk Raab would pilot the second DC-3 with three other crew members. The instructions from their CO had been crystal clear and they'd follow them to the letter—except for a small detour.

When they were ready for take-off, the men noticed a crowd slowly forming along the runway. Rumours of their plan had reached the other members of the unit and some of the staff. Norman had been unable to keep his mouth shut about it. The Australian RAAF men were on the runway, ready to wave off their Dutch allies.

As the engines of the Lodestar and the DC-3s roared to life, the men and women along the runway pulled out handkerchiefs, waving and shouting good luck. Rearing into the skies one by one, the three planes settled into formation and circled back to the airfield, soaring above the cheering crowd for the last time. A couple of higher-ranked officers came out to see what the fuss was about. For fear of being called back, the pilots quickly turned for Sydney.

No one uttered a word as they flew. Silent anticipation and excitement emanated from all as unit leader Gus Winckel took the lead. The rhythm of the engines worked like a monotonous chant. The men settled into their flying routines and their passengers could do nothing but wait.

Hours later, the shimmering suburban spread of Sydney came into view, guiding them in like a vast sea of lighthouses. Nearing Sydney Heads, the three aeroplanes held their formation with Gus's DC-3 just a nose in the lead.

Minutes later, Tom's heart skipped a beat when he suddenly recognised their target. He'd only ever seen the Sydney Harbour Bridge in a photograph Norman had shown him, but now, as they approached it, the sheer immensity of its structure was brought home to him. Its concrete pylons, faced with granite, stood like four proud miniature castles; its arch glittered in the sunlight. The bridge's reflection was dark and loomed like a sinister counterpart on the surface of the water below. Cars crept like a chain of coloured beads along the six lanes; pedestrians, no more than moving specks, ambled along the bridge's footpath.

This was their destination, the place they had chosen for their statement. They'd undoubtedly be noticed. Tom Derks smiled. He knew they could do it. During training, Gus and Guus Hagers—whom everyone called Hagers to avoid confusion—had shown an American general on Java just how good they were at flying in formation. They'd tied a rope between their planes before they took off. It was a dangerous thing to do: if either plane had pulled the rope too tightly, both would have crashed. But Hagers and Gus had been confident of their skills; they took off with the rope and landed with it still attached. The American general had shaken his head in disbelief.

Pedestrians on the bridge stopped to look at the planes approaching from the east. Perhaps some of them wondered if they were enemy planes coming to bomb Australia's largest city, but no one ran away or appeared to be alarmed. Most simply stopped to look at the aircraft for a moment then nonchalantly resumed making their way along the footpath. When the roar of the aircraft engines could be heard above the rumble of the cars, drivers started to slow down and stop.

As the three planes advanced towards the arch, cars and people came to a complete standstill. On the bridge, people started pointing at the aircraft, realising the planes were Allied. The mood now turned to excitement. When all three planes sailed under the bridge in formation, Tom could see people waving and shouting; he smiled, knowing the show was not over yet. Emerging from the other side, they soared upward, made a wide turn and then flew under the bridge again, now in single file. The men couldn't hear the cheering, but they could see the excitement on the bridge increase. They were finished. They had made their point and would now fly on to Wagga to hand over their aircraft. The spectators had witnessed a fine show.

Saluting each other and Sydney from their cockpits, they felt relieved, elated and euphoric as they headed to their final destination. This was something they'd always be able to boast about and tell their grandkids. They were all more than willing to endure whatever punishment was dished out to them. 'Then again,' Tom asked his brother, 'what can the authorities do? Lock us up?' He'd already experienced that and the prospect didn't daunt him too much. The only one with any stars to lose was Gus. Given the prospect of being short of good pilots when the new planes arrived, now that the larger part of the squadron had moved to Jackson, Tom didn't think that even Boot would consider standing them up before a firing squad and shooting them.

So as they taxied up to the hangars at Wagga later that day, the zinging exhilaration still ran through the men like an electrical current. Emerging from their cockpits, even their steps felt bubbly and weightless. Rapt smiles were smeared across their faces as they walked down the runway in unison.

'The best fun I have had in quite a while,' Norman said to Tom.

The pilots and crews made their way to the US Air Force office next to the hangars at the end of the runway to hand over their paperwork. They signed some documents and the

American officer on duty thanked them, a grin on his face. As they gathered up their belongings and turned to leave, the officer said, 'By the way, magnificent piloting, gentlemen.'

They turned back to him with questioning faces.

'Sydney,' the American added.

He already knew; the news had travelled faster than they had. Noticed at last. If nothing else, the stunt had given them a face.

When they arrived at Fairbairn later that day, they were met with admiring stares and appreciative smiles. While they were still talking to the American who needed to register their arrival, they saw Captain Boot striding towards the office and knew there'd be hell to pay. When Boot entered, they snapped to attention and quietly listened as he barked, bellowed and roared at them. After being pounded by the captain's relentless harangue for what seemed an eternity, they were surprised to find Major Jan van Haselen suddenly walking into the office at the very height of Captain Boot's anger. As the highest-ranking officer, he sent the captain off to cool down, and told the men to stand at ease. He ordered the Dutch to meet him in the officers' quarters after they'd finished their paperwork; Norman and Hutchinson he told to report to their own commanding officer.

'I think our careers just went down the drain,' Tom said.

The major was in command of the aviation school at Mallala near Adelaide. 'Why is Major Van Haselen here?' Gus wondered aloud. 'He's supposed to be in South Australia. We only flew under the bridge five hours ago, so he can't be here because of that.'

When they reported to the major, he explained that Major General Van Oyen had asked him to intervene because of the current situation with the men. What he didn't tell them was that the general had heard rumours of their dispirited frame of mind and wanted to douse the lurking flames of discontent before things got out of hand. Because the general was preparing to leave for Jackson and could not come himself, he'd sent Van Haselen to restore order and find out exactly what was wrong with morale.

The major said nothing about their little show in Sydney. After talking to all parties involved he was to send his conclusions and recommendations back to the general. In the meantime, he'd been talking to the men at Fairbairn and had also had a conversation with Boot. 'It would appear that the men don't get along very well with the captain,' he said, intoning it like a question.

Gus gave vent to all their feelings. They disliked and mistrusted Boot. He disciplined the men in a random fashion and nearly all of them had spent some period in detention, often for no apparent reason, but sometimes for insubordination and sometimes just to set an example. The major listened silently as the flying officer and unit leader carefully explained their misgivings.

Van Haselen appeared to understand the situation. When Gus had finished he removed his cap and pulled a hand through his hair. 'Now, about today,' he said.

The men cringed, waiting for the inevitable.

'Regrettably there is not much I can do to discipline you on today's misconduct,' the major said.

Gus raised a surprised eyebrow.

'It appears there's no official law against flying under the Sydney Harbour Bridge, so technically you've done nothing wrong.'

Tom shared a look with Gus, relieved.

'However,' the major continued, 'you did disobey orders, and I'd seriously think twice about pulling a stunt like today's in the future. You won't get off so lightly next time.'

That was it. All he added was, 'Dismissed.'

The men saluted him and headed for the door in a state of disbelief and silent wonder. They'd expected everything except this; for the next hour they had no idea how to react, so they just sat in their quarters for a while, silently staring at the ground as if an explanation would suddenly sprout from the floorboards.

A few days later, Major Van Haselen sent a letter to Major General Van Oyen telling him that he found Captain Boot a sober individual who demanded and expected the same from his men. 'Due to his severe disciplinary regimen, his men have come to distrust and dislike him. I would recommend replacing Captain Boot with a new squadron leader, preferably a man these pilots will trust and can identify with, whose authority they will accept.'

Soon news came through that Captain Boot would be replaced by Major Ben Fiedeldij, who had been scheduled to leave for America but had given up the chance to go to Jackson at Major General Van Oyen's request. Captain Boot would now leave in his place.

The new wing commander was of half European and half East Indies descent. It had been a tricky decision, but the Dutch high command believed their own men would have greater respect for him. They were unsure what reaction they could expect from the Australians, given the White Australia policy was still in force, but the wing commander had an immaculate reputation. He'd been the head of flight operations of the military air force in Bandung and, during the three months it had taken the Japanese to conquer the archipelago, had proved himself a very able and dedicated soldier. He was to become the first commanding officer of the new Dutch–Australian 18th Squadron.

Quite a few of the pilots had served under the major before and knew what to expect from him, but some of the other men doubted the new CO would actually be an improvement. Like Boot, Fiedeldij had brought his family out of Java, using his seniority to evacuate them before the island fell. This discredited him in the eyes of many of his men, but they decided to give him the benefit of the doubt.

That evening they celebrated. Boot was gone and they had left their mark. Their flight under the Sydney Harbour Bridge had made headlines in the Sydney morning papers. They were no longer just a nameless group of military men who'd accidentally stumbled into the country. Very soon they'd officially bear the title of RAAF 18th (Netherlands East Indies) Squadron. It would make them part of something. Give them significance.

When Tom prepared to go to bed that night, he ran his fingers over his breast pocket. The wattle was still there. He pulled the wilted strands from their hiding place and caressed them gently.

'What's that?' Bob asked.

'A woman.'

'I should have guessed,' Bob said shaking his head. 'Sana?'

Tom was momentarily confused—his memory of the girl on Java had almost faded. 'What? Who? No, not Sana,' he said. 'This one's called Grace.'

Bob tossed his brother a mocking smile.

It was real love this time, Tom assured him, but Bob knew from experience that Tom's love for a particular woman would wilt almost as quickly as the flower he'd plucked from his pocket.

Tom returned the wattle to his breast pocket and asked, 'Do you think of Colette much?'

'Every minute of every day.'

Tom thought he owed it to Bob to get her back. When the first B-25s arrived, he decided, they'd get those big birds up into the skies and chase the Japanese off the islands. 'I promise you we'll find her,' he said.

9 FAIRBAIRN AIRFIELD, CANBERRA

It was the end of May and the weather was turning. Tom began to realise, not without some concern, that it could be very cold in Australia. He'd always dreaded the cold winter back home, and for these Dutchmen who'd lived in the East Indies for most of their lives, the frosty, wet weather at Fairbairn was not a pleasant experience. They dreaded the wintry months to come, which the Australians described as 'cold as charity'.

Bob appeared to be one of the few who did not hate the prospect of cold; he became quite excited when he learnt that Canberra's streets sometimes welcomed snow and ice. Clapping Tom on the shoulders, he said, 'It'll be like home—snow, ice and leafless trees. We might even get to skate.'

'We don't have skates,' Tom replied bleakly, nonetheless knowing that his brother could improvise skates by embedding the blades of two sharp knives in pieces of wood tied to his feet with rope.

To their pleasant surprise, the five B-25 Mitchells finally arrived, although only two were operational and ready for flight training. The other three arrived by train and in parts. After assembling them, the maintenance crew and technicians found some vital parts missing, so they'd have to wait until they arrived.

Gus and Bob ducked into the first B-25 just after it had taxied into a hangar. For the very tall and burly Gus, getting into the pilot's seat proved a major operation. The cabin roof of the Mitchell was fairly low, and the pilot's and copilot's seats were very close together, which meant he really had to squeeze himself in. Once seated, the two men started to read the manual. With no previous experience of flying a Mitchell, it was all they had.

The B-25 was very different from any other aircraft the men had flown. The Lockheeds that had served them as transport planes stood on tail wheels, making the nose slant upward when parked. The B-25 Mitchell, with both wing and nose wheels, stood horizontally.

Take-off and landing wouldn't be easy, Gus realised. 'The nose will block your view when you land,' he said. 'It'll take some getting used to.'

Luckily, the throttles were where they expected them to be, and most of the switches for starting and for fuel management were on the control panel just in front of the throttles. The two men were eager and more than willing to spend hours learning to find and operate all the buttons and levers. Once they were up in the air, it would be vital to locate them without looking. Sitting in the aeroplane, they repeated the sequences continually, all the while running through emergency procedures and making imaginary touch-and-go landings.

Both men had passed all the pilot exams at Andir and Kalidjati air schools. Their training had been thorough, and they could fly single- and double-motor aircraft. They were no rookies. After reading the instructions for the hundredth time, Gus turned to Bob and said, 'I think we can try flying this thing.'

Standing ready for take-off at the beginning of the runway that day, Gus would never forget the feeling as his hand wrapped itself around the two throttles, the plane's two big radial engines, with 3200 horsepower, roaring at him from the wings. The noise this big lady made was unbelievable! When the wheels lifted off the ground and the plane bounded into the air, Gus watched Bob gulp. Gus had loved the Lodestar, but the B-25 was like no other. To him the beautiful bomber was like a fascinating woman—teasing him, testing him and leading him on.

After flying over the practice area a couple of times, he signalled for Bob to take over. But when Bob took the yoke, the nose suddenly dropped. Bob automatically pulled the yoke back—or at least he tried. He was flying with his left hand, his right resting on the throttles, and he found he didn't have enough strength to pull it up with just one hand.

'Gus, help!' he shouted over the noise of the screaming motors, 'I can't pull the yoke back!'

Gus, seemingly unfazed by the sudden nosedive, calmly told Bob to release the throttles, then brought his other hand over to help him pull her up. Sure enough, the lady straightened herself, resuming a horizontal position. Bob smiled a painful smile, sweat dripping from his face. For a moment, he'd expected the plane to start rolling, and God knows what could have happened then.

Bob and Gus finally understood why some of their colleagues had been shipped off to America for flight training—this was a headstrong bird. But they and the other pilots who had stayed behind in Australia would have to go on intuition, the manual and their abilities. The B-25 had so many peculiarities that Gus silently wondered how many would even survive their test flight.

Bob started to feel like he was getting the hang of the aircraft. He pushed the yoke back to keep the nose from dropping again, but didn't protest when Gus took over. Soon afterwards they decided to call it a day and to bring the aircraft down.

Landing the Mitchell proved another thing altogether. Gus started his descent, taking a long approach and giving it lots of power. As they approached the runway, Bob thought they were going to make a high-speed pass over it because Gus suddenly started to bring the nose up. Gus kept pulling upward until the plane's nose was on an alarmingly steep angle, so high that it blocked their view. Bob, thinking they might crash, started to sweat again.

An audible groan of relief escaped him when he felt the wheels suddenly make contact with the runway. As Gus gently applied the brakes, the rollout was arrow-straight.

'The brakes are very sensitive,' Gus shouted above the din. 'I'm afraid I'll lock them if I apply too much pressure.'

The brakes had double discs and just needed a whisper of pressure to stop the wheels. Trying to taxi smoothly proved a near impossibility, but the plane finally came to a reasonably straight standstill.

Men who had gathered near the hangars to watch the spectacle had witnessed the difficulty the pilots had experienced when climbing. At some stage it would be their turn to scramble into the skies with the B-25, something that gave them cause for concern. Tom had hardly taken a breath when the plane's nose appeared to dive; for a few anxious moments he'd feared that his brother might fall from the sky.

'She's a pussycat when she's up in the air. Agile and quick,' Gus reassured them stepping from the cockpit, 'but you'll need guts and brains to get her there. This plane could kill you. Remember that when you start flying her.'

In the weeks to come, the weather conditions in Canberra made it difficult for the pilots to practise. There were no sealed runways at Fairbairn, and the constant rain made the runway soggy and unfit for the heavy Mitchell. The force needed at take-off made the nose wheel dig into the top layer of runway, ruining it. As a result the runway needed constant repairs. Frequent fog was also a problem. One or two pilots had only just managed to avoid running the aircraft into the hangars after landing in dense mist.

Again, the men were forced to hang around passively. Some of them had formed a band to pass the time. Wil Burck, a great musician, became the leader, playing trumpet. His friend Adriaan Scholte played guitar and others filled in the gaps, making drums out of pots and pans. Hagers wasn't a bad piano player, and the officers' mess at Fairbairn had a piano. Evening parties were organised to entertain the men. On those evenings, Chugga Parson would pass around his infamous jungle brew made of sugar, malt, Marmite, potato peelings, salt, hops and a dessertspoon of Parisian essence, all thrown into a kerosene tin filled with water, brought to the boil, left to bubble and simmer for some time, then strained and bottled. The men all agreed it tasted 'bloody awful', but it got them where they wanted to go in a hurry.

Chugga's brew, however, caused a merciless hangover and a great deal of regret for ever having touched the stuff. It soon lost its appeal. The 'brewery' was shut down after half of Fiedeldij's men drank the lethal brew one night and missed rollcall the following morning. Chugga never found out who ratted on him, but nobody except Chugga himself actually experienced a sense of loss.

When he was off-duty, Tom would usually head for town, mostly with Wil Burck and Adriaan Scholte; on occasion Norman and Bob would join them. Norman wasn't much of a drinker and Bob was a one-woman man, so they didn't benefit from the two things that made the city appealing to their friends. At times Tom, Wil and Adriaan drank at a local bar and were at a loss as to why all the Australian bars closed at six in the evening. They explained to Norman that in the Dutch East Indies bars closed when there was no one left to serve. They reckoned that closing the bars so early only compelled the customers to drink faster as closing time neared.

Many of Norman's Australian friends in the force did not get on as well with the Dutch as he did. Bill Hutchinson was quite chummy with Hagers, and Gerry Wiggers occasionally took time to teach the Australians the basics of the Dutch language. Many of the Australians, though, thought the Dutch had a poor work ethic, and quite a few of them asked to be assigned elsewhere.

About 271 Australians had joined the 18th Squadron at the beginning of May, but their numbers were dwindling fast. Almost 70 had left, complaining that they felt out of place. Those who'd trained in India with the British were used to a very disciplined regimen, following rules without question. The Dutch appeared to constantly question their superiors and seemed to have little regard for authority; that the authority came from a Dutch–Javanese officer did not help matters. 'Last week, when we were on parade, Fiedeldij spoke to the men in English, Dutch and Bahasa. Made me feel like a flamin' foreigner in my own country,' one of the Australian mechanics moaned.

The Dutch taste in food did not go down well either. Their dislike of mutton and their preference for rice and vegetables spiced with just a tablespoon of meat drove the Australian cooks mad. There was a major incident in the mess hall when one of the part-Javanese NEI men went into the kitchen demanding to cook dinner. Norman watched with some alarm as the man landed on his bum in the aisle of the mess after being thrown out of the kitchen by the Australian cooks, who shouted, 'Get out of here, you bloody wog, and stay out!' It wasn't so much the colour of the man's skin that had rubbed the cooks up the wrong way, but him barging into their kitchen and criticising the food they were serving.

Tom and a couple of others rose from their chairs, but before anyone could say anything a fight broke out between the Dutch airmen and the cooks. The Australian and Dutch men, who had been eating together side by side just moments before, began punching each other and all hell broke loose. By the time everyone had calmed down, chairs and overturned tables lay in disarray. There were blood spots on the floor and walls, and the air was thick with animosity. The differences in attitude and the difficulties in understanding one another seemed settled by the fist fight that day, although animosity and misunderstandings continued to surface occasionally.

Because the weather in Canberra was so poor for flying, Fiedeldij requested permission to use the airfield at Moruya on the New South Wales south coast for operations and practice. Closer to the coast, with milder weather conditions, Moruya would be the perfect location for his pilots and crews to get some flight training. The men would also be able to take part in anti-submarine patrols and protect Allied convoys. Sydney and Newcastle had previously been attacked by Japanese submarines, so no one in Moruya would object to the extra pilots and aeroplanes.

The men, glad to be on the go, could not wait to be in the air and doing something useful. Gus's wife was in a Sydney hospital, almost ready to give birth to his second child. Taking part in patrols from Moruya felt like being closer to her. He was among the first pilots to be sent. Because Bob had been forced to leave Colette behind, and Charlie's wife and child had died escaping Java, Gus had always felt slightly apprehensive about having his family in Australia. No one ever reproached him or blamed him, but he still rarely talked about it for fear it might touch a tender spot among the men.

Wil Burck, however, questioned Fiedeldij's arguments for the move. 'Anti-submarine patrols? What is the man thinking? We're not even operational, and we only have five aircraft. It's crazy.'

Gus didn't agree. 'What does it matter if we have one or twenty planes? No one knows and no one cares. Anything is better than sitting here in the cold and rain waiting for better times.'

So at the beginning of June a number of pilots and crew made a temporary move to Moruya. The submarine attack earlier that year had left Sydneysiders in a state of shock, and the public was demanding preventative action. The men of the NEI 18th Squadron were summoned to commence patrolling the coast as soon as possible.

In the early hours of 4 June, while patrolling the Sydney Heads area, Gus noticed something sticking out of the sea close to the coast and decided to take a closer look. With Bob at Fairbairn, Hagers had come along as second pilot and Tom was in the front turret, supposedly on bombsight duty. The day before, their regular bombsighter had called in sick and Tom had volunteered to replace him.

The night before, Hagers and Gus had gone to the hospital in Sydney to visit Gus's wife, but Tom and Wil Burck had gone to a nightclub. Tom had drunk a good deal before returning to their base, not really expecting much action. He thought sitting in the turret would be a lot more relaxing than being second pilot. After a late night and an early morning, he now lay curled up, snoring.

Gus's voice booming through the aeroplane's intercom brought a rude awakening: 'Damn it, Derks, what the hell are you doing down there!'

Cruising above the surface of the water, Gus had sighted a submarine. It was quite a clear day and even at a great height he could make out the white feathers of foam spreading from the bow as it broke the water. The first attack run had failed because Tom had been asleep, so costly minutes had been lost.

Gus was not in a good mood as he pulled out of the first dive and was forced to fly the plane over the sub at mast height again. It had already spotted them and was crash-diving into the depths, but it did not dive quickly enough.

Bumping his head hard on the roof of the turret as he sat up, Tom, now suddenly wide awake and alert, peered through his Estoppey sighter. He dropped a full stick of six heavy bombs at just the right moment, then watched intently as they crashed in line along the submarine's deck. After they exploded, the sub disappeared. The men held their breaths in anticipation, waiting for the telltale cloud of oil to surface.

Tom could see nothing but rippling waves on the surface of the sea. 'Did we get it?' he shouted through the intercom.

Just a few seconds later, about five feet of the vessel's bow suddenly shot out from the surface like a black whale breaching for air. It stood for a moment at an angle above the sea, oil pouring copiously from its damaged hull, and then instantly sank back into the water.

'I don't think she'll ever see Japan again,' Tom said.

They cruised the spot where oil had spread and now covered the sea like a blanket, knowing without a doubt that the sub had taken its last dive. When the realisation slowly dawned that they had sent a complete submarine crew to their deaths, it became oddly quiet inside the aircraft. Gus finally opened his window and saluted them. At Broome he'd witnessed how the Japanese pilots had saluted their victims, and now he thought he might pay them the same respect.

Moments later, he started to transmit the victory to shore: 'Japanese submarine sunk. Coordinates 35.22 degrees south 152.36 degrees east, course 205 degrees, this morning eight o'clock, June 4th 1942.'

That evening Gus was already asleep when a knock on his hotel room door woke him. It was the press. They'd heard of the Dutch intervention and wanted to interview him. Dressed in nothing but his nightgown he told them in his own casual and unperturbed way what had happened. The moment they left, he went to bed again, falling fast asleep as his head touched the pillow.

The next day the story about the sunken submarine made headlines. The *Sydney Morning Herald* ran a front-page headline in big, chunky letters that read:

TWO SUBMARINES SUNK OFF COAST

The population of Sydney was jubilant because this was the third submarine to be sunk in a matter of days, the RAAF claiming the other two. People suddenly wanted to know all about this unknown ally, the Dutch. Who were they? What kind of unit did they belong to? The 'Forgotten Squadron', as the

18th had started calling itself, now found itself in the public eye, and even the Australian Government was forced to take note.

Australia's prime minister, John Curtin, invited Gus and his men to tell their story to Parliament. Rumours that Curtin wanted to award Gus a Distinguished Flying Cross (DFC) for his heroic actions had spread. The House of Representatives was astonished when they heard the 18th Squadron owned just five planes and had barely had any practice using them. For a moment they were the talk of the town, and now the Dutch NEI command in Melbourne also began to take notice.

10 THE MAKING OF THREE TRAITORS

Tom, Gus, Bob and Hagers had seen them coming that morning. Nine determined Americans, in polished boots with a sturdy step. After the soldiers had shown their credentials, they reported they were there to pick up the two operational B-25s. Leaving behind a confused guard and the warrant officer who had signed them in, they headed for the hangars at the other end of the base. But this time the 18th Squadron was not just going to hand over their aircraft; although they had no illusions about the outcome, they resolved to put up some kind of fight.

Warning the others, the four men sauntered out of their quarters and casually strolled into the hangars before the Americans got there. Working fast, they took the igniters out of the planes, rendering them inoperable. The Yanks would probably confiscate them anyway, Tom thought, but they could make damn sure that they'd have a hard time getting them out of the air base.

Moseying out of the hangar, having safely hidden the igniters, they saw Major Fiedeldij arguing with the Americans on the tarmac. Heading towards their CO, they kept their distance, making sure they were close enough to hear what was being said. Tom and Gus lit cigarettes while Hagers and Bob stood nonchalantly, hands in pockets, staring at nothing in particular as they waited for things to unfold. Tom noticed that Fiedeldij had a look of determination he hadn't seen before; he was arguing loudly.

When he clearly heard their CO say, 'I don't think you'll be taking these planes today, gentlemen,' Tom drew a breath, choking on the smoke he'd just inhaled. Coughing the smoke from his lungs drew the attention of the Americans, who noticed them for the first time.

The Yanks protested to Fiedeldij, claiming there was a contract to ferry the aircraft to Charters Towers in Queensland; but the major demanded to see it. The confused men couldn't produce one. They hadn't expected to encounter any difficulties.

'I'm in charge here. The planes will remain where they are,' Fiedeldij told the annoyed men. 'Go find the contract.'

One of the Americans stepped away from the group, turning his back on the major. The American took a few steps towards the hangar, but Fiedeldij made matters clear by saying loudly, 'If anyone comes near one of those planes they'll be arrested. Do I make myself clear, gentlemen?'

The pilot turned back, eyeing the major and the four men standing a few feet away, deliberating on what to do. Fiedeldij outranked them all. Dutchmen spilled from the barracks and surrounded the Americans, making it clear that they stood behind their CO and were ready to take any kind of action he'd order. The stand-off lasted all of five minutes.

The pilot decided not to create a scene and, giving Fiedeldij a reluctant salute, the Americans turned and marched off. A muted cheer rose from the men who could barely contain their joy. They felt triumphant—the retreat of the Americans was another victory. Fiedeldij had gained his men's admiration and respect. He was a leader who could stand up for them, fight to keep what was rightfully theirs.

'He's all right,' Tom whispered to Gus.

But Fiedeldij wasn't finished—he made sure that the baffled Americans also heard his orders to guard and protect the Mitchell bombers. 'Don't let anyone near them.'

By order of the Dutch command in Melbourne, on 17 September eighteen new B-25 Mitchells were delivered to the squadron. The attack on the enemy submarine, and the media attention that had followed it, had sped matters up. The men's spirits lifted. Rumours spread that Gus was to be awarded an Australian DFC for his actions but, to Gus's dismay and Prime Minister Curtin's annoyance, the Dutch command in Melbourne decided it was appropriate for them alone to reward their own men. Gus was promoted from flying officer to flight lieutenant and, as far as their Melbourne command was concerned, this ended the matter.

With plenty of new aircraft the pilots were finally able to practise flying in formation, working in conjunction with other fighter planes, bombing and shooting at air and ground targets. By the time Major Fiedeldij left for the Dutch NEI headquarters in Melbourne to discuss the reorganisation and the future of the squadron, morale had improved.

The Dutch were issued with new uniforms, identical to the Australian ones, making them look and feel sharp. The uniform was the same air force blue, but the badges and stripes were Dutch—every man had a golden lion, the Dutch national symbol, embroidered on their sleeve. All was going well, relations with the Australians had drastically improved and, as spring progressed, the RAAF's 18th (NEI) Squadron prospered.

—■—

A new detachment of Dutch pilots and personnel arrived from Bangalore, India, and were attached to the 18th Squadron, boosting the number of pilots by eleven. One of them was Lieutenant Ed Timmer, who'd brought along his wife, Betty. Strolling through the barracks, her breasts bobbing in her ruby-red dress, Betty turned quite a few heads, including that of Tom Derks.

Hers was a hard beauty, and the way she walked and talked betrayed that she'd been raised on the streets. Born in Rotterdam, in a neighbourhood of dockworkers and sailors, she'd fought her way through life, using her looks and her sharp tongue. She had seven siblings, a father who didn't care and a mother who cared even less. Never having any reason to be optimistic about her future, she'd used the only asset she had—her looks—to get what she wanted.

From an early age, her appearance had attracted a whole string of boys. She'd lie on the cold damp bench of a little concrete structure standing at the edge of the river that spilt into the North Sea, and the boys would fumble their way into her and apologise on their way out. She had no illusion that this was love, but it was as near to affection as she'd ever come until that time.

The shelter was a dismal spot. The people living in the small housing block along the docks called it the 'Tear House'. Women who'd bid their seafaring husbands goodbye sat on the cold concrete benches of the hut shedding tears after their men had left. At night, after yet another boy had groped his way around and into her, Betty would lie feeling soiled and miserable on one of those hard cold benches, wondering if the dampness creeping up from the bench and chilling her body was the result of all those shed tears. That thought comforted her somehow—knowing she was not the only one shedding them. By the time she was sixteen, though, her doubtful reputation had become public knowledge and she decided she'd had enough of boys—she wanted a man.

Ed Timmer stumbled out of a café one night straight into her arms. Although there was not a religious hair on her head, the seventeen-year-old Betty considered it an act of God. Ed was ten years her senior and a week later he asked her to marry him. His leave was ending and he wanted her to come with him to the Dutch East Indies. She said yes, packed her bag and left. She'd never looked back. It was her ticket out of that miserable life and she'd grabbed it, wanting it so badly it hurt.

Ed was a big burly man, a rough man, a fighter. He'd come from a wealthy background—his father had earned his money in the sugar industry on Java. Those who'd known his family said Ed had inherited his old man's callous ways and his inflammable temper. You didn't want to get into a fight with either man—they were known to be brutal. Strangely enough, both father and son were good observers and both had a knack for drawing. Ed always carried a pad and some pencils with him. His illustrations of naked women were renowned.

Ed and Betty lived in the Tourist Hotel in Queanbeyan near Canberra. It was standard procedure not to have married couples living on the base. With so many new men arriving from Bangalore, options to live on the base were limited, so some bachelors also got to live in the Tourist. Two of them were Eric de Lyon and Harry Kelder, who occupied the room next door to Betty and Ed.

The moody and often depressed Wil Burck formed a friendship with Eric and Harry. All three had families in the Indies and shared the same sentiments about having to leave them behind. They sought comfort from each other around the airfield, and spent many a night fantasising about stealing a plane from the base and returning to Java with it to save their families. Tom and Norman had run into them in the city once or twice, and Tom had ended up at Eric and Harry's hotel room on occasion, too drunk to make it back to the base.

On one such a night, as they made their way noisily down the hallway, Betty had emerged from the adjoining room, cigarette smoke meandering from her cherry lips. She eyed Tom boldly, pressing her mouth into a seductive flower. When she licked her lips, Tom's legs almost buckled and he cursed himself for turning into a damn quivering fish. All four men gawked at her. She looked down and nonchalantly pulled at her nightgown, covering her breasts which had fallen free of the garment. Pulling on her cigarette, she eyed them as the smoke left her mouth in soft puffs that turned to mist in the corridor.

'You boys might keep the noise down,' she said, her husky voice captivatingly coarse. 'There are people trying to sleep.'

Tom's body felt hot. His face flushed and time stood still as he watched her cigarette smoke drift slowly towards him. He thought of a hundred things to say to her, but his tongue felt paralysed, leaving him speechless. A smile meant for him glided from her lips. He loved her. In that instant he knew she was the woman he'd waited for all his life.

An annoyed bark erupted from the hotel room behind her, breaking the spell. Tom took a swaggering step back as Ed pushed his way through the door. Pulling Betty roughly back into the room, Ed smiled at Eric and Harry, but directed a sneer at Tom. After the door closed, muted laughter drifted to them from inside the Timmers' suite, followed by the sound of someone stumbling and an internal door closing.

The door of the suite opened again momentarily and Betty appeared. When a toilet flushed somewhere inside the room, she blew the men a kiss, flashed another smile at Tom, and then her body, graceful as a lioness, slipped back through the door and disappeared into the suite.

The next day everyone had heard about the encounter at the hotel. Eric de Lyon had come to the base early that morning and had told his mates about their flirt with Betty Timmer the night before. Men gossiped and laughed while they ate their lunch in the mess that afternoon. The tall blond pilot was going to get himself killed and Timmer's wife, well, who knew what that crazy madman would do to her?

Finally the rumour reached Bob. He was furious. He knew his brother had a habit of letting the wrong part of his body do the thinking for him, but this was dangerous stuff. Ed Timmer was a loose cannon, Bob thought, and he'd most likely kill Tom if he dared mess with his wife. When he found his brother in the tent, sleeping off his hangover, he had four words to say to him: 'Keep away from her!' When Tom gave him an innocent look, Bob knew he wouldn't be able to.

Betty would sometimes visit the barracks when it was Ed's turn to take part in patrol flights from Moruya. Her booming laugh would bounce though the base like a tennis ball. She didn't care what people thought. Nobody had ever cared about her or her feelings, and all Ed cared about was her loyalty to him. He never asked if she was happy, never told her outright that he loved her. She was his trophy. That had made her feel important for a while, but the way Tom looked at her made her feel so much more than somebody's prize. She also knew that Ed wouldn't be robbed of her without a fight; although that frightened her, still she toyed with the flame, knowing it would turn into a fire at some point.

Tom, thinking she was beautiful and exciting, became reckless and imagined he was in love. As the game between the handsome Dutchman and the woman with the big breasts and pouty lips dragged on, the men placed bets on how long it would take 'brutal' Ed to find out, and on Tom's survival if he did. For the men on the base it was all just entertainment.

Rumours spread that whenever Ed was away Tom would visit Betty at the hotel. Eric and Harry were probed about it, but they only smiled evasively and gave the men meaningful looks. Wil, when asked, enlightened them with nothing but the sound of his trumpet. Everyone suspected it had all gone beyond flirtation, and that it was now for Ed to find out. Some said you could feel disaster coming. It was like being in the eye of a storm and knowing that the worst of it was yet to come.

—■—

But life went on, and with eighteen B-25 Mitchells at their disposal, the men could take part in submarine patrols along the Australian coastline. Many of them still fretted about their families, and they could not help but show their distress and anger. It didn't go unnoticed at the NEI headquarters in Melbourne.

Captain Simon Spoor was sent to Canberra to assess if the situation was acute enough to justify some course of action. Spoor was a military man at heart, but he was also somewhat of an intellectual. He'd published articles in military magazines about politics in the Dutch East Indies and, after his escape from Java, had become an intelligence officer working for the Netherlands Forces Intelligence Service (NEFIS).

By late October, Wil Burck was so depressed that he'd shut himself up in his barrack, covering his windows with blankets to block out the daylight. Hagers had tried to talk to him, but

Wil fretted about his family and lay awake almost every night, wondering if his children were going hungry. His plan to escape to Java in an aircraft became an obsession.

Wil, Eric and Harry held secret meetings in the hotel room at the Tourist to discuss how they could hijack a plane. When Adriaan Scholte first attended one of these meetings, he was so alarmed by what he heard that he informed Captain Jessurun of the plans. Reinier Jessurun, a navigator and bombsighter, had fled from Java and been appointed second in command after Fiedeldij. A no-nonsense man, he sent Adriaan away, telling him he shouldn't believe everything he heard on the base. Adriaan had then turned to NEFIS and found in Captain Spoor a willing ear.

Adriaan Scholte admired Captain Spoor, who had promised the unassuming and dull private an interesting position within the army after the war, a prospect that made Adriaan particularly eager to please his superior. Succeeding in his mission would earn him respect and admiration from the NEFIS headquarters, so he wasted no time in briefing Spoor about the nightly discussions and alcohol-induced plans to hijack a plane. Adriaan revealed in detail how the men planned to surrender to the Japanese, hoping they'd be rewarded for their efforts by being reunited with their families.

Many of them at Fairbairn knew about the nightly meetings—it was no secret. Eric de Lyon had mouthed off about them, treating the whole affair as a joke. It was no more than a wild daydream, he told them, conjured up after a night on the town, something to keep the unhappy Wil occupied. Everyone else treated the story as no more than drunken nonsense but

Spoor was not so sure. He was tempted to believe that three of his men were planning an act of treason.

On the evening of 10 November, the four men came together in their hotel room to talk once again about deserting and escaping to Java. Adriaan had urged Eric, who had wanted to go to bed early, to take part in the meeting, which he did rather reluctantly. Adriaan was particularly adamant about meeting up that night and stood waiting outside the hotel, almost dragging Wil out of the cab when he arrived. After a few beers and some chit-chat, Adriaan steered the conversation towards escape and hijack.

Earlier that evening, Captain Spoor had knocked on the door of Betty and Ed Timmer's hotel room. It took a while for Betty to open the door, but as soon as she did, the captain identified himself and briskly pushed his way inside, leaving an astonished Betty standing in her nightgown at the door. Spoor wrongly assumed that the man in the bed must be Betty's husband. The captain did not know Ed Timmer so, when Tom's head emerged from under the covers, Spoor did not bat an eyelid.

'I'm here on a case of national security,' he said to the startled couple as he sat himself down at the dressing table. With an air of secrecy, he opened a small suitcase and Tom, surprised and annoyed by the interruption, sat up and watched as the captain opened it and took out an electrical gadget.

'Can I ask what this is all about?' said Tom.

Spoor, handling the device with care, stuck it to the wall. Putting on earphones, he told them to be quiet because he was going to listen in on the men next door. Tom, not sure what to think about this, asked if he and Betty could leave, but the captain ordered them to stay where they were.

They heard the faint sound of voices when the men entered the hallway. Tom thought he recognised Wil's voice. Someone opened a door as Wil jokingly asked if he could fly the stolen plane to Melbourne before leaving for Java.

'I'd like to throw a bomb on the Dutch headquarters there,' he said. Tom, realising that whatever was happening wasn't good, was tempted to get up and warn his friends. Spoor had casually placed a gun next to the suitcase on the side table. Tom and Betty exchanged concerned looks as their friends' laughter seeped through the crack under the door.

The captain's self-assured smile sent a shiver through Tom's body as he slowly began to grasp what was going on. He felt like shouting at them, warning them; he contemplated dashing out and banging on their door. As soon as Wil had shut the door, only faint muffled sounds from the adjoining room oozed through the thick walls.

Tom bit his lip as Spoor fidgeted with his listening device. A wire ran from the device to the microphone on the wall; the captain turned some dials in the suitcase, but he began to swear when the microphone picked up no comprehensible sound. The walls of the Tourist wouldn't leak a whisper. Often, when Betty screamed uncontrollably as they made love, Tom had secretly thanked God for the impenetrability of those walls.

Unknown to Spoor, the men in the next room had rolled out a map of the Pacific and were now in the process of trying to assess how many miles Canberra was from Java.

'We'll probably need additional fuel tanks,' Wil said. 'The B-25s won't get us there without extra fuel.'

'I can get them,' Adriaan assured the others.

It didn't occur to them to ask how he could do this unnoticed, given there were always other mechanics busy in the hangars. Discussing tactics, their fantasies became bolder. They debated ways to surrender to the Japanese without getting themselves murdered; Eric suggested they become spies for the Japanese, so they could be rewarded by being reunited with their families. Given their knowledge of the Allied forces, Adriaan thought they might become the heads of a deserters' air force group under Japanese command: 'There are more of us out there. With families in the Indies.'

Harry shook his head in doubt: 'The Japs will probably chop off our heads before we even get a chance to explain.'

This whole conversation, however, did not leave the confines of the room, because all Spoor could tape while sitting in Betty Timmer's suite was inaudible mumbling. Relieved that the captain's mission had not succeeded, Tom now sat on the bed smoking nonchalantly. He remembered having seen Captain Spoor snooping around the hangars at Fairbairn the day before and finding it odd.

Tom, however, knew nothing about Scholte's double role, and Adriaan knew nothing about the failed attempt at taping the conversation. Giving up, Spoor finally removed the microphone from the wall and packed his devices into the case. His short agitated movements did not go unnoticed and, when Tom gave the man an amiable smile, Spoor turned to him a face that appeared to have been set in stone.

He wouldn't fail, Spoor thought; he couldn't fail. He was there to set an example and he'd already informed his superiors of the traitors in their midst. He'd been unable to get what he came for, but that wouldn't keep him from fulfilling his objective.

The lives of three men were about to be destroyed.

11 NOTHING IS FAIR IN LOVE AND WAR

Years later, no one could recall exactly what had happened that day. Some said that Lieutenant George Cooke had arrested Wil Burck, Eric de Lyon and Harry Kelder cowboy-style: that with their hands up and a gun at their backs, they were marched off to Captain Spoor to be interrogated. Lieutenant Cooke could only remember bringing in Eric, using a gun to do so, but Eric himself couldn't remember a gun. It all became a muddle of conflicting memories.

It seems certain that Eric rode to the base by bus that morning. When he headed for rollcall, he ran into George Cooke, who had a gun in his hand and told him he was being arrested.

'What the fuck is going on?' Eric asked.

'Sorry, mate, I really have no idea,' Cooke answered. 'I'm only following orders.'

Eric was marched into Major Fiedeldij's office, where Spoor was sitting beside Captain Jessurun, an intimidating Colt pistol lying between them on the table. Fiedeldij stood behind them, his face ashen and confused. Eric raised an eyebrow at his commanding officer, still puzzled by what was happening, but Fiedeldij looked away, shaking his head.

Spoor's voice broke the silence. 'We know what you were planning and there's no use denying it,' he said, tapping his pen on the wooden table to emphasise his words.

Eric searched the captain's eyes and, finding no mercy there, decided to keep his mouth shut—at least until he knew what was going on. It was, however, beginning to dawn on him that it could all have something to do with what had happened the previous night. Just as Wil and Adriaan were about to leave, and he and Harry were getting ready for bed, Tom Derks had knocked on their door. He explained that an army intelligence man from Dutch headquarters in Melbourne had been trying to tap into their discussions through the wall next door. He reassured the four of them that the man had failed miserably. There had been drunken laughs and smirks as the men praised the hotel walls and sneered at the incompetence of Dutch intelligence. Adriaan Scholte had only smiled weakly.

'You fellows aren't really serious about this flight to Java business, are you?' Tom had asked, wondering why intelligence would send someone just to verify rumours.

Harry had breathed alcohol into Tom's face and said that, as long as they were drunk, they were serious. Meanwhile Adriaan had looked at Tom as if he'd swallowed a pig.

'You okay?' Tom had asked.

'Headache,' Adriaan mumbled.

Unable to rely on his legs to hold him, Harry had clutched the doorframe and swerved towards Tom before he suddenly appeared to think of something: 'What were you doing next door?'

Tom had cocked his head, chucking a knowing smile towards his drunken friend.

'Fucksake, Tom,' Wil burst out. 'The bloody intelligence bloke saw you in there with her!'

'He thought I was her husband,' Tom mocked.

'Crazy bastard,' Wil had said.

Now the captain's voice broke into Eric's recollections: 'You're unusually silent, De Lyon. Let me tell you that we have ways of obtaining the information we want from you.'

It sounded like a line from a crappy movie and Eric felt a sudden urge to laugh, but he remained stoic and kept his mouth shut.

'If you prefer to keep silent, that's up to you, but let me inform you that we have a sound recording of what was discussed in the hotel last night.'

From the information Tom had given him, Eric knew this was a blatant lie, so he kept his mouth shut. Spoor, now becoming frustrated, ordered Cooke to lead the silent prisoner away. Eric was placed in an adjoining room for the time being.

Captain Van Lochem later claimed to have witnessed Wil Burck's arrest that morning. They'd all been eating breakfast in the officers' mess when the door burst open and Captains Spoor and Jessurun rushed in, pistols at the ready. Within seconds, they arrested Wil, who let himself be led away without much resistance.

Through the door of the room where he now sat, Eric could hear Wil, and sometime later Kelder, being taken into the office and interrogated. He thought it strange that Adriaan wasn't being interrogated and wondered what could have happened to him. After all, he'd been the most eager to arrange a meeting the previous night.

Later that day the three prisoners were driven in separate cars to Queanbeyan police station. Being kept in separate rooms and interrogated by Captain Spoor individually meant they hadn't had a chance to speak to one another at all. But locked up in their cells, they could communicate for the first time—by shouting through the open shutters of their cell doors. Wil, like Eric, wondered where Adriaan was. Had he been shot? Or had he fled? They spent the long night in lockup, believing they'd soon be set free due to lack of evidence. They had no idea that Adriaan, after reporting to Captain Spoor, had been shipped off to Melbourne. His immediate promotion was to a job at NEFIS.

The next morning, having spent the night at the barracks, Captain Spoor marched through the airfield to a waiting car. The previous night he'd been busy composing a written confession for the three men—all they needed to do was sign the document, which he'd take back to Melbourne with him. The confession stated that the three of them had been conspiring together in an act of treason. Spoor would explain to them that signing the document was just a formality and that they'd be able to clarify the situation before the court later on. His main goal for the time being was to get the confession signed.

During his stay at Fairbairn, Spoor had found the attitude and insolence of the Dutch far from acceptable. He seemed oblivious to the fact that Fiedeldij had painstakingly gained the trust and respect of his men. Although his approach may have looked far from perfect to an outsider, the major had slowly but surely managed to get his men organised and positive. Spoor, however, viewed things differently. He feared it would all turn to anarchy if something drastic wasn't done. He needed to set an example, and he had to do so in the most frightening way he could think of.

On his way to the car, Spoor ran into Tom Derks, who was strolling along with a group of men. Some of the men had been on duty at Moruya, among them Ed Timmer, who'd arrived that morning. Tom was to be one of the Moruya replacements and Ed's group had just finished briefing the new unit.

Tom jumped when the captain smiled and said amiably, 'Well, Mr Timmer, I hope my intrusion on you and your lovely wife last night didn't upset her too much.'

The men turned to stare at Tom, who produced a couple of inaudible words while forcing a smile. But the smile faded when Ed pushed his way through the group. All six feet six of him faced the captain. '*I* am Ed Timmer,' he said.

Puzzled, Spoor replied that he'd been at the Tourist Hotel last night and had intruded on his wife and . . . Then he stopped, realising his mistake, looking from Tom to Ed.

There were a few smirks and an uncomfortable silence as everyone grasped what had happened. Ed tore his eyes away from the captain but, before he could do anything, Tom took off. They watched Ed's throat constrict just before his legs came to life. He bounded over the runway, chasing the fleeing Tom.

The men didn't know whether to laugh or be shocked. Most of them knew about Tom and Betty, and most of them knew the game they were playing was stupidly hazardous. Something like this had been bound to happen eventually. Ed Timmer, although somewhat stupid, wasn't a total idiot, and they were surprised he hadn't caught on sooner.

The men watched as the agile and much lighter man outran his pursuer with ease. Disappearing behind one of the hangars, Tom left Ed heaving and trying to catch his breath in the middle of the runway. There were laughs and shouts from the men, but this only infuriated the agitated Ed even more. He swore loud enough for all of them to hear. He'd get the bastard, he knew he would, and he hoped Tom Derks was shitting his pants in fear in a small and dark corner of the base.

Visions of his wife fucking the sinewy airman replayed themselves in his mind like a film loop. Drawing a hand across his eyes, he tried to erase the image, but all his fingers wiped away were his tears—not of sadness, but of frustration and anger.

On the other side of the tarmac the men scattered. With Tom gone, the spectacle was clearly over for the moment. Feeling self-conscious about the whole affair, Ed kept his back to them and made his way to the side of the hangars. He'd find his motorbike, he thought, and go back to the hotel to have a little talk with lovely Betty. The images he had of Betty with the tall blond Tom Derks made him livid with rage. He needed to calm down, he thought, or else he might kill her.

As he headed towards the base's parking area, Ed spotted Tom again. He was standing in the alleyway between the two hangars, his back to the looming danger. Relieved, and thinking he'd got away for the moment, Tom stood smoking a cigarette in the shade of the second hangar, oblivious to the approaching Ed.

After the men had sauntered away, Norman rushed to find Bob. He'd watched the scene from a distance and, although unable to understand a word that had been said, he knew what could happen if Ed got his hands on Tom. He found Bob in the officers' mess with Gus.

'Idiot, idiot, idiot,' Bob mumbled as the three of them dashed out.

The first punch smashed Tom's nose, the second his eye socket; when the third connected with his face, Tom believed he was going to die. He'd barely been able to defend himself at all after Ed launched his surprise attack. Now a strange sense of resignation took hold of him as his mind and body ceased to function. He slumped, the blows making his limp frame jerk like a puppet. The beating seemed to go on forever but, oddly enough, he didn't feel any pain, just the movement of his body as Ed drove his fists into it. Somewhere far away he could hear shouting and screaming.

Then everything changed, and the fist holding him up lost its grip and he felt his body hit the ground. The screaming was louder now. Someone had told Tom once that your hearing is the last thing to stop functioning when you die, and he couldn't help wondering if sound was the first thing a child noticed when it was born. It was a curious last thought, he supposed, and he tried to smile as he slipped into nothingness.

When Bob, Gus and Norman saw what was going on, they shouted and ran as fast as they could towards the punching Ed

Timmer. Gus was a big burly bloke, but when he jumped on Ed's back, the man shook him off like a rag. Then Bob and Norman both jumped on his back at once, trying to get hold of his arms, while Gus kicked one of Ed's legs from under him, making him lose his balance. Ed toppled and finally let go of Tom.

The noise and shouting attracted others, and now a group of men was trying to subdue the furious Ed, who still kept fighting. It was like trying to restrain an enraged bull, and it was all they could do to avoid his flying fists. In the end it took ten men to control him—five to hold his arms and legs and another five to sit on his body, trying to keep their balance as Ed squirmed beneath them.

Tom lay on the ground like a fallen tree, his arms and legs splayed like branches. Bob crawled towards him and threw up when he saw his head. Tom's once beautiful face resembled a bloodied knot sticking up between his shoulders. Bob howled as he grabbed one of Tom's hands. 'Don't you dare die!' he shouted. 'Don't you dare!' Then he realised his brother might already have done so.

When the medics came, Tom was still breathing and had a pulse. They rushed him to hospital and Ed was escorted away.

The next morning, Burck, De Lyon and Kelder were picked up from the police station. A heavily armoured vehicle brought them to Fairbairn, where a Mitchell bomber, one of the B-25s, stood prepared for take-off. It was scheduled to transport them to Melbourne.

Captain Spoor was also on the plane, and the three shackled men sat silently, waiting for take-off when another man, escorted by two guards, also boarded the plane. It was Ed Timmer, and when Harry Kelder opened his mouth, Spoor's harsh voice silenced him. 'All of you will keep your mouths shut for the duration of the flight! Understood?'

The men tried to catch Ed's eye, wondering what he'd done. He certainly hadn't been involved with any of their plans. For heaven's sake, Wil thought, the man hadn't even been in his own bedroom the other night. He'd been at Moruya—what could he be suspected of? The world had gone mad, he concluded, but he did not know just how mad things had become.

When they disembarked at Essendon Airport, the three men were immediately surrounded by detectives from the Australian Criminal Investigation Division; two detectives were assigned to each prisoner. But there was no detective for Ed. Wil noted that Ed was escorted to a taxi and its door was held open by another man until he was seated, whereas the three of them were firmly shoved into separate police vehicles, with two guards for each man. They never saw Ed Timmer again.

The next day, while doctors fought to save Tom's life, Betty Timmer came to the base. Wearing a scarf and sunglasses, she strutted across the tarmac, her head held high. She leant against the wall of the officers' mess and listened, a cigarette between her heavily painted lips, as Major Fiedeldij filled her in.

The men who were watching later said she'd looked stunning, like a movie star. Her high heels clacking on the concrete, she strode off after the talk was over. She never looked back.

12 PICKING UP THE PIECES

The day Tom Derks encountered Ed Timmer's fists, Norman, who had initially helped contain the furious Ed, ran for the base ambulance, picking up two medics on his way. There'd been little dispatch work for Norman at the base, so he'd busied himself working as a refueller, fire tender and ambulance driver. He truly feared for his friend's life and sped back to the scene of the fight, driving the ambulance himself as fast as he could. The medics, 'Bluey' Emmerson and Eric James, found a pulse, but there seemed to be no airflow through Tom's nose and very little through his mouth, so they inserted a tube in his throat and rushed him to hospital, hoping he'd still be alive when they arrived.

The surgeons operated on him for hours. His body was badly bruised, but the only real damage it had suffered was a couple of broken ribs. His face, on the other hand, had suffered the worst of Ed's wrath; his jaw, cheekbones, eye sockets and nose were broken, and the doctors had to reconstruct his face.

They told Bob there was a possibility Tom had suffered brain damage—they'd all have to wait until he regained consciousness to find out.

Bob stayed with his brother those first few days. Heartbroken, he sat waiting to see how things would turn out. Believing he'd lost his fiancée to the Japanese, he now feared he'd lose his brother over a stupid brawl about a woman. He wondered if Tom would ever wake up, and confided in Norman that his worst fear was that he might not 'fully return' if he did. The doctors had already told him that Tom would never look quite the same: they had done all they could to reconstruct the bones in his face, but if he survived the scars would remain. No matter how his brother came out of this, Bob resolved he'd always take care of him.

———■———

The winter in Canberra was icy and the RAAF boys had slept in their overalls in an effort to keep out the cold. They were sleeping twenty to a barrack with just one fuel heater to keep the frost from their noses. It was one of the coldest places Norman Harris had ever experienced and even the five blankets he'd been issued didn't keep him warm enough. Luckily, the days were gradually warming and on some days the men could even wear their summer outfits.

Norman and his fellow Don Rs were issued with peak caps and the distinctive dispatch rider's blue and white armband. An authoritarian and pushy Dutchman, Lieutenant Schelling, was now in command of transport, and the Australians didn't much like him. 'You can order an Australian soldier to do something, but you can't push him,' Norman explained to Bob.

In mid-November, the 18th Squadron was informed they'd be moving to MacDonald Airfield north of Pine Creek in the Northern Territory. The Japanese were becoming a real threat near Darwin, so it was thought that the squadron would be of much more use there than down in Canberra. They were almost a full-strength squadron now, with some 700 men. Moving all of them and their equipment would take a lot of logistics to accomplish, and 'The Move', as it became known, was planned to take place in four stages.

The first group would be sent to do the preliminary preparation work, which meant making the terrain accessible. MacDonald had already been roughly developed into an airfield by the Americans, but it would now need to accommodate a much larger group of men. The initial group would have to flatten the area with bulldozers and put up tents for the main group, which would follow a few days later with 750 tons of equipment. As soon as the base had a take-off and landing area, the air echelon would leave Fairbairn. The fourth and last group would be shipped to Darwin over sea, bringing bulk goods and the squadron's personal belongings with them.

The Dutch boys were euphoric. Any move closer to Java meant being closer to family. At Moruya they had practised 'skip bombing'—a low-level bombing technique—and 'shadow shooting'—shooting at their own plane's shadow in order to hit the enemy—and at Nowra some air-to-air firing; they were now more than eager to put what they had learnt into practice with a real enemy. Most of them wanted to leave as soon as possible. Up north they'd get a chance to fight the Japanese. They might even be asked to fight in the Dutch East Indies, in an attempt to liberate the islands.

Smokey Dawson briefed the RAAF men, warning them about the harsh conditions up north. There would be dust and mud to deal with, and guts and determination would be expected from every one of them. If any of them had doubts about the move, they could come and see him later and he'd get them posted to another unit. A few took up their commander's offer; those who remained all received their shots for cholera and plague. Dawson's brows furrowed when a couple of the men keeled over while waiting their turn in the line.

By the end of November everyone at Fairbairn became immersed in preparations for the move. Returning from their final leave, men found themselves facing the task of loading tons of equipment onto pallets to be transported to MacDonald. Everyone hoped to get settled in at the new base in time for Christmas.

It wouldn't be an easy relocation. The airfield was very remote and they'd have to cover thousands of miles by train and then on by army truck over outback tracks and through riverbeds. The Australian boys knew the heat out there could kill you. No one was expecting a picnic, but NEI and RAAF men alike were glad to be on the move, and an optimistic buzz ran through the air base as men and equipment were moved from one end of the airfield to the other.

The pilots would be the last to go, and Bob and Gus were glad they'd be able to keep an eye on Tom for a little longer. He'd awoken from his coma, but hadn't reacted in any way to their questions. He couldn't talk in any case, because his jaws had been wired together, so Bob had given him a pad and pencil, hoping he'd write something to show he still had all his marbles. So far, though, he'd not shown any sign of intelligence. This was nothing to worry about, Gus joked to Bob, because Tom rarely had. This was meant to cheer everybody up, but it was lost on Norman and Bob as they watched Tom drooling and staring into space in his hospital bed. Gus paced the room and Bob became ever more worried. The doctors huddled together at Tom's bedside, whispering medical speak neither Bob nor Norman understood.

The first sign that Tom was aware of anything occurred when Bob and Norman discussed the fire at the Tourist Hotel in late November. An article in a local paper said it was caused by a smouldering cigarette butt. It was no surprise to either Norman or Bob.

'The Tourist was always a bloody fire hazard with all the smoking and drinking going on in the rooms,' Norman said. 'It was bound to cause a disaster sometime or other.'

Apparently, the fire had started in the lounge, damaging only the upper portion of the hotel. The residents all scrambled to escape, and luckily there were a couple of firemen staying there who had assisted in the evacuation. One resident had to escape through a window onto the cantilevered awning and another had to be treated for the effects of smoke and shock. The damage exceeded 10,000 pounds. 'It's a miracle no one got seriously hurt or died,' Norman said.

Norman, who did not smoke and only drank moderately, was discussing the pros and cons of smoking when he suddenly noticed a reaction from Tom. Neither Norman and Bob, bent as they were over the newspaper to read about the fire, had noticed Tom taking the pad and pen from his bedside table. To their astonishment, he was now waving the pad wildly at them. They took it from him and read the childlike letters he'd scrawled across the pad: 'I'm dying for a smoke.'

It was the first sign of Tom's recovery, and as the days progressed he became ever more alert. When the bandages were removed from his face, Bob thought he didn't look all that bad. Yes, there were lumps and scars, and Tom's face had become unusually flattened, as if he'd driven it into a wall. The flatness gave him an Asian appearance, but he didn't look hideous and anyone who had not known him before might not even notice.

Norman wasn't as positive as Bob. Although the features in Tom's face were flattened, there were still lumps where the bones had been stuck together. To him Tom's face looked like it had been made up of spare parts, with dents and bumps in places where they hadn't been before. What worried Norman most was the vacancy in Tom's eyes. It was as if all the life had been beaten out of them.

When the wires were removed from his mouth, Tom was finally able to talk and eat again. He initially ate a lot, mostly porridge because he couldn't chew, but he hardly spoke. He appeared introverted and sullen, and his face had become almost devoid of expression. The doctors said it was due to nerve damage and that they'd have to wait and see if it healed. Bob could only hope that his brother would return fully, given time.

Tom soon began to hate the porridge he was forced to eat, but when he was finally offered solid hospital food, he changed his mind about the porridge—it hadn't been all that bad. Although Bob and Gus brought him fish and chips or Chinese noodles on occasion, the horrible soggy pieces of hospital meat and crumbling potatoes swimming in a sea of tasteless gravy was still part of his diet. He told Bob there was a morbid irony in the fact that while Ed Timmer's fists had been unable to kill him, the hospital food just might.

At the beginning of December, the hospital decided they'd done all they could and were ready to release him. Although he'd need to wear a face mask for a while to protect his damaged bones, he was a young man and the doctors expected him to make a full recovery. His face, however, would always bear the scars Ed had inflicted. Tom refused to look at himself in the mirror, afraid of what would stare back at him, but the doctors appeared very pleased with their handiwork, complimenting each other whenever they came in to check on his progress.

During his time in hospital, he'd asked about Betty just once. Bob told him she'd left, that Ed had been moved to Melbourne, and he suspected she'd joined him. 'Forget about Betty, Tom,' Bob warned. 'She was bad news from the start.'

But Tom couldn't. This woman had an edge to her, something he'd never come across in others. He'd paid dearly for his obsession, but he'd never forget her. That was something he kept to himself—he never told Bob.

Tom also wanted to know what had happened to Ed, but he might have been jailed or hanged or given a medal for all they knew. All Bob could tell him was that they hadn't seen him since that day. There were rumours that he'd been taken to Melbourne along with Wil, Eric and Harry, who stood accused of treason. Weird stories about the men had begun to spread. A newspaper article said the three men were thought to be German infiltrators who were planning to destroy the Australian Parliament building.

All the Dutch knew this was ridiculous. Hagers, who'd got to know Wil Burck quite well because they had been roommates for a while, sent a letter stating as much to the Dutch authorities. 'The plans were no more than talk from a few frustrated men, and it had nothing to do with treason,' he said.

In honour of Tom's discharge from hospital, the men in his unit decided to give him a proper welcome-home dinner. It had to be something special, something that would make him forget all that appalling hospital food. Gus suggested shooting some ducks. On the lakes near Fairbairn he'd seen hundreds of them swimming around and Tom loved poultry. The problem was that the damn birds sat in the middle of the lake and, without a dog to retrieve them once they were shot, there was no way to reach them.

Debates raged on what might be the best course of action. Some advocated shooting at the ducks from a distance to drive them over the land, where a couple of other men could shoot them as they flew overhead. This seemed such a good option they tried it. But the ducks flew too high or in the wrong direction, or they moved to another part of the lake, always out of shooting range.

The ever-enterprising Gus finally came up with a simple solution. The B-25s had inflatable dinghies on board, in the event of a crash at sea. They could use the dinghies to paddle up to the ducks, shoot them and retrieve them. Gus made a frame from thin tubes that he mounted over the small boat. 'We'll cover it with mosquito netting and float the dinghy slowly towards the ducks while we sit concealed under the netting,' he explained. 'They might think it's an island floating towards them.'

The others couldn't help but be sceptical, but they were willing to give it a try.

'The big problem, however, is the weapon,' Gus argued. 'One shot from a 12-calibre rifle will chase all the birds away and I don't think one duck will do a good job of feeding the lot of us.' But he thought his 22-calibre Mauser might do the trick if he could get a silencer for it. The local gunsmith told Gus he was willing to make a silencer for him but it would take a few days. When Gus went to pick it up, it fitted perfectly on his Mauser and looked great. And when he tested it by firing the gun into the air the noise was minimal.

The four-man hunting party set off early on the day Tom was due back. They loaded the deflated boat and their makeshift floating hide onto a truck and took off to the lake, which was about a fifteen-mile drive from the base. When they arrived, they could see hundreds of ducks on the water. For five minutes they stood taking in the view before inflating the dinghy and erecting their hide. Bob and Gus got inside and the other two pushed off their odd-looking craft in the direction of the ducks.

Hagers and Bill Hutchinson were staying ashore with the responsibility of shooting any duck that flew overhead. It all appeared to be working like a charm as Gus and Bob floated very slowly towards their unsuspecting prey.

About ten feet from their quarry, Gus aimed his weapon and fired. Nothing happened. They saw the bullet drop into the water just a few yards in front of the dinghy and sink to the bottom like a mini bomb. The silencer worked wonderfully—not a sound was heard—but it drastically reduced the velocity of the bullet. Gus cursed himself for not taking the time to test the thing properly on the shooting range. In the end, the four men decided on a surprise attack with their conventional 12-calibre rifles and the unsilenced Mauser. In all, they managed to shoot seven ducks.

Returning to the base, they proudly presented their prize to the Javanese cooks. Tom was guest of honour that evening. But even though the ducks had been stewed for hours, their flesh remained too tough for Tom to chew—he ended up only eating the potatoes and beans.

By this time Norman and a large group of RAAF and NEI boys had already headed north. The air echelon was due to join them soon, and for the first time in months Tom's thoughts returned to Grace. He'd really thought he loved her, but that was before Betty. Still, remembering the lovely girl now lifted his spirits a bit. Betty was, and would always be, off limits. He didn't want to lose his life over her.

He didn't know if MacDonald was close to Stapleton. Probably not, but he found some comfort in the thought that Grace was up there, somewhere.

13 THE MOVE NORTH

At the beginning of December 1942 the first small reconnaissance unit from the 18th Squadron had travelled north to MacDonald. Norman left about a week later, together with most of the squadron. They were to travel by train as far as Alice Springs and then onwards through the desert by truck. The men had worked hard at getting everything onto the rail trucks in Queanbeyan, and it had taken them a couple of days to load the 750 tons of equipment.

After travelling for three days, they got stuck in Tocumwal, on the New South Wales border with Victoria, where they had to change trains because of the difference in rail gauges between the two states. Moaning and groaning, the men set to work. Everything had to be taken out of the first train and moved from one side of the platform to the other, then loaded onto the second train. As they sweated in the midday sun, they knew they'd have to go through it all again at the next border town before they reached Adelaide.

They were especially annoyed because they were also hungry. The bad and irregular meals served on the train had done nothing for their stomachs or their spirits. The only pleasant surprise had been at Jerilderie, where the ladies had done their utmost to show their appreciation for the troops by providing them with a wonderful meal. The women had come aboard carrying large plates stacked with sandwiches, meatballs and mutton chops. They'd even come around to give many of the men a second and third helping.

'My word, you're as skinny as a poor man's wallet,' one of the women commented on seeing a very slight boy. 'Don't they feed you chaps in the army?'

Now their arduous journey continued. Travelling through Shepparton later that night, Fredrick Bowering suddenly opened one of the train's windows and shouted: 'Hi, Mum! Freck here— I'm doing all right.'

He was a red-headed, round-faced freckly boy, with ears that stuck out like taxi doors. He'd been nicknamed Freckles by his family—Freck for short. He looked like a cheeky fifteen-year-old schoolboy, but he was actually 25. 'She can't hear me, but somebody else might,' he shrugged when Norman raised an eyebrow and others started moaning that his shouts had woken them up. 'They might tell her I passed through.'

Freck had grown up in Shepparton, a town located on the floodplain of the Goulburn River in northern Victoria, and worked as a bank teller before enlisting in the army in 1940. He'd first served for fourteen months in the 10th Battalion, based at Warradale in Adelaide. Life in the 10th Battalion, with little action going on, hadn't really lived up to his expectations, and he became bored. He applied to join the RAAF and was soon accepted as a trainee wireless mechanic, but his secret wish was to eventually become a pilot. Freck was known to be impulsive and slightly brash, but he was also good for a laugh or two.

—■—

Eight days after they left Canberra, their train pulled in to Alice Springs. It was their last stop before heading inland by truck. They'd have to unload the train there, but after that they were due for a rest. The three days in Alice Springs did not seem very promising, though, given the Alice was little more than a couple of streets laid out in the middle of the desert and their base was a makeshift camp on the outskirts of town.

The Stuart Arms Hotel and bar run by Joe Kilgariff was a good spot for some entertainment and a drink or two. Before taking over the hotel, Joe had been a silent movie projectionist in Barmera in South Australia's Riverland. He'd brought all his equipment with him when he left Barmera, and he now held screenings in a shop across the road from his pub. When the pub closed, the men would take their drinks to the other side of the street to watch a picture show.

The Ghan, the train from Adelaide to the Alice, arrived fortnightly, bringing with it reels of film and cases of beer. The bottles were packed in straw inside wooden crates that Joe would haul into the bar and cover with bags of water to cool them. After three days of drinking in the Stuart Arms and strolling along Alice Spring's dusty streets, none of the men was sorry to leave. Norman and Freck together drove one of the trucks; after passing through the dry desert landscape of South Australia, they were pleasantly surprised by the tall green grass and the wildflowers of the Northern Territory. The wet had settled over the land and at times rain fell from the sky in torrents. Silver sheets of it poured down mercilessly and they'd have to stop for hours because they couldn't see a thing. Farm boy Norman noticed how rich the soil looked. 'If there was more water you could grow anything here,' he told Freck as the rain pounded them. Freck looked at the drenched scrub and gave him a confused stare.

Passing through Elliott after hours of driving, Norman fell asleep behind the wheel and their truck drove off the road and landed upside down in the scrub. The Dutch boys driving in the truck behind them jumped out to see if anyone was hurt.

Gerry Wiggers was the first to stick his head inside the window and assess the damage. Freck had toppled over Norman, and they were a tangle of limbs. Gerry helped Freck free himself and another Dutchman pulled him out of the window.

But when Gerry stuck his head back into the truck to offer Norman a hand, he quickly pulled his head out again. White-faced, he vomited on his mate's shoes.

'Oh my God,' Gerry moaned. 'His brains! His brains!' Freck stuck his head back into the truck and held out his hand to help Norman, but his hand slipped. When Freck looked at his hand, it was smeared with something red. Gerry looked on in horror as he watched fingers from inside the truck grope at the edge of the windows. Pulling himself up, Norman popped

Members of Blackforce, a brigade made up of Australian and American troops, with their armoured car transport, on their way to Batavia to cut off the Japanese advance in Java, 1942. AUSTRALIAN WAR MEMORIAL (043856)

Australian troops inspect the damage after a Japanese air raid on Darwin, 19 February 1942. The Darwin Post Office and Post Master's residence were both destroyed and the Post Master, his wife and daughter as well as members of the postal staff, including four female telephonists and two postal officers, were killed. AUSTRALIAN WAR MEMORIAL (042870)

After the bombing of Darwin, Broome became the main port for flying boats and planes fleeing the islands, but it was not equipped to accommodate such a sudden influx of aircraft. Flying boats had to wait for hours on Roebuck Bay to be serviced. Officially, no civilians were allowed to travel on Dutch military aircraft but many pilots, understandably, disregarded the order. On 3 March 1942 nine Dutch Dorniers and Catalinas carrying hundreds of Dutch refugees landed on the bay. In the early hours, nine Japanese Zeros flew over Broome, attacking both the airport and the bay. Many Dutch refugees, thinking they had finally made it to safety, died.

Dutch aircraft in a hangar at Fairbairn Airfield, Canberra, in 1942. The Dutch pilots and crews who fled to Australia initially regrouped at Archerfield Air Base in Brisbane, but in June 1942 they were transferred to Fairbairn to form the No. 18 (NEI) RAAF Squadron.

At the end of 1943 the No. 18 (NEI) RAAF Squadron moved to the Northern Territory to be closer to their targets—Timor and the Tanimbar Islands—and also to help defend Australia's almost defenceless northern coastline. Seven hundred and fifty tons of trucks, goods and men were loaded onto trains but, due to the difference in rail gauges, the men had to reload the trains twice. It took sixteen days to arrive at their new destination—MacDonald Airfield.

Dutch and Australians in line for inspection after finally arriving at MacDonald Airfield. Note their somewhat shambolic approach to wearing a 'uniform'.

The No. 18 Squadron was a mixed Australian–Dutch one and both countries provided their own commanding officers. The CO for the RAAF in 1942–43 was Leslie Roy (Smokey) Dawson (left) and for the NEI it was Major Benjamin Fiedeldij (right), who was of mixed European and Javanese descent. AUSTRALIAN WAR MEMORIAL (NWA0299)

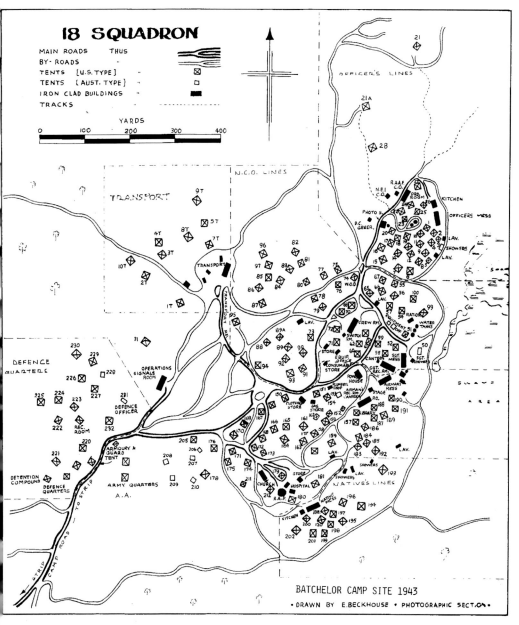

No. 18 Squadron's camp site at Batchelor, 1943, drawn by Sergeant Errol George Beckhouse 60641, RAAF Photographic Section, from a composite aerial photograph.

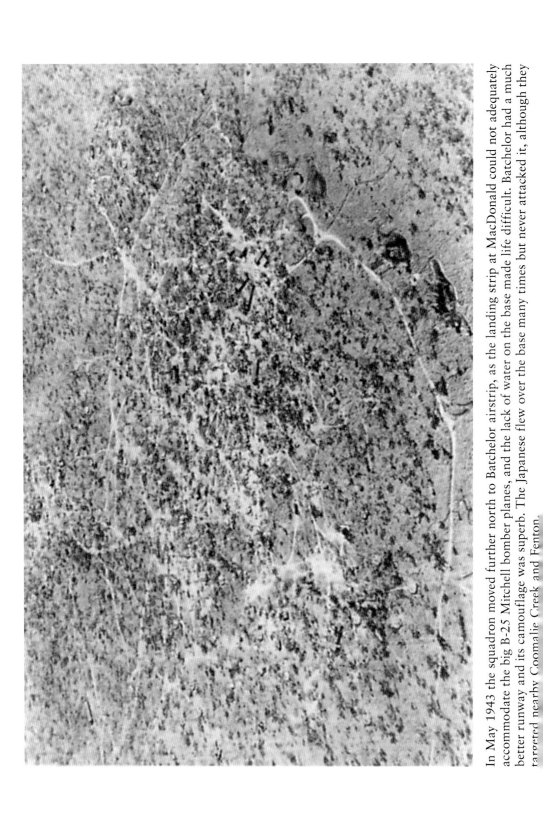

In May 1943 the squadron moved further north to Batchelor airstrip, as the landing strip at MacDonald could not adequately accommodate the big B-25 Mitchell bomber planes, and the lack of water on the base made life difficult. Batchelor had a much better runway and its camouflage was superb. The Japanese flew over the base many times but never attacked it, although they targeted nearby Coomalie Creek and Fenton.

Although Batchelor had a better airstrip as well as water in abundance, the accommodation was no better. COURTESY OF GUS WINCKEL

Sometimes accidents occurred during landing and take-off. Usually only the planes suffered damage but there were some fatalities.

Gus Winckel (second from left) standing in front of Fredrick Pelder's plane. Pelder is third from the left. Notice the name 'Pulk', Pelder's nickname, written on the side of the plane; it means 'to tinker' in Dutch. Pelder, thought to be the last Dutch pilot to escape the Dutch East Indies, was always tinkering with radios and motorcycles. COURTESY OF DIRK STELLEMA

The cockpit of a B-25 Mitchell bomber.

At Batchelor a small tractor was used to move the bombs from the bomb dump to the airfield, where a trolley (shown) and lifting device hauled them onto planes.

The planes were serviced under large camouflage tarps attached to trees. From the air it was almost impossible to notice the aircraft below. COURTESY OF BRIAN COLEMAN

Horse races were organised to amuse the troops and distract the townspeople of the Northern Territory. The war made it difficult to provide racehorses so both farmers and cavalry regiments 'lent' their horses for a day. AUSTRALIAN WAR MEMORIAL (061565)

Regular parades, such as this changeover parade of the Electricians, Instruments and Armourers unit, were held at Batchelor. Brian Coleman can be seen in the front row under the red dot. COURTESY OF BRIAN COLEMAN

Dutch B-25 Mitchell bombers flying in formation above Darwin. Note the Dutch flag on the side of each plane. COURTESY OF BRIAN COLEMAN

The aircraft guns were cleaned after each mission.

To amuse the men at Batchelor, a makeshift movie theatre was improvised on the base. Every man had to bring his own seat and some would climb up a tree to guarantee a good view. The projectionist, however, had his own bench as well as a table for the projector. Note the sign, OUT OF BOUNDS TO ALL RANKS, on the projector shed. COURTESY OF DIRK STELLEMA

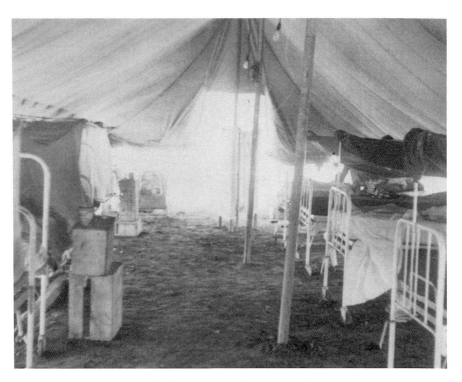

First stationed at Fenton, the hospital ward (1 Medical Receiving Station RAAF) was later moved to Coomalie Creek. On 13 August 1943, 1 MRS at Coomalie was attacked by the Japanese. Twenty-six bombs exploded on and near the hospital grounds but miraculously there were no casualties. AUSTRALIAN WAR MEMORIAL (P0I923.009)

Guus Hagers (the flying officer third from the left) and his crew. Hagers was a highly respected and gifted pilot: while taking part in secret missions on Merauke he was able to locate entry and escape routes for the Allies. COURTESY OF DIRK STELLEMA

The shores of Merauke. The No. 120 (NEI) RAAF Squadron arrived on the island in May 1944.

Guus Hagers in a B-25 bomber above Merauke. Note the name of his wife Lienke on the side of the aircraft. COURTESY OF B. BOGERS

Conditions in the Japanese internment camps on Java were appalling. Tjideng, the largest, was populated solely by women and children; boys over the age of twelve were sent to camps for men. Each house accommodated up to twenty people. The camp had no running water and there was an open sewerage ditch next to the gate. AUSTRALIAN WAR MEMORIAL (305356)

The badge of the No. 18 Squadron—the image of a Dutch girl with a mop. After sinking over 24,000 tons of Japanese ships around Timor, Ambon, the Kai and Aroe islands, the squadron earned the nickname 'The Dutch Cleanser', a term that originated from an Australian advertisement for a Dutch cleaning liquid.

Brian Coleman (second from left) leads the No. 18 Squadron on Anzac Day, 25 April 1998, in Melbourne.

ANZAC Day Parade, 25 April 2003, Brisbane. Gus Winckel can be seen second from right.

his head out the window mumbling, 'Could someone give me a bloody hand here?'

Men from the other trucks had by now crowded around the overturned vehicle and, when Norman's head appeared, they all recoiled in shock. It appeared to have been split open by the blow of the overturning truck. Red blood and what looked like brain matter were oozing from his head and running down Norman's face. A couple of the boys ran away and others turned their heads, unable to watch as Norman rose from the truck looking like something from a freak show.

Freck, slightly confused because of the commotion, looked at his hand and then at his friend. It took a second for the penny to drop, but he suddenly started to laugh. A couple of men screamed for a medic while carefully lifting Norman from the truck.

When Freck grabbed one of the NEI boys and tried to explain, they pushed him aside and told him to sit down and take it easy, they'd take care of his friend. The injured dispatch rider looked dumbfounded as he was carefully placed on the ground. When he tried to get up, firm but gentle hands forced him back.

'What?' he asked. 'What the fuck is wrong?'

The men spoke reassuring words, setting off all his alarm bells, and when the medic raced towards him, pushing everyone aside, Norman became genuinely frightened. Meanwhile Freck was sitting in the dirt, laughing and looking like an idiot as he wiped the tears from his eyes.

Gerry Wiggers, having recovered from his initial shock, came over to pat Freck on the back sympathetically. Men shook their heads, thinking the poor kid had gone nuts at the sight of his friend dribbling brain matter. The medic was now wiping away most of the blood and brains from Norman's head, trying to locate the wound. Norman lay wide-eyed and terrified.

'Spaghetti!' Freck managed to cry. 'Spaghetti!'

Getting up, he shrugged Gerry away and ducked into the truck. Gerry shook his head in pity as Freck's body disappeared from view. He thought the poor bloke was trying to retrieve his friend's brains from the truck. But he reappeared holding high a can of Heinz spaghetti, a big grin over his face. A moment of silence settled over them as they tried to grasp what they thought they'd seen.

Freck explained: 'I was eating this when the truck overturned. Must have spilt most of it over old Norm's head when the truck rolled.' It was hard to tell who felt more relieved—Norman or the men who thought he'd lost his brains. Norman almost cried when he realised he wouldn't die after all. The men simply grinned, embarrassed and relieved at the same time. The vehicle had survived the accident with no more than a dented rear bumper bar and the loss of one of its headlights. Minutes later the truck was back on its wheels, but now Freck was the driver.

It took them sixteen days to travel from Canberra to MacDonald. From Alice Springs, the roads were mostly non-existent or in very bad condition; on a good day they managed to make about 200 miles, but on most days they travelled a much shorter distance. It was hard going. During the day the heat was intense and the trucks were often so hot that the men could burn themselves if they accidentally touched the hot metal. Then the rains would come, making travelling through the riverbeds almost impossible. And the flies were a constant nuisance.

By the time they passed through Pine Creek late one evening, the men were tired, dirty and dispirited. The last few miles to MacDonald Airfield were especially gruelling because the trucks got hopelessly bogged in the mud, their wheels sinking so low they were barely visible. The wet clay sucked hungrily at their wheels and sometimes up to three other vehicles were needed to pull out a marooned truck, only to find that another truck had become stuck in a pothole further on. When the men tried to push a truck, they'd get a mud bath from the wheels spinning frantically. Emerging from the back of the vehicles, the soldiers looked like moulded clay manikins. With no running water to wash off the grime, they resigned themselves to the inevitable and waited for the clay to dry and crack then peel from their clothes and bodies like old skin. It seemed to the men that nature had turned against them.

When they finally reached MacDonald Airfield, nothing but crickets and eerie silence greeted them. The English and Australians who had used the field before them had left weeks ago and the site was now abandoned. That first night most men slept inside the trucks or under them. It was much too late to put up a tent. All they wanted to do was sleep.

They settled into their sleeping bags, men and equipment hidden from view by the grass, which had grown six feet high in the rich soil. The only thing that betrayed their presence was the sound of their snores.

14 MACDONALD AIRFIELD, NT

MacDonald Airfield wasn't much of an airfield; Norman Harris didn't think it was much of anything. The base was one of the most barren airstrips he'd ever come across. When they woke that morning the men realised it would take a lot of effort to make it usable, let alone liveable. As the men looked around the area for the first time in daylight, most hearts sank in disappointment.

The English and the Australians had constructed an airstrip, but it was unsealed and much too short for the B-25s that were due to land there in a few days. When the Brits and Aussies left, they had taken everything with them, leaving behind only a short airstrip and a lot of rugged outback.

Norman, Gerry Wiggers and a couple of RAAF boys examined the short, crude landing strip in dismal silence. Norman was no pilot but even he could see the strip wouldn't facilitate their bombers. Those at RAAF headquarters who had allocated MacDonald to the 18th Squadron had demonstrated little understanding of the needs of a B-25.

'My brother said that the Brits and our lot flew English Beauforts and Hudsons to fight the Japs off while they were here, along with a couple of Aussie Boomerangs,' one of the mechanics muttered.

'Well, the strip would have been big enough for them,' Gerry said, scrutinising the runway and spitting into the dust.

'Maybe they haven't read the manual,' the mechanic said.

If the RAAF had a B-25 manual at headquarters 150 kilometres away in Coomalie Creek, then they certainly hadn't got around to reading it, Norman thought.

Recovering from their initial shock, the men went to work. With scrub to clear, trees to chop down, and roads, taxiways and dispersal areas to construct, as well as a runway to extend, there was no time to mooch and moan. So they rolled up their sleeves.

But they didn't know half of what awaited them. All the work had to be done out in the open, with temperatures rising to 40 degrees Celsius; as soon as a space was cleared, tents fourteen feet square had to be erected. With six men to a tent, they'd have to put up more than 100 just to provide a bed for each man.

The main problem, though, turned out to be the constant lack of water. No one had bothered to explain that there was no drinkable water on the site. It had to be carted in from Katherine about 60 miles away. The Brits and Australians who had previously used the base had been a relatively small group, but the 18th now had about 700 men. There was a bore only a fifteen-mile drive away, but to supply each man with just a few gallons of water per day someone would have to drive the water wagon back and forth continually. Water, being so precious, was soon rationed: two gallons each a day, for cooking and drinking, as well as washing themselves and their clothes.

Suspecting there might be water right underneath them, Norman asked permission to sink a bore. 'There's got to be water somewhere down there,' he said to Smokey Dawson.

Having been brought up on a farm, Norman knew about artesian bores, which were vital to crop farming in most areas. A group of volunteers took turns at drilling, but the soil turned out to be hard, rocky and merciless. Sweat, flies, heat and an occasional downpour got in the way.

It seemed to take forever and they could only drill a foot at a time. After days of work there was still no water bubbling to the surface. Norman wasn't one to give up easily, but he began to wonder if he might have got it wrong.

Just when they were deciding whether to throw in the towel, however, they struck water at 90 feet. A loud cheer surfaced along with the water, and Norman threw his hat in the air like a Texan striking oil as he danced under the flowing fresh water. Norman and Freck volunteered to be guinea pigs for the rest of the squadron and tested the water, drinking a cautious pint each. They both wished they hadn't a couple of hours later.

Freck thought it tasted a 'wee bit briny', but it had looked clear enough and it was pleasantly cold. An hour later, however, Freck's rear end felt like it was going to explode in his pants and he dashed into the scrub in a graceless manner with one hand on his buttocks. Crouching behind a bush he managed to lower his pants just before he let go. His sigh of relief rose from the scrub above the explosive noises. Before long, Norman followed suit. They were sick for a day and a half, and when the new Dutch base doctor, Herman Storm, declared the water unfit for use, that was that. The flow of water didn't last anyway. It had initially come in a rush but that had soon died down to a trickle and all the hose did a few days later was drip water onto the thirsty sand.

Being so low on water, you'd think that the men would have welcomed the wet, but the torrential rain was a dubious blessing: it turned the dust into mud, which made extending the runway an arduous job, the trucks and bulldozers constantly getting stuck in the soft slush. The granite gravel on the airfield washed out during the heavy rains, leaving potholes. When there was a downpour, they did at least collect some water in the tanks they'd erected, but in many ways the rain was a disaster.

Nonetheless, somehow a fortnight later the base was ready to receive the air echelon. What had seemed impossible when they started, they'd managed to accomplish. In Canberra, 162 men and eighteen planes, waiting patiently for the okay, at last received orders to head towards the Northern Territory. It would take two days for most of them to get to MacDonald.

Some of the planes left early because they had to first make a detour to the Laverton air base at Melbourne. To ensure they'd have enough fuel to fly great distances in Asia, these planes were to be fitted with bomb bay tanks. Because there were not enough tanks, not all the planes were fitted with extra fuel tanks—some would fly to Melbourne at a later date. It took two days for the mechanics to install the tanks and for the men it was a nice break. Not long before Christmas, Bob, Gus and seven other pilots flew their B-25s south to Laverton.

Returning to the airport two days later to pick up their planes, Tom and Gus stood at the hangar's entrance, waiting for their aircraft to be towed out. It had started to rain that morning and the weather had gone from bad to worse, with no sign of clearing up. Peering out through the rain, Tom noticed someone running towards an aircraft on the runway. The bulk of the man and the way he moved seemed familiar. For a split second he thought it was Ed Timmer. But it couldn't be, he realised, touching his face gently with his hand—surely the man was sitting in a cell somewhere for what he'd done.

—■—

Two days before Christmas, Gus and his crew were the first to reach the new enlarged MacDonald Airfield. They flew in at about eight in the evening; it was dark and a slight dribble of rain had petered out after a downpour earlier. As Gus approached, he saw the reassuring flicker of a row of storm lanterns escorting them in.

'Almost home,' he said to Tom as he proceeded to land, hitting the lever that would release the plane's wheels.

'Fuck!'

Gus rarely swore and Tom looked around in alarm. He saw the problem just seconds after Gus had and braced himself as

Gus pushed the throttles in an attempt to pull the plane up. As they shot past the runway, their Australian radio operator pushed his head into the cockpit and asked what was going on.

'The bloody lanterns are on the wrong side of the runway,' Gus explained.

Contrary to normal procedure, the lanterns had been placed on the right-hand side of the runway, almost making Gus land beside the strip. Landing on the soft shoulder could have killed them: it had been piled up with tree roots, branches, and all kinds of rubble that had been cleared when the runway was extended.

On the second attempt to land, Gus put his plane down as carefully as a parent would put a baby to bed, but inside he was fuming. He took his anger out on the temporary commanding officer, Captain Jessurun, who'd directed the placement of the lanterns. Jessurun was not a pilot, and apparently no one had corrected him. Gus stomped out of the officers' mess and no one ever placed the storm lanterns on the wrong side of the runway again.

On Christmas Day, they awoke to the sound of rain pelting down on the tent roof. The Christmas Day cricket match had to be called off, but the men all received hampers from the New South Wales division of the Australian Comfort Fund (ACF)—the contents included a cake, plum pudding, cream, cheese, toothpaste, razor blades, some tobacco and chocolate.

The ACF raised money through various activities to buy food and make items they sent to the Allied troops. The Australian boys also received parcels on a regular basis from their parents or other family members. Norman felt sorry for the Dutch, who hardly ever received a package because their families were interned or suffering in wartime Europe. If they were lucky, they'd receive an occasional letter from loved ones.

Except for the hampers, Christmas came and went without much sparkle. On such a remote base, there wasn't much to do anyway. MacDonald did not have women, beer or anything to entertain the men. A picture show had been set up just outside the camp and, if it didn't rain, they'd screen a film. *Cisco Kid* was on just a few days after Christmas. You had to bring your own seat; the boys who didn't have a seat found a spot in a tree.

Determined not to let New Year's Eve pass by unnoticed, a party was organised so the Australians and the Dutch could celebrate the event together. A few days before, beer was flown in from Darwin and some clandestine bottles of whisky arrived as well. With Wil Burck and Adriaan Scholte gone, the former band had lost its main members, but plenty of men could play some instrument or other, and seven of them formed a small band, practising whenever they could.

The evening would be a memorable one, but it started off innocently enough with the band playing 'Dixie'. A boxing match followed, but Tom could not really appreciate it, as each blow made him cringe. The Hawaiian Ensemble—six men in grass frocks and flower chains, attempting to transport the audience to the beach at Waikiki—were good for a laugh and some insinuating remarks. With enough beer to go around, everyone seemed happy. The treacherous jungle brew had also suddenly reappeared from nowhere, concealed in jerry cans labelled 'Open with caution'.

The pace at MacDonald was slow because the constant downpours made any kind of work or flying almost impossible. To create another water truck, the pilots sacrificed two of their bomb bay fuel tanks. Because there was little dispatch work, Norman had been driving the water truck full time but, with a second water truck now operating, he was assigned part time to Signals, where he joined Freck, who worked as a radio operator. Norman was on duty there for 36 hours every four days; the remaining time, he'd hop on his truck and make his way to the bore.

Tom, who was still recovering, spent most of his hours in the recently established air base library. He'd never really liked to read, but in the library he discovered Lawson. Rather ignorantly, he hadn't realised Australians wrote books, and Lawson's prose and poetry appealed to him. His vivid descriptions of the country read like miniature movies.

MacDonald was a far cry from the comforts of Fairbairn. At night the men would sometimes hear Japanese Zeros fly over. The whole base was in blackout and there was also radio silence. The food was mostly tinned and the water lukewarm. Flies were rampant, and the tents became hot and muggy at night, especially when it rained. They started to wonder if the cold of Canberra had been so bad after all.

In the first weeks of January 1943, the 18th Squadron was fully operational and more than ready for action. The men were itching to go. They couldn't wait to fly to the islands and chase off the Japanese.

15 FIRST OPERATIONAL ORDER

The last group of men finally arrived at MacDonald early in January. They had come by sea, travelling on an American Liberty cargo ship that was attacked by the Japanese near Thursday Island. They'd had quite a scare and some of them had been injured, but the damage hadn't been substantial. Shaking his head at hearing this, Hagers said, 'It's time to go and do something about it. What's everyone waiting for?'

Fiedeldij assured them that their first official operational order would be arriving soon. The squadron's role would be to strike the Japanese airfields day and night, carrying out low- and ground-level strafing attacks, and also to attack enemy vessels at masthead height. Mainly they were to up the pressure on Timor and Ambon. Additional tasks would be making photo-reconnaissance flights of special targets in occupied areas of New Guinea and dropping provisions for the Allied guerrillas fighting in occupied areas.

The operational order came in on 17 January 1943; on the next day three planes finally took to the air. Gus Winckel was the patrol commander on that first assignment. Lieutenant Hagers and Sergeant-Major Louis Schalk flew the two other Mitchells. They were to make a reconnaissance and bombing flight to the Tanimbar Islands, part of the Dutch East Indies.

That morning Bob flew with Gus and Tom flew with Hagers. Adrenaline cascaded through them, filling them with a strong desire to fight. It was as if all that dull and monotonous waiting in the rain had to be driven out, and the only way to do that was by putting their lives at risk. They dropped a few bombs on Dili in Timor and were chased away by Japanese Zeros. One of the Japanese pilots appeared especially zealous and wouldn't leave them alone until they headed back.

Gus openly admired this pilot's expertise and nicknamed him 'Willy from Dili'. 'This bloke can fly,' he said. 'He knows his stuff. Hope we don't run into him again.'

During the flight back they had time to let their adrenaline subside; no one shot at them and they came across no great enemy movements on land or sea. The initial thrill had worn off and Tom couldn't help but feel slightly disappointed. Yes, they had been attacked and yes, they had dropped a few bombs, but somehow it hadn't been enough. It was as if they'd been sent on a fishing trip and hadn't even managed to catch a sardine.

Many more sorties followed, and from that moment on they flew out across the Timor Sea on an almost daily basis. In the coming months, they'd see more action than they'd bargained for. In February and March, the squadron flew 87 missions above enemy targets, attacking Japanese ships and air bases. Some crews lost their lives in the process.

There was still a constant fuel problem. If they were being chased by enemy planes or had to engage in air fights, the return flight became quite hazardous. The distance from MacDonald to the North-West Area of the East Indies was too far for the B-25s, and they'd sometimes run out of fuel on their way back to the base. Even with the added bomb bay tanks, most planes only just made it back to the air base, and a fair number touched down with their fuel gauges on empty.

The first accident with a Mitchell occurred due to fuel shortage. One of RAAF patrol leader Lieutenant George Cooke's planes, flown by Captain De Jongh, made an emergency landing near Alligator Creek on the Daly River. On the flight to and from the Timor Sea, they'd lost a lot more fuel than they'd bargained for; all the combat flying guzzled up most of it. On the return trip, they decided to refuel in Darwin, but the town had raised the alarm, making it impossible to land there. Not wanting to get caught in the crossfire, they headed for Port Keats, wasting even more fuel.

With just a drop left, the crew flew inland, heading for MacDonald, but before they could get there, they were flying on empty and the plane started to descend. Spotting a nice flat outback area they could land on, De Jongh decided to bring the plane down. He kept the wheels tucked in and the landing went incredibly well; the crew were very surprised that they felt hardly a shock or jolt when they touched down. Once they were out of the plane, it became clear why their landing had been so smooth: they were in the middle of a swamp. The five crew members climbed onto the plane and waved to Cooke circling above, to let him know they were all right.

With insufficient fuel to make it to MacDonald, Cooke turned back and just managed to land at Port Keats where he immediately gave orders for a plane to be sent to the area where De Jongh had landed. It would supply the crew with food for a few days until they could get to them by boat. The rescue plane found the men soon enough and threw out the packages with a note attached. The supplies, however, were too heavy and sank as soon as they fell into the swamp, vanishing between the reeds and the mud. A couple of men saw a crocodile taking off with what looked like one of their parcels. The beast swooshed about, finally going under and taking the loot with it.

No matter how hard they tried to locate the packages, they couldn't find them, and the men didn't much care for taking a dive into the water. They weren't that hungry, yet. But after a couple of days, when the food shortage had made them desperate, De Jongh gathered his courage and took a dive into the swamp. It resulted in nothing. He didn't find the parcels; they were gone. 'Hope the bloody croc chokes on them,' he spat as he hoisted himself back onto the plane's wing.

They waited for days, hungry, dehydrated and bitten by mosquitoes. They tried to shoot a bird, but it landed in the middle of the swamp and became just another free meal for the patrolling croc. The swamp water tasted briny and gave them the runs so they stopped drinking it. Just when the men thought everyone had forgot them and they'd surely perish, they heard the sound of a motor.

When Cooke returned to MacDonald he thought the men had already been plucked from the swamp, but the pilot had only dropped food and was under the impression that Cooke would make sure his men were picked up when he got back to the base. After two days, with none of the stranded men turning up, Cooke started to get worried. When he phoned Keats, it became apparent that they were still in the swamp and he knew it would be hard to get to them by plane.

It was Tom Derks who came up with the idea of using a motorboat to rescue the men. He arranged to hire one at Adelaide River and took with him a tracker and another Aboriginal man. They knew the area and would make sure he didn't get lost. They drove from the Adelaide to the Daly River and began their boat ride. Tom was mesmerised by the wildlife on the river— crocodiles, buffalo, bats as big as dogs, and of course the birds. Galahs, magpies, parakeets and lorikeets were abundant in the lavish bush. He loved it.

The men were stranded in the swamp for four days before they saw the motorboat leisurely making its way up the creek. They almost wept with joy.

As the boat came closer, De Jongh recognised Tom Derks and waved.

'Bet you thought we'd forgot you?' Tom said, throwing them the food and water he'd brought with him.

De Jongh guzzled at the water, took a bite of a sandwich and asked, 'What took you so long?'

Tom told him he'd taken his time to enjoy the view. 'This is Albert, by the way,' he said introducing his Aboriginal guide. 'He'll be making sure we don't get lost finding our way back.'

Getting back to MacDonald took another three days. When they arrived, their joy at having made it was overshadowed by the news that nine men from the squadron had been killed.

———————

It was Sergeant Louis Schalk and eight of his crew. They had taken off on 5 February in their heavily packed Mitchell. To be able to fly the route, the Mitchells were filled to the brim with fuel; they were also packed with crew, firearms and bombs. This meant they were well over their maximum take-off weight. A drizzle made visibility poor, and in the early evening the ground temperature was unusually high, which adversely affected the motor's speed. Radio silence was in place, and with no lights to make trees visible, it was always difficult to avoid them. The gumtrees around the runway had been left untouched because they provided natural camouflage.

Bob and Norman had been standing near the edge of the runway as the plane prepared for take-off. The motors had revved in anticipation as the captain pushed his plane into gear. The B-25 sped along the runway; Bob remembered later that he hadn't waved the plane off, which he always did when watching one of their own leave. He and Norman had been deep in discussion about the possibility of Gerry Wiggers resuming his Dutch lessons. The sound of the plane caused Bob to turn around; he could already see it was not making enough height.

A sharp crack sounded as a branch tore from a tree, and Bob knew things were about to go horribly wrong. The plane struck the top of the gumtrees.

'Fuck,' Norman whispered as the plane zigzagged across the terrain just beyond the runway.

The wheels were still out and Bob shouted, 'Pull in the fucking whee—'

The last word was lost as the plane hit the ground, exploding on impact, just as Bob and Norman ducked into a trench. It was the first of many explosions, because the loaded bombs went off one by one. It seemed to take forever and, when silence finally returned and they dared raise their heads, both knew that no one in that plane could have survived. Fire trucks were already rushing to the scene, but all the men could do was watch as the plane burned out.

It was not the first time a take-off had gone wrong, and it would certainly not be the last, but this crash would go down as the most devastating. That night Norman stuffed his ears with Tom's tobacco, trying to block out the sound of sawing and hammering as the squadron's carpenter, Johnny de Lille, worked all night preparing coffins for the burial. The next day the remains of the nine crew members were put to rest in the small cemetery at Adelaide River.

Major Fiedeldij was furious and sent an angry letter to his superiors at the RAAF No. 79 Wing. The conditions at MacDonald were simply not good enough for the heavy bombers his squadron was flying. Based too far from their targets, the B-25s didn't have the required range to hit Japanese objectives on New Guinea. Low-level and ground strafing attacks exposed the Mitchells to enemy fire, making it more than likely that the planes would have to return home with damaged engines. This and their limited range would increase the danger of losing planes and crew. Fiedeldij suggested that either the planes be modified for long-range flight or the 18th be transferred to the North-Eastern Area, near Port Moresby.

HQ rejected his suggestions. Air Vice Marshal Adrian Cole thought the Dutch pilots lacked dash and initiative: 'You're not flying a commercial airline,' he retorted. Fiedeldij, fearing for his men's safety, wrote another letter to his RAAF commander, Air Vice Marshal Frank Bladin. This time he did not mince words: the heavy losses were unacceptable to the Dutch Government.

Not wanting a Dutch–Australian dispute on their hands, RAAF HQ backed down. The planes would be modified at Eagle Farm near Brisbane; they'd be fitted with more weapons of a heavier calibre, and their under turrets would be replaced with 300-gallon drop tanks. It would, however, take until June for all the planes to be modified, so accidents and near accidents still occurred. In time, the squadron would also be leaving MacDonald for Batchelor, a base further north.

—▪—

There were a few scares when Japanese planes flew over the area at night. They never dropped anything, but everybody took to the trenches anyway. After rain the trenches were often full of water, because they were situated in the low-lying areas of the base. To avoid a drenching, some of the Australians would take to the hills whenever enemy aircraft flew over; the Dutch started calling them 'Dawson's hillbillies'.

Sometimes, for reasons unknown, someone in the camp would go 'troppo'. One day Jack Douglas went crazy. The mozzies had been driving the men mad and they'd sprayed the water in the creeks with oil in an attempt to get rid of them. When they still buzzed, droned and whined around Jack's head, he set fire to the swamp. There was a general panic when the fire spread. Men scattered, running around the base, salvaging their possessions from the flames. Jack stood among the tall grass laughing hysterically; they had to pull him out of harm's way as the fire raged towards him. Just a day later a Dutchman who was peacefully playing the guitar suddenly, for no apparent reason, picked up a gun and threatened to shoot his roommates. Men from the other tents came looking for the cause of the commotion, but backed off when they saw the gun. A couple of them tried to reason with the man, but he claimed that no one appreciated his music and that he'd kill them because of it. Storm, the base doctor, finally managed to calm him down.

With no women ever visiting the base, the whole male squadron went slightly bonkers when three showed up unannounced one day. They were nurses from the hospital at nearby Coomalie Creek on a tour of the air base. Fiedeldij and Dawson, who had polished their boots and faces for the three ladies, marched them around the base, all friendly smiles and courtesy.

But it was Norman who attracted the attention of one of the nurses—sitting on his Indian-brand motorbike, his hair combed back, with the beginnings of a moustache, 'looking like bloody

Errol Flynn', Freck thought. When she walked up to Norman, he almost fell off his bike, steadying himself as he blushed. He wasn't brash, and he wasn't one for smart repartee or bold pick-up lines, so when she asked him if he'd take her for a ride on his motorbike, he was somewhat stuck for words.

''Course he will, sweetheart,' Freck intervened, coming to his rescue. 'And if he doesn't, I will.'

She hopped on the back and Norman revved his bike to life. He moved off without a word, her arms wrapped around his waist. Watching him disappear into the distance, the men almost died with envy.

Norman took the girl, whose name was Olivia, out a couple of miles. The road was a bit boggy but the bike ploughed through it all right. The girl was thrilled when he stopped at the nearby creek, where a group of Aboriginal children were splashing and shrieking in the afternoon heat, swinging from the paperbarks into the cool water. They stayed for an hour talking and watching the kids show off. On the way back, Olivia snuggled up to him with her head on his shoulder, and Norman felt as if he'd won first prize in a lottery.

Ten minutes from the base Norman's bike ran into a mud pool and they were stuck in the middle of it. As she dismounted, Olivia's shoes sucked into the mud, and she lost her balance and toppled over. Watching the girl rolling around in the treacherous mud, trying to gain a foothold, Norman leaned over to give her a hand and accidentally let go of his bike. Now they were both stuck. Norman honked the motorbike horn, hoping it would attract attention. They were only half a mile from the base.

They had just managed to get out of the mud pool when a truckload of men from the base found them. Looking awkward and uncomfortable, Norman tried to regain his composure, acting as if he was in complete control. Four men jumped down and retrieved his bike but, as soon as they'd hauled it to dry land, they turned their backs on Norman, leaving him standing there with his bike. All of them turned their attention to Olivia, apologised for their clumsy mate, helped her up into the truck's cabin and drove off without even a backward glance at the forlorn dispatch rider.

A couple of the motorbike's sparkplugs had got wet and the thing refused to start, so Norman was forced to walk it back to the base. For days, there were jokes about the mudwrestling contest between the nurse and a certain Don R.

Sometime later, to his surprise, Norman received a postcard from Olivia thanking him for the ride and saying she hadn't had so much fun in ages. She was based at Coomalie Creek, near Fenton, and, if he were ever in the neighbourhood, she'd love it if he looked her up.

'Looks like you've got yourself a sheila,' Freck said after he snatched the card from Norman and read it out loud.

'She's sorry for me, that's all,' Norman said, snatching the card back. He thought about visiting Coomalie, but told Freck it would be too far by motorbike. Freck argued that it was just up the 'bloody' road and he could think of no reason why Norman wouldn't take his bike and ride up there on a day off. For some reason Norman felt self-conscious about the whole thing, suggesting to Freck that Olivia may not actually want to see him and the postcard was her way of being nice. Freck feared it would be a long time before Norman ever saw Olivia again.

'Ah well,' Freck told him. 'You wouldn't be able to get into the place, anyway. I hear the nurses are guarded by the soldiers as if they were precious jewels. Any man trying to get to them would be shot on the spot.'

16 ACROSS THE TIMOR SEA

In March 1943 the 18th Squadron flew 46 sorties and in April they took off 57 times. Despite the Japanese striking at Guadalcanal, Oro Bay, Port Moresby and Milne Bay in April, it was actually looking as if the Allies were winning the air battles. The Japanese suffered a devastating blow when Admiral Yamamoto, their adored leader, was killed in April. American Lightning pilots took down the plane he was travelling on. It seemed the enemy was close to defeat, but the Allies lacked the forces to deliver the final blow.

In the course of all this Bob was feeling very depressed. He discovered that the only way to take his mind off Colette was to volunteer for duty, grabbing every chance he could get to fight the Japanese. He was in the air for weeks on end.

'Your brother up there, doin' the Japs in again?' Freck asked Tom.

For almost every day that month Bob had been involved in some kind of action, sometimes as first pilot and sometimes as second. He didn't care, as long as he could do something that made him feel he was making a difference. His eyes had become hollow, expressionless and vacant. Tom was worried and thought it might have more to do with the bennies (Benzedrine) his brother had been popping than the amount of combat time to which he was subjecting himself.

After a week of continual flying, Bob had gone to Dr Storm complaining of fatigue and loss of concentration. The doctor had given him a bottle of pills, telling him to take one when he felt exhausted, but Tom thought his brother had been taking more than one lately. Bob was unusually thin and had no appetite; while some of this could have been due to worry about Colette, Tom suspected that most of it was to do with drugs.

It was a strange responsibility for Tom to worry about his brother. For the whole of his life he'd been the one to cause concern; now he was at a bit of a loss about how to act as the sensible one. When he confronted his brother, he felt like a right idiot; Bob threw him a sceptical glance and simply walked off. Tom decided to let it go; he just wasn't example material.

Like Bob, many of the men were moping around the base, jumping at every opportunity to grab some action. Hagers, who had a fiancée in the camps on Java, had been flying as many missions as he could, using Benzedrine to keep him on his toes.

Hager's friend and mechanic, Bill Hutchinson, had come back from leave one day with a puppy for his mate. Bill's parents owned a cattle farm near Katherine and when one of the farm dogs had pups, he thought one might help take Hagers mind off his girlfriend and give him something to take care of.

This appeared to work. The little dog followed Hagers around wherever he went and the grieving pilot grew quite attached to it. When he was away on a short mission, he would always see to it that someone else took care of the dog. Hagers and Gus even managed to make a small parachute for the animal and, when he went away on any longer mission, he'd fly over the Hutchinson property, drop the dog and pick him up later.

Tom considered a dog for his brother, but he doubted Bob would appreciate it. Stray dogs sometimes came into the camp looking for food, but Bob never felt sorry for the animals and shooed them off if they came too close. Norman said the dogs were dingoes, and that the local Aboriginal people sometimes kept them as pets. Spotting a mother with her pup one day, Tom had pointed her out to his brother, but Bob had been less than interested, claiming the dogs only brought fleas and ticks to the camp. When he threw a stone to send the two dogs on their way it was quite clear he didn't want a pet. Tom left it at that.

One evening Bob wandered into the scrub and stood watching the brief Australian twilight fade, his thoughts as ever turning to Colette. As the sky turned from purple to dark grey, he heard a plane preparing for take-off. There were always planes coming and going, but for some reason Bob noticed an off sound as the plane picked up speed. Here we go again, he thought, the memory of the last crash still fresh on his mind.

It was Captain Ekels' plane racing along the runway. Captain Jessurun was on board as navigator, perched in the B-25's nose, sharpening his pencil so he could note the exact time of take-off. Halfway down the runway Ekels realised his aircraft was not lifting off. In an attempt to abort, he shut down the fuel supply as he sped towards the end of the runway. Bob watched as the plane skidded into the scrub, crashing its way into no man's land. It ploughed along on its belly then came to a sudden halt. The impact catapulted Jessurun out of his seat between two 50-calibre machine-guns and through the turret's glass, spitting him onto the ground.

It took Bob two minutes to get to the aircraft. When he found Jessurun, he wished he hadn't. The first thing he saw was the sharpened pencil sticking though the navigator's throat, its lead tip emerging from the other side; Jessurun looked like a speared fish. But he was alive. Bob poked his head into the plane's cockpit to check if there were any other wounded. Ekels gestured that they were fine. They were knocked about a bit, but apart from a few bumps and bruises everyone had survived.

Jessurun wasn't someone Bob particularly liked. His involvement in the affair with Wil, Eric and Harry had not earned him points in the popularity department, and neither did the lighting incident on the runway that had almost made Gus crash. Nonetheless, Bob rushed over to the man and tried to console him as he moaned in agony. Jessurun's arm was strangely bent, most likely broken, and his knee was bleeding, but it was the pencil that worried Bob. By now, men were arriving from all directions and Dr Storm pushed Bob aside, yelling for a stretcher, which arrived a minute later. When they carried the captain away, Bob feared the worst.

Miraculously, Jessurun's pencil hadn't damaged anything vital. The doctor set his broken arm, stitched his knee and a few days later the men saw him limping around the base again. Captain Ekels and the three other crew members had come away unharmed. Because of the accident, a new rule was introduced, forbidding anyone to sit in the front turret during take-off.

—■—

Life at MacDonald settled into a daily rhythm. Planes would land and planes would take off. Whenever a plane didn't come back, morale would drop. Pilots often had a sixth sense that a plane had gone down. At night there were regular scares as enemy planes searched the outback for signs of landing strips. MacDonald was hard to spot from above, and even the pilots who knew exactly where it was had been known to fly past the field on occasion.

Darwin was under constant attack and there was not much of it left. The government feared that it might cause panic if it were known further south that the Japanese were bombing Australian targets on a regular basis. The news that was sent out was mostly positive, proclaiming the many victories of the Allied and Australian troops, but the truth was much more alarming—Zeros bombed Darwin repeatedly, sometimes using daisy-cutter bombs to maximise the blast damage.

The 18th Squadron did all it could to keep the Japanese busy on their own occupied territory and keep them out of Australia, but there were strikes and attacks on strategic targets from both sides. In a show of tenacity, the enemy forces sent regular high-flying reconnaissance aircraft over the Darwin area.

At the beginning of May, when flight commander Gus Winckel's unit bombed targets on Timor, they met up with an old acquaintance—'Willy from Dili'—who came to greet them as they made their way to Fuiloro. The little troublemaker's propeller had been painted red, but even without this distinctive feature, they would have known it was Willy. He was a master in the air and flew his plane like an acrobat. Bob, who was second pilot to Gus, held his breath as he saw him coming. 'Willy' recognised his equal in Gus and immediately targeted the plane. Four other Zeros headed for Hagers and Tom's plane. The Zeros were so agile it made the B-25s appear awkward and ungainly, but that was an illusion—the B-25 was a safe and forgiving aircraft and the bombers were also sturdy, taking a lot of bullets to bring one down.

By now Zeros appeared to be coming from everywhere and they attacked with vehement intensity. Hager's air gunner, Ronnie Horridge, managed to down a Zero with a direct hit. The plane spiralled, leaving a black smoke plume as it disappeared into the Timor Sea. But with another Zero attacking Hagers' plane from above, there was no time to rejoice.

Through the intercom Tom heard Horridge yell, 'Oh shit! My damn guns have jammed!'

Gus chased the Zero off, his gunner spitting bullets at the plane like hailstones. Tom gave his commander and his brother a big thumbs-up when they passed, but then a radio call came in—both aircraft heard a cry for help from Lieutenant Gummels: 'Mayday, too many planes attacking. My starboard engine's been hit.' Zeros were coming from everywhere.

Gus told Hagers to keep close and to attack the enemy with his front machine-guns, but before they could get there, a Zero flew up to Gummels and shot at the pilot through the cockpit at '12 o'clock high'. Gummels and his nose gunner, Tyler, were killed instantly.

Gummels' second pilot, Fischer, took over the controls, screaming into the mike that his commander was dead. Wind blew through the cockpit window of the badly damaged plane and Fischer could hardly keep his eyes open as it slapped into his face. The plane lumbered on, steadily losing oil, pressure and power. Fischer knew he'd have to ditch the plane before it got out of his control.

The fight had taken them out to sea, and the Zeros started heading back to land one by one as their fuel ran out. But Willy did not intend to head back and he pounced on Gus's plane. Bob had seen him coming and mumbled a low but sincere curse that made Gus sit up—'We've got the fucking march fly on our tails again.'

Picking up speed, Gus ducked and came back behind the little Japanese, but they lost him when he somersaulted his aircraft above their heads.

'Where did he go?' Bob asked, nervously checking the airspace for a trace.

Willy had pulled his plane around and now began attacking them from the rear. It was a split-second decision that made their top turret gunner, Bill Maks, turn his weapon and launch a direct hit, pumping 'blue-nose' ammunition into the unsuspecting Zero. It exploded right behind them, killing Willy.

By now Fischer was in real trouble. Tom, Hagers, Gus and Bob could only watch as his bomber skidded into the sea, tail first. Gus circled overhead on the lookout as Fischer and the mechanic crawled out of the sliding side windows near the pilots' seats. The mechanic released the rubber dinghy from the roof compartment and it launched itself in seconds. Fischer frantically tried to break the glass of the top turret with his hands. There were two gunners in the turret—one had been killed and the other was wounded.

'Get out of there!' Tom yelled, even though he knew Fischer couldn't hear him. Fischer was struggling to break the glass before the plane sank. Taking his Mauser out of its holster, he frantically started to attack it with the butt. All Gus and the others could do was circle above them, letting the men know they were there and that they wouldn't leave until they'd organised some kind of help.

Just moments before the plane sank to the depths, Fischer managed to pull the second gunner free and hoist him into the dinghy. 'Tight call, damn tight,' Tom said to Hagers as the dinghy drifted away from the aircraft.

'Go back to base!' It was Gus, ordering his men on the radio. 'I'll call it in and stay as long as I can.'

The wounded gunner was bleeding profusely. The circling airmen could see the bottom of the dinghy turning red as blood mixed with sea water. They knew these waters were infested with sharks and that any blood that escaped into the sea would attract them. Tom swore under his breath—if a shark bit into the boat, the three men would drown or be eaten.

'Go!' Gus ordered the rest of the squadron again. There was nothing they could do, so reluctantly they headed back.

Gus's radio operator sent a coded signal to Darwin, giving the position of the dinghy: 125 degrees east, 9.40 degrees south. Three Hudsons immediately headed out with supplies for the castaways, and a note telling them a torpedo boat would soon be on its way to pick them up.

Circling one more time, Gus saluted his men and they waved back. The sea was becoming choppy and the waves were sprouting white caps that looked like sharks' teeth. Bob hoped they'd be all right; he felt exhausted and wondered if he should take another 'wonder pill' as they headed towards Australia's shores. Deciding against it, he rubbed his eyes and slapped his face.

Low on fuel, they stopped at Darwin, where they were told that a boat was already on its way to pick up the men. Gus, deeply concerned, reminded the radio operator that the wind had changed and that the boat could have drifted a considerable distance from the coordinates he'd sent earlier. The man told him he was on it and not to worry.

It was almost dusk when they took off from Darwin, and the sky was feathery with pink clouds. Now and then they saw a lightning flash beckoning from the horizon—an atmospheric lighthouse blipping them in. They didn't talk. The toil of the day had left them speechless and Gus noticed how Bob's eyes drooped. Below, he watched the Australian mainland pass by under them while the plane's propeller sang a high note in the headwind. As the sun surrendered to the twilight, they left the green and woolly mangroves, and the purple cliffs behind them.

They'd made it through another day, although others had perished. It wasn't the first time and it wouldn't be the last. Gus knew it might even be their turn next. Cliffs gave way to scrub, and the tiny roofs of homesteads, still discernible in the vague light, resembling a collection of random stamps on a strange postcard. In the last light, the tired pilot caught a glimpse of a silver river slithering through the land like a giant snake.

For a brief moment, Gus's thoughts returned to Willy. He'd admired the man's skill and he could imagine how the two of them might have discussed manoeuvres and tactics over a beer had they not been enemies. It was the war that decided who you liked and who you didn't, who would become a friend and who wouldn't, who was good and who was bad. But there was no logic to it, Gus thought, no logic at all.

Landing at MacDonald felt like coming home, and they'd rarely been happier to have made it back. On inspection, the plane had quite a few bullet holes and would need repairs. Gus patted the beast's belly and sent his second pilot staggering through the night in search of his tent and a bed. 'Good shot, Bill,' Gus said to his gunner.

Maks nodded in acknowledgement. 'More a lucky shot than a good one ... Too bad about Willy, though. He was a pest, but a very talented one.'

Gus was famished and headed towards the officers' mess, hoping for some kind of meal. He'd need to debrief, but it could wait until morning. All he wanted now was to eat and, after that, go to bed. He might even have a shower before closing his eyes, he mused—perhaps the water would be a reasonable temperature. During the day, the water in the tank usually became so hot that it was impossible to stand under the spray. Now that it was well into the evening, it might have cooled down, Gus thought.

Tom and Norman sat outside the tent they called 'Walsh's Bar'. They were out of beer or any other kind of alcohol, so there was nothing to justify it being called a bar. They were drinking lukewarm lemonade, pretending it was something else. They knew beer would come eventually—not tonight, but someone would soon take a plane up to Darwin or fly to Sydney and bring crates of beer and maybe some whisky back with them.

As Gus walked by, his face was drawn and tired but his back was straight and his head erect. He didn't notice them and they didn't call him. Tom was relieved to see him, although he'd never doubted that his commander and his brother would return safely. Gus had so much confidence, not a trace of hesitation in his gait as he walked by. He led his unit with the same confidence, heading straight for the target and not letting anything distract him.

Gus was a hero of sorts, Tom thought—it wrapped around him like a well-fitting coat. His men claimed that if you flew with Gus you had a greater chance of coming back from a mission alive than with anyone else.

Tom believed it. 'He ordered us to leave while he stayed,' he said to Norman with a glint of admiration in his voice. 'I didn't even doubt that he'd return safely. Life clings to that man like a damn lover.'

17 BATCHELOR, NT

Batchelor, where the squadron was now to be based, was further north, near Victoria River. Although one of the men who'd been stationed there at the beginning of the war described it as 'a place God created while suffering from a hangover on a wet Monday morning', the men didn't care. They weren't expecting paradise, but nothing could be as bad as MacDonald. No one had the slightest regret at leaving.

The prospect of Batchelor excited Bob—it would bring them much closer to Darwin. Timor would still be a long way off, but those couple of hundred miles closer would take the edge off the fuel shortage and make reaching Java a possibility instead of a daydream.

It did mean, though, that they'd have to move again. All 750 tons of equipment—everything they'd dragged with them from Canberra—would have to be packed and loaded onto twenty-odd trucks and unloaded at Batchelor.

Norman knew what the future had in store for him because he was to be part of the advance party. That meant he'd have to do most of the work, which didn't make him at all happy. 'It's always us, the ground troops, that have to do the hard work,' he moaned to Tom. 'All you pilots do is wait until your bed is made and then you fly over.'

Tom raised an eyebrow. 'Okay, Norm, here's the deal: you go fight the Japs above the Timor Sea and I'll set up camp and have coffee ready for you when you come back.'

Norman weighed up the options for a moment before deciding that being a mover had more appeal than being a fighter pilot. Freck, however, watched the pilots with envy when they returned; he saw their look of exhilaration, caused by the rush of adrenaline and the realisation they'd survived. For them, surviving worked like a strange drug. He knew it was a stupid life-or-death game, but he wanted to be part of it. It was a way of thinking Norman couldn't comprehend—all he wanted was to get through the war alive.

What Freck didn't know was that the pilots would have rejoiced had he offered to become a pilot and fight with them. Now that a number of pilots and crews had been lost in action or to accidents, there was a shortage of able crews. The 18th had started understaffed and didn't have ready replacements. A lost plane could simply be replaced—you just ordered a new one—but a lost pilot was a much harder gap to fill. Fiedeldij sent letters to Jackson, where the Dutch pilots were still being trained, begging for back-up. A reply from Jackson explained that training hadn't reached the stage where the men could act as a relief unit. Decent training took time; the 18th would have to wait.

Most of the RAAF and NEI ground troops arrived at Batchelor by the end of March 1943. A year earlier, at the beginning of February 1942, President Roosevelt had ordered General MacArthur to evacuate from Corregidor in the Philippines. With the rapid advance of the Japanese in the area it had been vital to get MacArthur to safety. The general and his staff managed to escape the Japanese cordon around Manila Bay in four PT boats and headed for Mindanao. Two B-17s at Delmonte Airport then took MacArthur and his staff south to Australia. With the Australian coast already in sight, the planes were redirected to Batchelor airstrip because Darwin was under attack. To the new arrivals at Batchelor more than a year later, this was a historical place, where the great warrior himself had once set foot.

So for the 18th Squadron Air Division, putting their planes down on the airstrip at Batchelor on 9 May 1943 was almost like landing on holy ground. The base had a much better airstrip than MacDonald, with a waterproof gravel runway long enough for the B-25s. At Batchelor, too, water wasn't an issue, although the accommodation was still quite basic, with tents and buildings that were no more than makeshift structures. Compared to MacDonald, though, it was a step forward in many ways. The base, spread out over a large area, appeared huge. Norman was stationed on the northern side with the other transport units, and the pilots were on the southern side close to the NEI and RAAF command posts. Tom mused that he'd almost need motorised transport just to visit Norman.

———

Batchelor was also almost 500 miles closer to Darwin, but Tom hadn't realised that Stapleton Station was also just a couple of hours' drive away. When he found out, he was itching to find a way to get there.

For him, Stapleton was as much like home as it got. It had provided his first acquaintance with Australia and its people. Like most of his countrymen he was homeless; whenever Norman talked about the farm his parents owned in Yarrawonga, Tom felt a strange yearning. Every now and then Norman would share a cake with Tom, or a tin of baked beans his mother had sent him. It was good to eat something baked for you by a loved one, even if it did make Tom realise he was something of a displaced person. Maybe he'd always feel like that, because he felt no urge to return to the Netherlands; even when the war ended, he didn't think he'd go back. There was no mother waiting for him there and nothing much else to return to. He was starting to like this country; it wasn't his birthplace, but he could make it his home.

On his days off, Tom would sometimes hitch a ride into Adelaide River. The small settlement had formed the backdrop to the fleeing Darwin population and had become a recreational base for the many troops in the area, who frequented its cinema and couple of lively bars. In one of them Tom met a local called Jim Maloney, a man in his sixties who had been a crocodile hunter in his youth. He turned out to be a regular visitor to Stapleton and knew Winnie and Harry Sargent well.

One afternoon, when Maloney was heading for Stapleton to load some merchandise onto the early morning train the next day, he offered Tom, who was on a long leave, a lift there on his truck. He said there was a train that went from the Stapleton property to very near the base, so Tom could catch it back. Settling into the passenger seat of the ute, Tom felt like the prodigal son returning home.

He knew they'd reached Stapleton Station long before he saw the house. He could smell it: swamp and peppermint. It was late afternoon when they arrived; Winnie and Harry had seen the vehicle climbing up the hillside and recognised it as Maloney's truck. When another man spilled out along with Jim, the Sargents noticed something familiar about his passenger—his build and the way he walked. It was unmistakably Tom Derks.

Harry vigorously shook his hand and Winnie kissed his cheek. She tried not to stare at his face. 'War scars,' Tom said self-consciously, tracing a scar with his fingers and grimacing.

Stepping into the house felt like coming home to Tom, and minutes later it was all laughter and food: potato salad and eggs, pickled onions and meat. The room lit up with storm lanterns and their talk as they reminisced about how Tom and Norman had come tumbling from the skies that night many months ago. Tom told them he and Norman were still together, serving in the same squadron at Batchelor.

Winnie said the Japanese were still flying overhead and Tom remarked that she still wore her guns. 'Just in case I find a live one on the property,' she said. 'Harry desperately wants to catch one alive, so he can hand him over as a prisoner of war.'

'Who knows what a Jap could tell about the enemy's plans?' Harry added.

In fact Winnie and Harry had found a number of Japanese on their property. Some were still in their parachutes, hanging from trees like strange pods, others were mangled in their damaged cockpits. They were all dead.

Fleeing Darwinians still crossed the Sargents' land whenever the Japanese raided the area. Winnie was surprised that there was anyone left in the battered town.

Harry also told Tom about a couple of blokes from Batchelor airstrip who'd combed the place and confidently claimed to have found gold. A fellow named Schwenke, who said he was a surveyor before the war, had shown Harry a pickle bottle full of nuggets and said he was going have it crushed at Maranboy battery.

Harry had laughed at them when they said they'd be back after the war to put in a claim. He and Winnie had been digging the land for years. 'There's lots of tin and some uranium, but no gold worth digging for,' he told Tom. Harry knew the country—a bloke could come up with a jar full of gold nuggets only to find out later that was all there was.

After many hours of lively conversation, the Sargents and Maloney went off to bed one by one. Tom stepped out into the evening breeze to enjoy a last coffee and a cigarette. In the shadows, he saw a figure he recognised.

'Grace?' The word dropped from his lips like a pebble. Calling her name again, he saw her hesitate in the shadow of the mango tree. A couple of dogs barked from the sheds in the distance.

Finally she emerged into the soft light that drifted from the window of the Sargents' living room. He held his breath as she moved towards him like a ghost. She didn't say anything and he couldn't remember if she'd ever said anything much to him. It had been a year ago. He couldn't remember her voice or what it had sounded like, and he thought he should have.

'Saw you comin',' she finally said. 'I wait longa time.'

She wore a cotton dress that hugged her body and a small hand-knitted jumper that was unravelling at the neck. Her long bare legs, incredibly black under the pale dress, were lost to the darkness, making her appear all the more like a beautiful phantom floating towards him.

When she stepped up to him and smiled, he took her chin and kissed her cheek. Her eyes met his; in that soft dark face they shone like moonstones. He'd created a memory of her in his mind and now he realised how true to life it had been. He'd been afraid that he might have embellished his image of her over time.

Grace touched his face, running her fingers across the scars, and he repeated the words he'd said to Winnie: 'War scars.'

Her incredible beauty took his breath away, but he couldn't help thinking of Betty as he stared into her eyes. He knew he could never love anyone the way he'd loved Betty, but he also accepted she'd never be more than a distant star.

He had to move on, and that night he did. Grace and Tom walked along in silence. Touched by a wind that blew in from the plains, they willingly let it sweep them away into the night.

18　WAR AND HORSERACING

When it was time to leave Stapleton, Tom rode back to Batchelor on the train that had been dubbed the 'Leaping Lena'. The troops travelling on it had given it another name—the 'Spirit of Protest', a pun on the *Spirit of Progress*, the famous train that ran from Melbourne to Albury.

The 'Protest' had a dubious reputation. Its main purpose was to pick up troops and stores at Larrimah railhead and transport them to Darwin. It did not have coaches; the men slept and ate in cattle trucks during the 24-hour trip. They were never sure if the old locomotive would reach its destination, because the unreliable engine had been known to run into difficulty climbing even the slightest of inclines.

Harry gave Tom a slap on the back when he boarded. 'You'll be fine,' he said reassuringly.

Very soon after it departed, Tom became painfully aware of the reason for the train's nickname. The soldiers travelling in the cattle wagons were bounced about like balls in a pinball machine. Whenever the rickety train screeched and puffed its way up a hill it was a harrowing experience, but it was going down again that scared the daylights out of Tom. Once the train had cleared the crest, it raced downhill at lightning speed, its nuts and bolts creaking and moaning.

Tom held on with white knuckles and, for the first time in his life, mumbled a prayer or two. He could only hope the damn train wouldn't come off its rails, taking its load of military men with it. One of the Australian soldiers tried to reassure him: 'She picks up speed when she smells beer.' Up in the air, with the Japanese on his tail, was like a tea party compared to this; when he eventually got out at Pine Creek, he almost threw up.

He hitched a ride back to base with one of the RAAF men, and decided he'd never, ever travel on that train again. He would, however, go back to Stapleton. There was Grace to consider, and the Sargents had made him promise to come back soon. Winnie had taught him how to ride a horse and chase after a cow; he'd busied himself putting up fences and socialising with the Aboriginal stockmen.

Settling into his new life at Batchelor wasn't hard. Everyone agreed it was a much better set-up than MacDonald. In June and July they flew many missions to and from the islands—Timor, Ambon, and the Kei and Aroe islands. It was a relief to be closer to their targets by some 500 miles and run a much lower risk of having to crash-land their planes.

Until now Tom and Bob had mostly served as second pilots, but as first pilots were becoming rare both men were promoted to flying their own B-25 with their own crew. The shortage of flying crew and pilots was becoming so desperate that everyone was called upon to volunteer for a position.

Freck was one of the first to step up, which didn't surprise Norman, although he did make one last attempt to talk his friend out of it. Being a radio communicator wasn't as exciting as Freck had hoped and, together with his friend the Dutch mechanic Jan Keesmaat, he'd talk for hours about his hopes of adventure in the skies. Keesmaat and Freck were delighted when they were selected as candidates. Gus Winckel was assigned as their mentor and, from that moment on, every free minute Freck had was spent studying flight regulations and procedures.

At the end of June a group of Japanese planes flew over Batchelor, with American Kittyhawks on their tails. Many of Batchelor's planes had departed the night before, heading out across the Timor Sea, so all the remaining men could do was duck for cover in the trenches and watch the Americans chase the Zeros across the Northern Territory. They cheered when one plane was shot down, spiralling in the air, its tail breaking away as smoke billowed from the hull. As the plane went down, Tom saw the pilot eject; he thought the floating foe might well end up in the Sargents' pandanus swamp and Harry finally get himself a prisoner of war.

Around this time the Royal Netherlands Military Flying School in Jackson finally decided to send six men who'd completed their training to Batchelor. The new pilots were well trained, and flying a B-25 Mitchell bomber wouldn't present them with a problem, but they had little or no experience at combat fighting.

Engaging in the brutal realities of warfare was quite different from making test flights above friendly territory.

A new operational order from RAAF headquarters came in just days after the new men arrived. A sighting of enemy ships off the coast of the Aroe Islands at Dobo was reported. The crews were ordered to attack the vessels at mast height, and Tom, Bob, Gus and Lieutenant Oudenraad were chosen as first pilots because of their experience. The pilots from Jackson were assigned as second pilots. Disillusioned and annoyed, they loudly protested this decision.

'You don't have any experience at actual warfare,' Gus explained.

When they persisted, bragging about their time as trainees at Jackson, they were told: 'That was a game. This is reality.'

De Knecht, who had had some experience of air battle in the early stages of the war, was assigned as Bob's second pilot, but he soon made it clear that he didn't fancy flying with 'the midget'. Derks was too small, De Knecht said, suggesting Bob's size had something to do with his abilities.

'He has no idea,' Tom mused to his brother, who wasn't upset. He simply shrugged.

After the briefing, they hoisted themselves into their gear and headed towards their planes. It was finally settled that De Knecht would fly with Oudenraad, and Ketting would take up the second pilot's seat on Bob's plane. Ketting apparently did not mind an undersized first pilot.

Targeting the ships near Dobo, the pilots flew in at mast height as ordered. The Japanese anti-aircraft guns immediately fired at them, spraying bullets at Bob's plane. He managed to pull the bomber up, but not before a few dozen bullets had smacked into its hull. No one was hurt, although he noticed that Ketting had broken out in a sweat and gone a strange shade of white.

Bob was about to tell him to relax when Oudenraad's plane was struck by a direct hit. Horrified, they saw the plane explode and go down burning. It disappeared into the sea with all its crew. Ketting almost threw up and sweat dripped from his head into his lap. *Damn*, Bob thought as he watched his second pilot become immobilised with fear.

The anti-aircraft guns kept firing, giving the men no other option than to drop their bombs, hope they'd hit at least some of the ships beneath them, then disappear into the safety of the clouds. Hours later, Bob, Tom and Gus managed to get their crews and planes home safely. On Oudenraad's plane they'd lost De Knecht, their radio operator De Jongh and two Australian turret gunners, Morris and O'Hea.

O'Hea, a former bank clerk from Kempsey and a friend of Norman's, had been badly wounded just a year before when he was assigned to a reconnaissance flight over Rabaul. Tom wasn't looking forward to telling Norman his friend had died.

The maintenance crew at Batchelor counted 107 bullet holes in Bob's plane. It would be out of action for a long time. Ketting, having recovered from his anxiety attack, apologised to Bob, who clapped him on the back and said robustly, 'It gets better when you've done it a couple of times.' Within weeks of their arrival, three of the six new pilots were killed in air fights with the enemy.

———————

Air Marshal Zomer replaced Fiedeldij as commanding officer in June 1943. During the operational period under Fiedeldij's command, the 18th Squadron had lost seven Mitchell B-52s, three of them due to crash landings. These statistics justified Fiedeldij's claims that the Mitchells didn't have the range to reach their targets. He joined the small Dutch planning staff in Melbourne with a clear conscience, knowing he'd done all he could to draw attention to the problems of his squadron.

Zomer had been head of training at Jackson. The disciplined and well-equipped training school and airstrip in America was a far cry from what he found at his new posting. The Batchelor airstrip was a sprawling, jungle-carved advance base; dotted around its edges were crashed and abandoned aircraft, to give the enemy the impression that the base had been abandoned. The hangars were no more than spaces between the paperbarks, and the planes were hidden from the enemy under camouflage netting.

The heavy bombs were kept a safe distance from the planes, as a small tractor would deliver them to the allocated aircraft. When Zomer saw men with lit cigarettes in their mouths using a petrol-powered lifting device to load bombs onto planes, he was shocked.

After all the efficiency and precision to which he'd become accustomed, Batchelor appeared horribly inefficient and disorganised. He observed his unshaven and dishevelled men relaxing in comfortable chairs in the midday heat and couldn't help wondering why Fiedeldij had put up with the situation. He was certainly going to do something about it.

Zomer expressed his misgivings to Smokey Dawson, but all he got from the Australian was a raised eyebrow and a shrug. Dawson had been with these men for more than a year now. Having lived among spick-and-span British soldiery, he too had once stared in amazement at these 'scruffy' men, mistakenly believing they'd need a few more years of hard training before they'd be of any use. During his time with them, he'd become well aware of their efficiency and amazing capabilities.

At MacDonald he'd witnessed the fearlessness of the Dutch pilots and their mixed crews as they poked out across the sea night after night to wreak havoc on Timor and beyond. Many of these men had come from the Dutch East Indies, and their pilots and navigators could fly over the islands blindfolded. Dawson had come to admire them.

One morning after the alarm sounded, any doubt Zomer might still have had about his men vanished. The air marshal watched in amazement as his 'lethargic' men suddenly came to life, scurrying to take off in anything airworthy. The duty roster Zomer had set became instantly inoperative. Every one of his men, without exception, leapt to life, clambered into their cockpits and began jockeying for a position on the runway. Most were clothed in nothing but their shorts and sandals. Tom Derks came rushing out of the showers in his birthday suit, with shaving cream sticking to his face like a Santa beard. Scrambling into a B-25, he took his place in the line of planes waiting to take to the air.

These men were excellent and fearless flyers; they knew their jobs and risked their lives on a daily basis. As they clawed their way up into the blue, Zomer felt a strange sense of pride. He never again doubted their commitment, but from now on smoking cigarettes during the loading of weaponry onto the planes was prohibited, and punished with a day in lockup.

In the months to come, Batchelor would become a vitally important dot on the map and, luckily for the men on the base, the Japanese had trouble locating it. The enemy spent hours droning about at night looking for strips and installations; often, after giving up, they'd unload their bombs on Darwin's RAAF and civilian aerodromes on their way back to Timor. They must have suspected that there were air bases well hidden in the scrub, but the Allied pilots and their crews knew they were very hard to find. Amazingly, under the daytime heat haze Batchelor resembled a lake from the air. Even its own pilots sometimes had trouble pinpointing it on their way back from a mission, despite their expert local knowledge.

In June, July and August, the Japanese kept bombing Darwin, unaware that the town had become nothing more than a refuelling station. Bombers from Batchelor touched down at Darwin to fill up their tanks and leave wheel marks on the tarmac before they left for the islands. The troops stationed there were under orders to maintain an appearance of life and activity, so dummy planes were constructed and wheeled about every day, and abandoned wrecks were propped up so they looked ready to go. For the time being this ruse succeeded, and Batchelor could carry on unscathed at full pressure while Darwin's strips were pounded day and night. If the runway was too badly damaged the fighter squadrons would sometimes use the highway to Darwin as a landing strip but the RAAF personnel became so adept at repairing runway damage with tip trucks and gravel, they could wipe out the effects of a heavy raid in twenty minutes.

The town of Darwin and its population were resilient. They'd witnessed disaster many times before, when passing cyclones had managed to destroy the town. The residents who'd been forced to leave knew that one day, after the Japanese had been chased away and had no bombs left to drop, they'd return to rebuild their town again.

Much to Tom's joy, Norman was assigned to drive the meat supply truck every week to pick up the rations for Batchelor from Stapleton Station. If Tom wasn't on duty, it meant he could drive up there with him.

One day Norman returned from one of his visits with some seeds. He was very enthusiastic about the quality of the soil in this area of the Territory, finding it very rich. 'There's about two feet of clay here before anything else. You could grow almost anything,' he told Tom. But there was one big problem with farming in the Territory that Norman hadn't taken into account: the weather. It was either too hot and dry for long spells, or way too wet for anything to grow. Nonetheless, he planted lettuce and radish seeds behind his tent and waited patiently for them to sprout.

Norm cared for his plants as if they were the most precious things on earth; his tent mates mocked him, but this didn't bother him. Looking after the budding plants was a way of keeping himself sane, if nothing else. The realities of war had hit home after he learnt that his friend O'Hea had perished. Night after night Norman would lie awake, listening to planes taking off or waiting for the steady drone of a Zero flying over in search of some sign of life. Knowing his friends could be lost in action, he'd anxiously await the return of the crews that had left earlier in the night.

On the base random accidents occurred almost daily. Boiling water spilling from a makeshift billy pot burnt one young man; a dispatch rider broke his shoulder jumping a log with his bike; 'Pop' Brouwer died when his gun went off accidentally during inspection; men drank jungle juice and sometimes tried to kill one another for no apparent reason. Sometimes it was a madhouse. So, to Norman, planting seeds was about as sane as things got.

Like Hagers with his little dog, Norman needed something to take care of. He always was, and always would be, a farmer at heart, so he did what people had done for millennia—he planted seeds. He watched his lettuces and radishes flourish, and he admired those once-tiny seedlings, knowing he'd never give up on small things.

At times he'd try to forget the war and remember Olivia, the nurse from Fenton. He thought he might just try to travel there with his bike one day, although he knew he'd need at least a day to get there and back.

A welcome distraction came when the Adelaide River races were organised especially for the forces. Jim Maloney acted as a bookmaker, shouting the odds and taking bets as he stood on a box. There were no real racehorses due to the war, but a syndicate had borrowed some horses for a day from the neighbouring station owners.

The small settlement of Adelaide River became the Mecca of the moment, with bushies and townies alike flocking to the local racecourse. People arrived in buggies, donkey wagons and cars, and on motorbikes; both black and white folk were excited by the upcoming event. Girls strolled around wearing sunshades and bright scarves, the men stalking after them.

Maloney waved to Tom as money changed hands. Tom placed his bets nonchalantly—there was nothing else to spend his money on and, if he lost, Maloney would win and he didn't begrudge the old bookie his loot.

The band, playing in a smattering of shade on a lawn nearby, suddenly stopped as the horses were paraded out onto the racecourse. Soon the starter's handkerchief dropped and the crowd roared so loudly that everything else was lost in its surge. The men threw their Akubras into the air and the girls waved their scarves.

For some, the excitement, beer and heat became too much as the horses started the last mad rush down the straight. The heart of Grant Morgan, a 72-year-old surveyor, stopped beating as the jockeys charged their horses over the finishing line. His was the only death that day. There were a few skirmishes and some fights over girls. Tom did lose quite a bit of money, but as he reflected on the drive back to Batchelor he thought it had all been worth every penny.

19 NEW RECRUITS

In August, the Japanese raided Fenton Airfield. It wasn't the first time the base had come under attack—its position close to Darwin made it an attractive target for the Japanese bombers. The enemy appeared to favour the full moon for their air raids; on the night of the attack, the atmosphere was clear and the moonlight cast bright shadows at ground level, which made it easier for them to hit their targets. They attacked at midnight and 26 of their bombs landed on the hospital grounds at Coomalie Creek.

When the news reached Batchelor the next morning, Norman panicked. Olivia was stationed at Coomalie, and all he could think about were the bombs that exploded in the hospital grounds. Although no news of casualties or deaths reached them that morning, he feared that Olivia might not have survived the attack.

It took all Tom and Freck's persuasive powers to stop Norman jumping on his motorbike and racing to Coomalie. After he'd calmed down a little, Freck suggested he ask Dawson for permission to head up there. He started off for the CO's office immediately, and the other two joined him.

Dawson's initial reaction was no. When Norman begged and pleaded some more, Dawson finally softened a bit. The dispatch rider's obvious distress changed his mind; Norman didn't have much to do in the way of work and Dawson did want to know first-hand exactly what had happened at Fenton and Coomalie. He allowed Norman to go, but only in his official capacity as a dispatch rider. He was to deliver a message, informing the hospital that it was welcome to any help or amenities Batchelor could provide. When Dawson handed him the message, Norman grabbed it so quickly he almost forgot to salute, then raced out to prepare his bike, Freck close on his heels.

Tom hung back for a moment. 'Maybe I should go along?' he suggested to Dawson. 'Norman's in a bit of a state and I could keep an eye on him. I'm not on duty again until tomorrow night.'

'His freckled friend?' Smokey Dawson asked.

Freck was due to do a compulsory commando course that afternoon and would have to stay on the base, Tom told him.

Dawson advised Tom to talk to his own CO. 'Is he engaged to this girl?' he added as an afterthought.

'No. He only met her once.'

Smokey raised a surprised eyebrow as Tom saluted and left in a hurry.

An hour later, the two friends were on their way, Tom perched on the back of the Indian, clinging to Norman, who rode like the wind, the message safely deposited in the inner pocket of his uniform. Before the war, the highway from Alice Springs to Darwin had been little more than a dirt track, infrequently used in the dry season and mostly impassable in the wet, due to flooding. The few people who lived there accepted such pioneering conditions. But when the army had begun making extensive use of Northern Territory roads and the old tracks had not been able to handle the constant and heavy military traffic, the army had contributed to the cost of upgrading many of the roads. The road leading to Darwin had been a priority and was now sealed.

Other frequently used roads had been upgraded without being sealed. That was the situation from Batchelor to the main road—conditions were reasonable, albeit dry and terribly dusty. But Coomalie Creek was on the other side of the main north–south highway leading to Darwin, so Norman had to drive through rough terrain, where some of the roads were no more than dirt tracks. To Norman's surprise it took them only two hours to get to the hospital grounds.

The official name of the hospital at Fenton was 1 MRS (Medical Receiving Station). It was a fully equipped hospital with 60 or more beds dispersed among four large marquees. The operating theatre was situated in its own large tent; those who'd had surgery and those suffering from tropical diseases and general illnesses occupied the wards. More substantial buildings were provided for the cookhouse and mess areas. The hospital staff consisted of several medical officers, along with nurses, a pharmacist and a radiologist. The wards were staffed day and night.

When Norman and Tom rode onto the grounds, they were shocked. The place was a shambles. Holes four or five feet deep dotted the area, and most of the marquees had been damaged by bombs landing in close proximity. Their canvas awnings were punctured and flapping about in the breeze. A trolley lay tipped over on its side against a tree, surgical instruments spilling from it and lying scattered in the dirt. Nurses, doctors and patients were busy salvaging what they could.

Norman stopped a man in a white coat, who looked more or less like a doctor: 'I'm looking for Olivia. I don't know her last name. She's a nurse.' Norman sounded out of breath.

The man told him the nurses were at work in the wards.

'Is she all right?'

The man shrugged, but told them he hadn't come across any casualties in the aftermath of the bombing. 'I know,' he added as Tom and Norman looked at him in disbelief. 'Twenty-six bombs hit us, and not one of them seems to have landed on a patient or staff member. It was a dreadful experience, though, especially for bedridden patients who couldn't make it to the slit trenches.'

As the doctor hurried off, they were left standing there, reluctant witnesses to a crime scene. Norman turned to search the grounds for Olivia and worried that he wouldn't recognise her if he saw her—it had been quite a while since her visit to Batchelor.

But when a girl appeared from behind a canvas flap, the doorway to the hospital ward, Norman immediately knew who she was. Her white cap and dress billowing in the hot wind created a strange illusion—as if she were sailing towards him as she made her way across the lawn.

'Well, well, Mr Dispatch Rider,' she said.

Norman suddenly felt shy, and a little silly. What was he going to say to her? She'd asked him to look her up, but months had passed without him even giving her a call, and now he'd shown up amidst all the chaos. His mind rummaged for the words to express some kind of acceptable explanation. Her arms slowly folded across her chest in a gesture that said she didn't have all day.

The wavering Norman suddenly remembered his CO's message. Pulling it out, he said, 'I've been sent to deliver a message to your CO.'

Tom made a face at Olivia behind Norman's back.

'Oh, I just heard from our general practitioner, George Simpson, that a very concerned young man had asked him the whereabouts of one Olivia!'

Norman stared at her folded arms, remembering the feeling of them as she'd wrapped them tightly around his waist months before. He had remembered her fragility as she struggled to get out of the mud, but now, standing here on her own turf, she appeared strong and determined. He remained silent, grappling to find the right words. He wanted to sound sincere, but was afraid of sounding indifferent, so he just stood there mutely looking at her.

She told him she had patients to nurse—boys and men who'd lost parts of their bodies, as well as parts of their souls. Tom casually lit a cigarette and wandered off, giving them space and privacy.

When Tom and Norman headed back that afternoon, Norman was in a state of wild bliss. He had a big smile stuck to his face, so Tom assumed he'd finally managed to impress the young lady, but his reckless driving made the bike splutter and spit. Between the main road and Batchelor base, it stopped with a bang. They were eight miles from camp, in the middle of nowhere, with the sun still very hot, even though it was steadily dropping behind the peppermints. Tom sighed and got off the bike.

'We'll have to try to fix it,' Norman said, 'although I wouldn't have a clue what to use. Looks like we might have blown something.'

Tom wiped the sweat from his forehead and stared into the distance, remembering what the two of them had previously been through. They'd once fled across the ocean together in a makeshift aeroplane; it felt like a lifetime had passed since then. Norman knew what his friend was thinking and together they mulled over old memories in subdued silence.

Finally Tom said, 'We've had tougher nuts to crack.'

So they set to work on the bike, knowing they'd repair it or die trying. It was dusk when they returned to the base. The bike had sputtered and protested the whole way, inching along the dusty tracks, but in the end it had got them home.

—■—

Also in August the new commander of the North-Western Area, Air Vice Marshal Adrian Cole, deployed the 18th Squadron to put more pressure on the enemy and wear it down. The men flew missions constantly. Ambon was attacked by the 18th and a 250-ton vessel was sunk off Larat. Koepang was bombed and two days later Dili was raided. By the end of the month, Squadron Leader Andrew Chirnside had replaced Dawson as CO of the Australian personnel.

By now Norman's garden was producing radishes and cucumbers, but he almost had to put a guard in place to protect them. As the sprouts had finally turned into something edible, they were suddenly of interest to some of the men. Growing fresh produce was not such a bad idea after all, they told Norman.

Tom made regular visits to Stapleton because he was allowed a 24-hour rest after every mission. He'd visit Grace, do odd jobs for Harry or go hunting with Maloney. Harry, who'd heard that the troops liked to send coconuts home, gave Tom twenty of them, from the coconut palms growing around the station. Apparently, you carved a name and address onto the coconut and, after the army censor had okayed it, you put a stamp on the coconut and signed your name. Then it would go to the post office at Adelaide River. The coconuts were only deliverable to an address within Australia, so most of the Dutch had no interest in them, but handing out coconuts made Tom very popular among the Australians.

Just before Norman's crop was ready to harvest, Tom returned from Stapleton with two goats. They'd make nice pets and they could also supply them with fresh milk. Norman would look after the goats when Tom left for a mission and promised he would return them to Stapleton if, heaven forbid, his friend didn't return. If the unthinkable did occur, Tom had asked Norman to give the goats and all his other belongings to Grace.

One night in early September, when Tom had set out on a mission across the Timor Sea, Norman came back from dinner to find his garden in chaos. The goats had managed to break free and had headed straight for the little vegie patch, destroying most of it. Norman found them munching away in the middle of his small crop: the cucumbers, riddled with bites and teeth marks, looked as if they had been strafed by bullets, and his radishes had all been eaten.

Norman was furious and blamed Tom for 'bringing the friggin' animals into camp in the first place'. He moped about, grieving for his loss and making a spectacle of himself for days. Tom tried to make amends and even presented him with one of his most treasured possessions—buffalo horns from the first buffalo he'd shot, but only after Tom took the goats back to Stapleton did Norman's fury subside.

Days later, Norman and Tom forgot about the demolished vegie patch when a large number of fully trained Dutch pilots arrived from Jackson with new crews. 'The Americans', as Tom called them, wore bright new uniforms and strode through the base looking like movie stars. Their thorough training gave them an air of confidence and optimism.

The 'old' 18th pilots observed them with some wariness. It was no secret that Air Vice Marshal Cole wasn't impressed with the 'old' 18th Squadron and had even sent a complaint to HQ a few weeks before the new arrivals came in, expressing doubts about the 18th Squadron as a fighting unit. He also observed that most of its pilots had been civilian pilots and still had a 'safety first' attitude. He expected more and better results from the new recruits.

Bob was furious when he heard about this criticism. The new Dutch recruits had come equipped with state-of-the-art Mitchells, but the old crews had been operating with planes that had had to be modified time and time again. Some had been fitted with extra fuel tanks and others hadn't, some had machine-guns but others hadn't; it was a wonder most of them survived the missions at all. 'We should stick Mr Cole in one of those planes without the extra tanks and send him out to battle the enemy. See if he can come back without trashing it,' Bob suggested.

To avoid further conflict, the Dutch command thought it wise to relocate the 'old' 18th Squadron crews. They still bore a grudge at not having been allowed to rescue their families and felt that they hadn't been taken seriously as a squadron. The overall assumption by the Dutch headquarters in Melbourne was that the general attitude of the 'old' pilots could be a bad influence on the new recruits.

Bob was among the first to be reassigned. He'd be involved in establishing a new squadron, the 119th NEI/RAAF, with its base in Canberra. This meant returning to Fairbairn, but with promotion to flight lieutenant and head of operations. He was actually quite pleased. Remaining involved in the fight for the Dutch East Indies was vital for him; his aim was, and always had been, to pilot one of the first Allied planes to re-enter the Dutch East Indies. In his fantasies, he'd fly over Java at mast height searching for Colette, and she'd wave her scarf as he swooped over the POW camp. It was a sugar-coated daydream and he knew it, but it comforted and motivated him. He'd put this new squadron together and, when they were ready, he hoped they might well become instrumental in fighting off the enemy.

The new head of operations for the 18th Squadron at Batchelor was Rene Wittert, who'd come in with the new recruits. He had also been trained at Jackson and would replace Gus Winckel as flight commander. Gus would stay on at Batchelor for another month to teach the new commander the ins and outs of the North-Western Area, but would eventually join Bob at Fairbairn as a flight instructor for the 119th. Gus didn't regret leaving either. He'd put in considerable time and effort, and he was now suffering from battle fatigue. His reactions weren't as sharp as they had been months ago, and he didn't want to put his crew in harm's way. Teaching men to fly, and staying away from the fighting for a while, suited him just fine.

Tom and Hagers were assigned to transport. Both had served seven months of operational tours, constantly fighting the enemy. Now they'd be shipping goods and officials from one part of the country to another, Tom flying a Lodestar, Hagers a Dakota. The B-25s had never been able to steal Tom's heart, so flying the Lodestar again was like meeting up with an old friend.

'Transport?' Gus Winckel exclaimed. 'You'll get really good at playing cards now.' He clapped Tom on the back good-naturedly. Flights from Batchelor to Dutch headquarters in Melbourne and back took four days; it was no secret that the pilots who flew the route would kill time with a game of cards.

Although still based at Batchelor, Tom wouldn't be part of the fighter unit and would see much less of his friends. The 18th as he'd known it would never be the same; the new men were already starting to take over.

In the following days, tents were cleared out and old beds handed over to new occupants. A leaving party was organised at Walsh's Bar. There the men had a 'goodbye' drink or two that resulted in shouts, laughter and a few ridiculous speeches in honour of the men who were leaving. There were also tears, both sad and joyous. Some shed them, realising how lucky they'd been to make it through those gruelling months of constant air battles. Most of them at some stage had doubted they'd survive their tour. Everyone in the bar that night had known someone who hadn't made it.

The 18th Squadron had once boasted eighteen complete crews, six of which had lost their lives. More than half of the initial aeroplanes, ten in total, had been lost due to accidents or warfare. In the following months, the 'old' crew dribbled off, new recruits eager and ready to replace them.

The new Mitchells were equipped with heavier tail and nose armaments and, of course, were inevitably better suited to their job. The new planes also had a new squadron emblem—a little Dutch girl sweeping with a broom. The picture, which was supposed to represent the joint RAAF/NEI nature of the 18th, had featured in a pre-war Australian advertisement for a Dutch cleaning powder.

At the beginning of November, Tom went to say his goodbyes to Grace, Winnie and Harry at Stapleton. He would return, of course, but thanks to his new job in transport, his visits would not be as frequent. Winnie and Harry were sorry to see him go. They'd become attached to the tall Dutchman who appeared to get on well with the stockmen, communicating with them in a way that made them work just that little bit harder and not mind it. Just before he left, Tom told Harry he was thinking of buying himself a spot of land when the war was over and would ask Grace to live there with him. Tom liked this wild northern country and thought he might try his luck at hunting and a bit of mining. Harry was sure he'd do well.

Tom and Grace stood silently in front of the little hut Grace called home. They felt at ease with one another, and their bond was one of silent comfort. Grace was ashamed of her pidgin English; Tom's difficulty in understanding it had resulted in her customarily responding to him in short sentences. If she had something really important to say, she'd slip him a piece of paper with a message on it, written for her by Winnie.

As Tom left, she slipped him a note, a tear leaving a wet scar on her black skin. He absentmindedly stuffed the note into his shirt pocket, hugging and kissing her, trying to console her, promising to return as soon as possible. That night, when he finally remembered the note, he took it from his shirt pocket and discovered that Grace was going to have his baby.

20 DEATH OF A FRIEND

When Bob left for Canberra, Tom told him he was soon to become an uncle. He did so with a grin on his face, in that carefree way Bob had always found so annoying when they were kids. He'd always regarded Tom's relationship with Grace as a frivolous and superficial affair; he doubted whether his brother was ready to take on any serious commitment, especially fathering a child.

Bob had only met Grace twice and she'd hardly spoken a word. She seemed a quiet, pretty girl. He was grateful that his brother was slowly becoming his old self again, although he would have been happy to see certain traits disappear forever.

In Canberra, Bob served under the command of Van Haselen, who'd been promoted from major to lieutenant colonel. Squadron Leader Rutter led the RAAF component of the squadron. It had been decided that the 119th would in time work jointly with the 18th Squadron at Batchelor. The RAAF, which was to deliver the ground crews for the new squadron, wanted the 119th to become a separate, fully functional squadron. The Dutch let RAAF headquarters know they didn't really care one way or another, as long as the two squadrons would be operating from the North-Western Area, where they could reach the Dutch East Indies.

It was proposed that the 119th would move to Darwin after it was fully operational, and in Darwin Lieutenant Gus Winckel would instruct the pilots and crews in anti-shipping techniques developed by the 18th Squadron. Vice Marshal Cole himself had recommended Gus as a war-training instructor to NEI headquarters in Melbourne. His more than fine record had won the confidence and admiration of Cole and his staff. In the past months, Cole had become very aware of Gus Winckel's capabilities; his judgement of the 18th had also mellowed considerably.

Within days of Bob landing in Canberra, it became evident that the 119th was going to suffer from a staffing shortage. There simply weren't enough crews coming from Jackson to service both the 18th and the 119th, and the Australians had limited the number of men they were willing to contribute to the Dutch units. Bob's heart sank when he went to inspect the planes that had been issued to them. Van Haselen pointed out to him the two Mitchell bombers and one Lodestar transport plane standing forlornly on the runway—this was all they had to work with for the time being. New Mitchells were supposed to be on their way, but for now the new squadron would have to make do with only three planes. It was a bitter disappointment.

—■—

With all the old Dutch pilots and crews gone, Norman and Freck looked on as the new lot went about their daily routine. In the early morning hours, the 'Dutch Americans' would emerge from their tents and head for the showers with towels from New York's Sheraton or Waldorf Astoria hotels casually draped around their shoulders; afterwards they'd carefully hang them out to dry, prized mementos of bygone days. Their long stay in America had given them a better than basic knowledge of the English language, so communication between the different nationalities was much easier.

Freck and Keesmaat were by now getting flight training from Gus, and both felt at home up in the air. Their enthusiasm didn't go unnoticed at the base, and the men in their units called them the 'pilots', although they still had a long way to go. Now they knew the basics, Freck applied for advanced training at the No. 5 Service Flying Training School at RAAF Station Uranquinty in New South Wales, one of the 'Wagga Flying Training Schools'. At the beginning of November, Freck's application was approved and Norman realised that he too would soon be moving on.

Norman still didn't understand why Freck wanted to put himself in harm's way by becoming a pilot, but Freck told him that pilot training would enhance his chances of a better job after the war: 'Imagine, mate, flying all over the world and spending time in Honolulu or Las Vegas.' Norman saw a totally different image: 'Imagine a plane spiralling into the ocean with its tail ablaze.'

At the end of October, an order for midnight training came from Australian HQ, and although it was not uncommon for crews to participate in training after sundown, this particular exercise came with a twist. There was a designated area for night training—a pitch-dark section close to the base, where planes and their air gunners could drop bombs on a target—and this night the B-25 crew was being asked to take photos of its actions. They were to test a new device called a photoflash bomb. It had the capacity to produce a flash equal to the light of about a million candles and would be able to illuminate the area as if it were daylight. It had to be dropped precisely ten seconds after the bomb so a camera could produce clear and detailed photos.

Because it was known that Keesmaat loved to fly but hadn't yet been allowed to join any flying combat missions, the crew offered him a 'free ride' and he gratefully accepted. Flight Sergeant Engels would be leading the operation, flying with three of his men.

Late that evening word came in that the exercise had gone terribly wrong. Norman was awake and sitting outside his tent when a communications officer rushed by, asking for Freck. He told Norman that a plane had gone down with Keesmaat on board. Although the captain and two crew members had wandered into Coomalie Creek, and a passing jeep had picked up a fourth an hour after the plane went down, Keesmaat hadn't reported back yet.

'He's probably still out there somewhere. He'll come wandering in, most likely,' the officer said, but you could hear the doubt in his voice. They'd have to wait for daylight before a search party could be organised. Driving around in the pitch-black bush would be a useless exercise.

As the first rays of light seeped above the horizon that morning, Freck and Norman hopped on the Indian and headed out to look for Keesmaat while Gus and a few others followed close behind in a truck.

Before they set out, Engels reported that the parachute carrying the photoflash bomb had entangled itself on the opened bomb bay doors of the aircraft. Keesmaat was in the lower turret at the time, making sure he got a good view of the bombing. The entangled burning device soon filled the plane with smoke and, when the 'bail out' sign came on, everyone scrambled for their parachutes at the back of the plane. One by one, the crew bailed out. By the time Keesmaat had clambered up from the turret, the plane was full of fire and smoke.

The last to jump had been Captain Engels. In the general panic he'd forgotten about Keesmaat, but he did catch a glimpse of him coming out of the turret at the last moment. As he fell to earth, Engels became worried when he saw no sign of the engineer emerging from the plane, and he feared he might not have been able to reach his parachute.

Freck and Norman, the first to arrive at the crash site, were shocked by what they saw. Gus arrived moments later, his burly frame scrambling out of the truck with unusual agility. Gus studied the marks the plane had made through the scrub and the way it was positioned. He shook his head as Norman and Freck ran up to the wreckage, already knowing what they'd find.

Keesmaat had managed to ditch the plane, just as Gus had taught him—the marks in the bush showed a perfect dead-stick landing. The plane had been kept in a horizontal position just above the ground, its wheels locked in, and the pilot had managed to skittle its body through the scrub until it crashed into a termite mound or two. But then something had caused the plane to explode. Maybe it had been the photoflash tube, or one of the remaining bombs; whatever had caused the explosion had reduced the plane to splinters and rubble, scattered for miles around.

Gus walked up to Freck and tried to comfort him by telling him he was proud of his pupil. Freck walked away in grief. Losing a man to the enemy was part of the job, but this was a stupid accident and Keesmaat shouldn't have been on board in the first place.

The next day both the new and the old members of the squadron held a funeral service for Jan Keesmaat at the Adelaide River cemetery. As he watched the men paying their respects, Norman thought it strange that he never detected any fear in these men's eyes. Just the thought of flying and facing the unpredictable, suicidal enemy—with their fast Zeros, their drop tanks and their zealous determination—was enough to send a shiver up his spine.

Tom had once explained to Norman that it was something you got used to, like when they'd crossed the ocean in that rickety aeroplane without knowing if they'd survive: 'We knew the danger but, having no other option, we just did it.' It was all part of the job and they did it every day, because they thought it was their duty and that the 'dying' part of it did not apply to them—that was someone else's plight. As long as they believed that, they could function. Living in the face of death almost every day was ridiculous, but there was no other way to tackle war.

—■—

Every Thursday Norman would drive up to Adelaide River to pick up a couple of tins of film for the picture shows at the base. He'd often take a detour to Coomalie Creek to visit Olivia, who scheduled her hours around his visits so they could spend time together. After a few hours Norman would depart with nothing on his mind but returning to her as soon as he could.

By now Batchelor had electric lights, which replaced the lanterns in the tents. The smell of kerosene and petrol in the tents had been awful, especially during those hot muggy days before the wet. Now, with the wet approaching, the arrival of electricity was greeted with much enthusiasm.

The Saturday-night picture shows at Batchelor were immensely popular, and not only for the soldiers; more and more local Aboriginal people wandered in on film nights. The theatre was no more than a large tarp rigged between two paperbarks at the edge of the camp. Word soon passed around the Aboriginal communities, and men, women and children would crowd into the area and watch. Mesmerised, and not wanting to appear ignorant or ill mannered, they seemed to laugh whenever the soldiers laughed. Some of them would walk for two days to reach Batchelor then sit at the edge of the camp for another two days, waiting for Saturday night.

It was during one of those Saturday nights that Tom told Norman Grace was pregnant. Norman didn't know if he should congratulate his friend or not. It was such a casual announcement that the only response Norman could muster was 'Oh'. He didn't mean to be rude; he was just at a loss at what to say. He knew Tom had been infatuated with Betty, but Grace ... well, Norman didn't really know what to think. Norman couldn't imagine them being a couple.

Later, sitting down with Tom for a Coke, Norman said, 'It might be best if you walked away, Tom. As you know, it's a hard world and Grace is coloured.'

Tom looked at him. 'I love her,' he said, and got up and walked away.

Norman's reaction had been genuine, but he realised it also sounded cruel and prejudiced. It was hard for him to understand how his friend related to the Aboriginal people, and he was afraid that his infatuation with Grace had more to do with flirtation than with love. He was only trying to protect Tom from making life very difficult for himself.

Freck was due to leave in December for Shepparton, where he'd enjoy a few weeks of Christmas leave at home before reporting to Uranquinty. He was eager to leave; he missed the farm and the smell of home. 'I want to sleep under a real roof again,' he said. 'I've seen enough tarp to last me, I'll tell ya.' Now that the wet had brought rain again, he was eager to leave the sound of dripping bush behind him.

The day after Freck left, Norman received orders that he was being dispatched into the transport unit in Bradfield Park, Sydney.

21 MOVING ON

On 1 September 1943 the 119th Squadron was officially founded at Canberra. But by November the squadron only had 25 NEI staff, to which the RAAF had added 35 men as ground crew. This was no squadron, Bob thought; it didn't even come close. If the Australians couldn't produce the requisite ground crew, he doubted the 119th would ever become operational. The two B-25 Mitchell bombers and the Lodestar transport plane had stood idle in their hangars ever since he arrived. Van Haselen claimed that Dutch HQ had ordered another 39 Mitchells, but no one seemed sure. Bob had no idea how this all would end, but it wasn't looking good.

Meanwhile, Tom was seeing more of Australia than probably any Australian ever had, delivering officials from one end of the country to the other. On 6 December he was back at Batchelor, bringing Major General Van Oyen, who was going to inspect the 18th and the new pilots. Batchelor would be Tom's home for two days before he was due to return the general to Melbourne. At last he had time to visit Grace again, and he rushed to Stapleton as soon as he'd finished the paperwork.

Tom had bought some things in Sydney he thought Grace would need. Baby stuff. He'd felt awkward standing in the shop—the woman helping him had grinned from ear to ear, asking nosily about the 'lucky lady' with a gleam in her eye. Wouldn't she like to know, Tom thought, and wouldn't she be shocked if she did. He couldn't help smiling as he left the shop with a small cot and a bag of baby clothes.

Grace was overjoyed by his unexpected visit, and he watched her caress the tiny socks and little woollen coat, fingering the items with great care. The puzzled look in her eyes as she held the coat at a distance told him something wasn't quite right. The clothes were much too warm, he suddenly realised. They would have done nicely for a baby born in the middle of a freezing Dutch winter, but this baby wouldn't even come close to knowing what cold felt like. The cot was okay, though. Grace loved the way it rocked on 'little boomerangs'. She smiled and asked: 'You stayin?'

'Yes.' he said, 'Till tomorrow.'

She told him she'd be leaving the next day as well. 'Meeting three uncles, blackfella business,' she explained.

'Oh,' he said, realising her life was a universe away from his. He suddenly felt that he hardly knew her. He knew every inch of her body—had memorised it—but he didn't know what she thought about, the things she liked or, come to think of it, what she thought about having his baby. It hadn't seemed important until now. *Damn*, he thought, *we're having a child and I know so little about her.*

He'd always felt a deep sense of relief at not having awkward words confusing things as they made love, or after. Just being intimate with her had been enough, but now he wondered if it would always be like this. Their lovemaking had resulted in new life, a life that would join them together. This realisation scared him no end. Fear pounced on him like a rogue dog. His hands felt sweaty and his kiss was insincere. It wasn't Grace's fault—she was as stunning as ever, with or without a protruding belly—it was knowing that he still secretly loved someone else more than her that worried him.

Grace's tiny shack was assembled from a variety of materials—canvas, corrugated iron and wood. Although it sagged in places and the iron was rusting and the wood nibbled by white ants, it had always felt cosy, their own little centre of the universe. But now its modest dimensions were suddenly stifling. The thought of living there, with a baby screaming in the midday heat, made Tom want to run.

Grace showed him the tiny sheets Winnie had made, patched together from old shirts. She stood in front of him as he sat on the bed, her belly sticking out from her body. It reminded him a bit of the turret on a Mitchell bomber. He'd never asked her before when she was due to have the child, so he asked her now. She only laughed. *Perhaps she doesn't know*, he thought.

Although he didn't show it, the pregnant Grace scared him more than any combat mission ever had. In battle, he was always in control. There was always a plan B if things didn't go right;

there were guidelines, rules and regulations. Maybe he didn't really control any of it, but there was confidence in knowing what to do and how to do it. This father thing had ambushed him; he hadn't planned it. Seeing his worried look, Grace took his hands and put them on her belly. He could feel tiny movements, like air bubbles trying to surface beneath her skin, and he smiled in spite of himself.

Later that evening, after they'd made love in the grey heat of the wet, Tom suddenly heard his father's voice for the first time in years, barking at him. He'd hated his father, and his father undoubtedly hated him back. Tom and Bob's mother had died giving birth to the twins, and the old man had always blamed Tom. Bob had been born without so much as a hiccup, and his mother had been very much alive as his brother squirmed in the hands of the doctor who delivered him. It was only then that the doctor realised another baby was on the way.

Tom didn't come willingly; they'd had to rush his mother to surgery and during the operation she died. The old man had always believed that Tom would come to no good and that he was destined to make a complete mess of his life, that he'd inevitably knock up some innocent girl one day, destroying her life along with his own. His old man might just have got it right, Tom thought dismally as he lay looking up at the roof of Grace's home.

Needing a cigarette, he stepped outside onto the wet grass and watched the clouded moon hover over the earth. He wondered if Grace would die giving birth, as his mother had. The thought terrified him and he didn't want to be present when she went into labour. Winnie and Harry were back, the light in the house bright and welcoming, but he couldn't face them. He was too tired, too scared.

Staying here was not going to help his peace of mind, so he jumped in the truck, drove quietly past the Stapleton house and snuck off like a deserter back to the safe haven of the base. That night his sleep was filled with sweaty nightmares and interrupted sleep. The next day Tom was thankful that it was back to business again, flying from Batchelor to Cloncurry, and on to Charleville and finally to Sydney.

On 10 December, Tom took Major General Van Oyen to Canberra. The formation of 119th Squadron was not going according to plan. The Australians had been willing to supply staff for the 18th, but the staffing of the 119th was proving problematic. Dutch HQ in Melbourne had suddenly raised plans to establish another squadron, the 120th, and, besides, there was also a personnel and equipment pool to be manned. The Australians let the Dutch know that they couldn't, and wouldn't, be able to staff four squadrons with an adequate number of ground crews; they just didn't have enough men. Major General Van Oyen, who'd talked to both the Australian HQ and the Dutch command, had now come to Canberra with a new proposal. Later that day it was announced that 119th Squadron would be replaced by the 120th and all staff and crews would be merged into the latter.

When Bob heard the news he shook his head in disbelief. 'I wish they'd make up their bloody minds,' he said to Tom as they had a drink together in the officers' mess at Fairbairn.

'First they want a squadron of bomber planes, and now they tell me we'll all be shoved into the 120th, flying Kittyhawks. Kittyhawks! Can you believe that? They're fighter planes, not bombers. They want us to operate from the North-Western Area with a plane that doesn't have enough range to get us to bloody Darwin, let alone Timor. How do they expect us to fly to the Indies in them?'

As his brother talked, Tom stared distractedly into his beer.

'You hear anything I said?'

Tom looked up. 'Sorry, things on my mind.'

Bob tried to sound casual when he asked, 'How's Grace?'

'Big. Like a damn balloon.'

'Well, that's what happens when women get pregnant,' Bob replied, glancing at him. 'Know what you're going to do, yet?'

Tom shook his head.

'Well, at least you're thinking about it. You treated the whole thing like some casual mishap last time I saw you.'

'It's hard,' Tom said, his eyes searching the wall of the tent for something he knew wouldn't be there. 'It's hard when you want something, but can't have it.'

Staring into his beer, he weighed up his options.

At Batchelor, things had gone unusually quiet. The Japanese appeared to have vanished, and Darwin hadn't been targeted at all since November. Now that there was finally a squadron with state-of-the-art equipment and well-trained pilots operating from Batchelor, the enemy seemed to have disappeared.

Norman thought they'd perhaps retreated or were just keeping their distance out of self-preservation.

A number of RAAF dispatch riders had already left for Bradfield Park, but Norman had been ordered to stay on in Batchelor for another two or three weeks. Nominated by his superiors as the welcome party for the new replacements, he would have the job of introducing them to the specifics of being a dispatch rider at Batchelor.

He would have headed to Coomalie to see Olivia, but just before Christmas she told him her shifts had been moved around and, due to staff shortages, she'd have to work through Christmas and New Year. So on Christmas Eve, Norman sat in his tent listening to the sounds of the bush and the sad sound of rain dripping on canvas.

His orders to leave finally came through at the end of January 1944. To compensate for his delayed departure, his CO told him he'd be travelling by plane. A Lockheed was coming in that afternoon and would be leaving for Sydney a few hours later. It was a great relief to Norman, who'd really dreaded the long train ride to Sydney. Being in charge of the dispatch rider service had its advantages, he thought.

Their busy schedules had made saying goodbye to Olivia especially difficult. He'd seen her only once, about a week earlier, after driving up to Coomalie on an impulse with two rookie dispatch riders. It had been hot, and her fringe hung in soggy strands as sweat dripped from her forehead. They couldn't say goodbye properly. The rookies revved their bikes impatiently, nudging one another as the couple exchanged clumsy kisses.

Norman's arms found it hard to let her go, and he clung to her like a lifebuoy. Self-consciousness made her push him away gently.

'Well, see ya,' she said, watching the two boys making eyes at them from their bikes. The finality of her words nonplussed him and he stood waiting for something more, but when she remained silent, only giving him a small twiddle with her fingers, he replied, 'Yeah . . . see ya.'

He thought about the way she said goodbye and assumed that the boys on the bikes had embarrassed her, so he phoned her later, trying to arrange to see her before he actually took off. On the phone, she found excuses, telling him she was needed at the base and she hadn't been feeling well.

'Might have come down with a spot of flu,' she told him. 'Wouldn't want you to get infected.'

He didn't believe a word she said and he was afraid that it was her way of saying their affair was over.

The day of his departure, a truck came to pick up Norman and his belongings. It drove him to the runway, where a Lockheed Lodestar stood, looking like a giant green grasshopper in the afternoon sun. The Lodestar brought back memories—hair-raising ones for the most part—and for a second, as the sun flashed in his eyes, he thought he saw a familiar figure standing next to it. Shading his eyes, he heard someone say, 'Oi! Hurry up. We haven't got all day you know.'

He knew that voice; it belonged to Tom Derks, whose image shimmered in and out of sight as the heat from the runway engulfed him. 'Thought you'd never get here,' he said, walking up to Norman and grabbing the bags from the truck. 'We work to schedules, you know. I almost left without you.'

'Tom!' Pleased but confused, Norman trailed after his friend.

'Come to think of it, you can carry your own bags,' Tom said, turning and shoving them into Norman's chest.

'But Tom . . .'

Tom told him he had a plane to pilot and to get on board. 'We'll talk later, in Cloncurry.'

When Norman climbed into the plane, he realised it had been fitted out for paratroopers and transporting goods. There were no seats, only benches. Ten men and a young nurse were already on board. Norman looked for a place to put his bags, finally shoving them under the bench. He sat down, nodding at a bloke in an American uniform who sat on a bag of mail, smoking a cigar and smiling up at him.

Tom stuck his head through the cockpit door. 'Norm, you've kept the lady over there waiting longer than necessary, so you'd better go over and apologise.'

Norman turned his head to look at the nurse sitting at the end of the plane. It took a moment to realise it was Olivia. Stumbling over bags and a couple of legs, he reached her and put his lips to her forehead, tasting powder and smelling perfume.

'Surprise,' she said simply, giving him a long and sincere kiss just as the motors of the Lockheed kicked in. The other men applauded.

Olivia's aloofness had been nothing but a ploy. She'd been busy arranging her own transfer. Getting them on the same plane together had been arranged by Tom and was meant to be a surprise. Of course she still loved him, she said. She gave him a cynical look and a push when he said her aloofness the week before had almost given him a heart attack.

Olivia had asked for a transfer to Yaralla Military Hospital in Concord, Sydney. Like Norman, she'd had enough of the heat and rain. She wanted to be somewhere where there were seasons. The hospital was much bigger than the one at Coomalie. 'It's a real building,' she told Norman, 'with bricks and concrete.' Built during the war to accommodate casualties of war, the place was huge, with a staff of 2000. The prospect of working there thrilled her, and excitement poured from her like air from a punctured tyre. She'd be nursing Australians, Americans, Filipinos and even Japanese prisoners of war. No doubt it would be tough. The men there suffered from severe wounds, burns, tropical diseases, even starvation. For now Olivia didn't want to think about casualties of war, though. All she wanted to think about was Norman. They touched, talked and laughed together, oblivious to the other passengers.

They landed in Cloncurry and stayed there overnight, spending the evening drinking a few beers with Tom. Norman avoided bringing up the topic of Grace. If Tom didn't want to talk about her, it might be best not to. So they laughed and joked and drank cold beer until it was time to go to bed. The only one not thinking about Grace was probably Olivia, Norman thought.

Early the next morning they flew to Sydney. An RAAF officer was waiting on the runway when they landed and, as soon as Tom came out of the cockpit, he was handed a telegram. It was from NEFIS, the Netherlands Forces Intelligence Service. As soon as his plane was ready, Tom was to fly to Melbourne and report to the Dutch HQ there. No further specifics were mentioned but the telegram was labelled 'Top Secret'.

22 THE HELL OF MERAUKE

When he stepped out of a taxi in front of the NEFIS building in Melbourne, Tom Derks was still puzzled by the strange telegram he'd received in Sydney. Dead tired, sweaty and in need of a bath, he dreaded what the air force command would have in store for him. Flying around the country for three days in a row, without much sleep, had left him exhausted.

Knowing NEFIS would have nothing good in store for him wasn't helping to improve his mood. He was well aware he didn't have the most impressive military record, so he was at a loss to imagine why he'd been summoned.

As he grabbed his bag out of the boot, he noticed a car, some 200 feet away, and caught a glimpse of a woman getting into it. Tom thought he spotted something oddly familiar about her. He'd only seen a flash of her back, her legs and her high heels, but the way she moved . . . For a second he felt compelled to call out and stop the car, but it had already pulled away from the kerb and was heading in the opposite direction.

An officer hurried down the path to meet him, shook his hand, introduced himself and accompanied Tom to the building. As the officer led him up the steps to the front door, Tom couldn't help looking back.

The car was gone, of course, and he realised now that his eyes had seen only what his mind had wanted them to see. It wasn't her; it couldn't be. Trying to clear the image of those legs from his mind, he stepped through the door, where Guus Hagers greeted him with a slap on the back and his most generous grin.

Tom was so relieved to see a familiar face that he almost fell into Hagers's arms. 'What is this?' he asked.

But Tom's relief was short-lived when his friend explained: 'You may hate me for the rest of your life for getting you into this, but I thought you'd be the best man for the job.' He led him into an office where Van Oyen sat behind a desk tapping a pencil.

Van Oyen came straight to the point; they were to go on a secret mission to Merauke in Dutch New Guinea (DNG). General MacArthur had plans to attack the capital of DNG, Hollandia, from the sea as well as overland from Merauke. He'd requested a reconnaissance flight to map both an attack route and an escape route. MacArthur wanted a Dutch pilot for the mission because he knew most of them were very familiar with the area.

The Dutch high command had recommended Hagers for the job. Born and raised in the Dutch East Indies, he knew Dutch New Guinea better than any man; he'd flown over it countless times and was also an experienced fighter pilot. Together with Tom as his second pilot and a photographer, Lieutenant Olsen, they were to investigate the possibilities of a land route from Merauke to Hollandia, as well as an escape route for Allied aircraft through the treacherous mountains.

'Hagers specifically requested you to be his second pilot,' Van Oyen said with a small smile. Tom looked from the general to Hagers and both of them stared back at him. He had no idea what to say; he had no idea where Merauke was, couldn't even point it out on the map.

Then there was Grace and the baby to consider. His fingertips could still feel the tiny quivers the baby had made as it moved under her skin. He'd take care of her in his own way, he thought, and send money to Stapleton. He'd be useless there anyway. Having a baby was a woman's thing and he'd just get in the way. Winnie was there to take care of Grace; she'd be all right. Choosing to go on an important mission seemed a legitimate reason for chickening out and, anyway, flying from Batchelor to Cloncurry and Brisbane and back almost every day was tiring him and he didn't mind a diversion.

'Okay. When do we leave?' he said at last.

Van Oyen and Hagers smiled.

It turned out to be the next day.

In February 1944, Bob and some new recruits from Jackson had been sent to the 2nd Operational Conversion Unit at Mildura in Victoria, an RAAF training unit that provided specialised training for a large range of aircraft. Bob and his men went there to learn the ins and outs of flying the P-40 Kittyhawk fighter plane. Bob remained doubtful about the Kittyhawk's suitability if the squadron was going to operate from the Northern Territory. To be able to fly deep into NEI territory, the plane would need at least an extra fuel tank.

By now the 120th Squadron consisted of 28 pilots and 213 RAAF ground crew, and was operating under the command of Major General Hans Maurenbrecher. From a Dutch family with a long military tradition, Maurenbrecher had been a training instructor at Jackson. Bob voiced his misgivings to his CO, in whom he hoped to find a willing ear. Maurenbrecher had seen a lot of combat, but he had little knowledge of Australia. Bob thought he probably had no idea how vast the distances in this strange, empty country were and most likely assumed that the North-Western Area was very close to their targets. Maurenbrecher listened intently to what Bob had to say and promised to take it up with the authorities in Melbourne.

The Kittyhawks were a disappointment right from the start. They could perform, but they fell short in most areas. They were American hand-me-downs and, by the time they were handed over to the Dutch had been stripped down to the basic necessities. They were slow, and climbing proved a problem; as single-engine aircraft, they had little power and Bob feared that if they encountered any Japanese, they'd have a hard time chasing them—the Zeros would outrun them easily. Trained as a two-engine pilot, he feared the single-engine Kittyhawk because, if its engine failed, there was nothing to fall back on. The first 24 American fighter planes would soon be at their disposal, with another 26 due to arrive later. Bob thought they were a waste of money, and they didn't even have enough pilots for them all.

Bob and his men finished their training at the beginning of March, but when they arrived back at Fairbairn they were in for a pleasant surprise. Maurenbrecher told them that the 120th would be stationed at Merauke, on the south coast of Dutch New Guinea. A big cheer went up; the news could not have made Bob happier.

At last, the Dutch would be operating from home territory. For the men who had lived in DNG, it would mean going home; even to Bob, who'd never set foot on Dutch New Guinea, it felt as though he'd be closer to Colette. She never left his thoughts. Every hour of the day she'd be there—sometimes small and unassuming, but mostly big and bright. If he thought about it rationally, he knew that operating from DNG wouldn't really bring him any closer to her, because Java was further away than the Kittyhawks could fly, but operating from Dutch territory would still make him and many of his squadron feel better.

Merauke had been a Dutch military post since 1902. Although the Japanese could reach Australia from the northern part of New Guinea, the south had proved impenetrable. Jungle and vast swampland surrounded Merauke. The area had suffered, though, having been bombed and strafed by enemy planes on numerous occasions. Despite all their efforts, however, the Japanese had been unable to conquer this one little piece of Dutch territory. The Dutch flag still proudly flapped in the Merauke wind.

The runway at Merauke was made from layers of perforated steel plates. When the wheels of Hagers' B-25 hit the plates, it made a terrible racket. 'They can hear us landing in Australia!' Tom shouted above the noise.

Once out of the plane, they were taken aback by the conditions. The constant bombing by the Japs had caused massive destruction in the area. Huts were in shambles, trees uprooted and Merauke itself was nothing but a big swampland. Their tent, like those of everyone else stationed there, stood under some coconut trees. The mosquitoes were rampant, and their enormous stingers penetrated almost everything. To ensure they wouldn't contract malaria, Tom, Hagers and Olsen were given Atabrine tablets before they left, but the Americans warned them that the pills were bitter and had some unpleasant side effects. Turning a bright shade of yellow was one of them.

'Great,' Tom mumbled, swallowing a pill. 'We have the choice between contracting malaria or looking like a banana.'

The air base had a radio station and a beacon, but radio contact on long-distance flights wasn't possible because the beacon's signal didn't reach very far. Tom realised that if they had to ditch their plane in the jungle, their chances of being found by a search party would be very slim. Hagers told him that there were also cannibals out there. It made him seriously question having given up his quite comfortable job in transport.

The next day, when they were preparing for their first survey of the area, one of the ground crew handed them their parachutes and emergency rations with a grin on his face. Inspecting the emergency kit, Tom found a bar of chocolate, a few small bullets ('to shoot birds with' was the helpful explanation), tinned fruit and meat, some small beads and a couple of shiny objects that looked pretty useless. The beads and shiny stuff were 'to trade with the Papuans'.

'You're kidding me?' Tom asked sarcastically, but the young bloke, who wore glasses and had a very strange haircut, just kept grinning at him. Tom felt a sudden urge to wipe the smile off his face.

'Why don't they just give us a gun with one silver bullet, so we can shoot ourselves if we live through a crash?' Tom asked Hagers as they stepped onto the plane, 'instead of giving us the illusion of being able to survive out there. Chocolate to eat and beads to trade with the bloody Papuans. If we're lucky, we might get to show them the shiny stuff just before they spear us and serve us up for lunch.'

Up in the air everything changed. The region was beautiful. To the north they mapped out an area of swampland some 200 miles long and wide. A massive mountain range ran like a back-bone across the island, with the highest peak sticking out like a colossal cake, iced with snow. Trapped between the mountains were humid clouds. It was obvious to them that massive rainfalls fed the swamps and the Sepik River on the other side of the range. Thunderclouds had developed on the mountainsides, and Hagers knew that sometimes these were known to hide chunks of ice. It was a beautiful landscape, but Hagers told Tom that it took a good pilot to fly through it safely. This airspace was no place for amateurs.

During the next few days they found a lake. Situated high up in the mountains, it had probably once been the mouth of a volcano. They carefully mapped out its location, realising it could serve as a sanctuary for the Allied flying boats because it was easily accessible.

'We'll christen it Hagers Lake,' Tom said.

They hadn't found a safe route to Hollandia through the mountains, but finding the lake wasn't bad for a first survey.

More days passed, flying over mountain ranges, through ravines and along rivers, surveying the land and taking photos, making the blank spaces on their maps come to life. Every day they were making more sense of this largely uncharted territory, their magical lines connecting the dots.

They saw places no one had ever set eyes on from the air before. Extinct volcanoes with huge mouth-like cavities gaping up at them; grasslands that looked incredibly fertile as they emerged from between the mountain ranges, spreading out like enormous green tablecloths. Sometimes Papuans could be seen emerging from the jungle and running into the clearings. The Dutchmen figured they'd never seen an aircraft; in their excited fury, they threw spears and shot arrows at the plane in a futile attempt to bring it down.

Flying low through the valleys and manoeuvring through the mountains was a hazardous game—one false move or misjudgement and they'd crash. Strangely, in all the time they carried out their surveys, they didn't come across a single enemy aircraft.

One day they found the Baliem Valley, the most beautiful place they'd ever seen. Olsen set to work, taking dozens of photos. A bamboo bridge spanned the river running through the valley, and oval huts bordered by fences stood in small clusters on the green plains. *The Papuans here must be farmers*, Tom thought, because the land had obviously been worked. Had it not been for the surrounding mountain range, from the air the valley would almost have resembled the neat rectangular fields back home in the Netherlands.

These Papuans, too, flocked into the fields when the B-25 flew over; judging by their appearance, they hadn't encountered Westerners before. While Olsen took his photos, Hagers and Tom threw their survival packs down to the locals, who were waving spears at them in warning. The people disappeared when the packs hit the ground, frightened by the objects falling from the sky.

Heading on through the valley, Hagers and Tom finally found the pathway to Hollandia they had been searching for. The river flowing through the valley was broad and the plains were wide; although the valley gradually turned into a gorge and the gap became narrower, it was possible to fly between the mountains and out to the sea at the other end. It was an escape route as well as an attack route. If they took this route, the Allies would no longer need to fly over the mountains to reach Hollandia. They were ecstatic, and Hagers' plane circled above the ocean like a happy gull, before heading back into the gorge.

Because clouds would often accumulate around midday, they always left the base in the early morning. In their excitement this day, they hadn't noticed that the weather conditions had started to change. Clouds as thick as cotton were gathering, and they suddenly realised they needed to head back fast, before the weather became unpredictable and flying difficult.

By the time they arrived at the base, the clouds had made it impossible to see the runway, and Hagers had to rely on his instruments to land. The landing strip only came into view when they were practically on it and touching down. It was then that they noticed they weren't the only ones to have landed there that day. The base was packed with Kittyhawks.

'Looks like a new batch of Americans just landed,' Hagers said. 'MacArthur isn't wasting any time and, boy, do we have some very good news for the general!'

While Hagers hurried to the debriefing office, Tom stopped on his way to the officers' mess to take a look at the planes. They looked a little worn and tired, and he wondered why the Americans were still using them.

'Hey, don't you dare say anything negative about our fleet!' The sound of that voice had been in his ears his whole life and he spun around to face his brother. Before he could speak, Bob went on: 'I was wondering where you'd got to. Thought you were still flying around Australia, but now I hear you've been sent exploring.'

Over lunch Bob told his twin about the new 120th Squadron. They'd been due to leave for Merauke almost two weeks earlier, but the Australian military command had suddenly become worried about their western shores coming under attack and that Perth might be a target.

'A US submarine sighted two Japanese battleships en route to Singapore, and RAAF HQ ordered us to make an emergency transfer to Potshot,' Bob said. Potshot was an Australian base near Exmouth Gulf. An attack by the enemy on Australia's western coast had always been considered a possibility. 'Now that the Japs are losing a few serious battles, there was a bit of a scare that they might make a move towards the Australian mainland to restore their faith.'

By the time the 120th had received its orders, the 18th Squadron was already transferring from Batchelor to Potshot with its Mitchells. When the 120th arrived, a cyclone was thrashing the Potshot area. 'Flying a Kittyhawk through those winds was like pushing a plane through concrete. I really had to push it to its limits to keep from being blown off the runway and in the end I had to do a vertical landing. Like a helicopter.'

Bob had bumped his way along the runway and eventually managed to land, although taxiing the aircraft to the hangars had proved almost impossible. Winds blowing 200 miles an hour did their utmost to prevent any coordinated movement, but he'd managed in the end.

The cyclone and its aftermath lasted three days and the camp was flooded out. Four feet of water covered all the supplies and equipment they'd brought with them. The heavy bombers were stuck in the mud, their wheels no longer visible. The lighter Kittyhawks had managed to get off the ground, and Bob had taken part in reconnaissance flights. They hadn't sighted any Japanese, though.

A week later they heard that the Japanese battleships the US sub had seen were fleeing their naval base at Truk, one of the small Micronesian islands. United States forces had successfully attacked the Marshall and Gilbert islands, and the Japanese thought they were getting too close for comfort. They fled Truk, looking for a place to hide their ships. They hadn't been in the least bit interested in attacking Australia. So ten days later than scheduled, the 120th was finally sent to Merauke. 'We're here to provide air defence and fly combat missions.'

The Kittyhawks weren't as bad as they looked, Bob reassured his brother. During training he'd discovered that they were solid and generally reliable. They'd actually been stripped of most of their gear to make them lighter, leaving only the basic instruments, but the radio and electrical circuits caused problems if they got wet or damp.

Tom thought the Kittyhawks and their pilots were in for trouble. 'Look around you. Nothing but rain, dampness and swamp.'

Bob shrugged then changed the subject suddenly: 'By the way, am I an uncle yet?'

Tom shook his head, 'I haven't a clue. There was no baby when I left.'

This was the first time it occurred to Tom that his child and his brother would be related by blood. In the silence that fell between them, Tom Derks forgot to tell Bob that Guus Hagers and he had found a safe way through to Hollandia.

23　ISLAND HOPPING

Olivia and Norman had both been issued with two-week tropical leave passes before they were to report for duty again. They spent it discovering Sydney and going up to Coffs Harbour for a couple of days to enjoy the beach. It was a bit like going on a honeymoon, Norman thought.

Their days together passed too quickly; although reluctant to leave Coffs Harbour, they boarded the train to return to Sydney. As they rattled across the Hawkesbury River Railway Bridge, the train's image was reflected in the water below, its shadow racing itself. They sat in companionable silence. Being with Olivia was much like spending time with his own family, Norman concluded—it was comfortable and she never made him feel uneasy. He wondered why such a bright, caring and cheerful person had chosen to be with him. For the moment he considered himself a very lucky man.

They said their farewells in Sydney and Norman travelled on to Bradfield Park, which turned out to be just a layover until Norman received his final posting later that week. It was an incredibly busy place, with soldiers and staff coming and going. When he received his final orders, he learnt that he was dispatched to Tocumwal near the Murray.

If Bradfield had seemed huge then the base at Tocumwal was gigantic. It was spread over eight square miles, although disguised as much as possible; the accommodation buildings had been constructed as normal houses, aligned with the streets of the town. It had four runways, about 100 miles of roadways, giant hangars to accommodate its 54 Liberator bombers and about 600 other buildings scattered across the area. The place was daunting to Norman after serving in relatively primitive outback locations.

Everything, including dispatch riders, was supplied in abundance at Tocumwal. Norman's transport section had sixteen dispatch riders, and their time was spent hanging around with little or nothing to do. Because the transport section was located a couple of miles from the main areas, its meals were supplied by field kitchens and a mobile canteen, where on hot days a long queue for ice-cream developed.

The dispatch riders' camp was near the flight practice area, and some afternoons Norman would sit on a dead tree watching Liberators engage in mock battles with Kittyhawks; or paratroopers jump from Dakotas, their parachutes blossoming as they fell from the skies above the town. By the very nature of their training, the pilots took massive risks. They flew on adrenaline and were encouraged to flirt with danger in order to develop the skills and reflexes needed for combat flying. They came to the base with little more than a suitcase filled with bravado. They'd need it—they had to be trained and ready for battle in eight weeks.

On one occasion, a mock fight between two planes almost caused a disaster when they missed each other by no more than a whisker. Norman held his breath as the young pilots skimmed past each other, realising a collision could well have wiped the town clean off the map. One of the Women's Auxiliary Australian Air Force (WAAAF) members on the base shouted into the skies: 'The silly bastards should flamin' well be knocked out of the air force, scaring everyone to hell and back like that.'

There were 400 of these women, and Norman was glad that only one of them had been standing next to him, because she'd shouted so loudly he thought he'd gone deaf in one ear. The WAAAF worked with codes and ciphers, analysing reconnaissance photographs and performing intelligence operations. Norman was very pleased that for once he was serving on a base with plenty of women.

Mentioning the presence of the WAAAFs in his letters to Olivia, however, appeared to arouse her jealousy, which Norman hadn't realised she possessed. He answered her suspicious queries, expressing his upset that she doubted his loyalty. In reality, he felt slightly flattered by her possessiveness.

The small town of Tocumwal had doubled in size during the war, and the impact of all the soldiers on the little town was enormous. It was now bursting with shops and pubs. There were cricket matches to watch, a sprinkling of cinemas and a couple of dance halls. Norman gobbled up life at Tocumwal with greedy delight. After all those months stationed in the middle of nowhere, this was like one big jamboree. Fearing the consequences, he never mentioned to Olivia that on occasion he'd visit the town and dance with the WAAAF girls.

The enormous hangars on the base would at times serve as a setting for concerts organised for the soldiers. A Gracie Fields concert aroused a lot of interest among locals and troops alike; it sold out within the hour. Norman failed to get a ticket, but one of the transport officers was called home because of a death in the family and left his ticket with the men. They held a lottery and Norman won. Squashed between masses of air force men, he watched Gracie perform some fifteen songs; the men went crazy as her magnificent soprano almost stripped the paint off the hangar's walls.

Serving up north had almost made him forget there was more to life than war, rain and heat. Tocumwal was not bad at all, Norman reckoned. Working a couple of weeks in a row would earn him a long weekend off, so every few weeks he caught the train to Sydney and spent his leave with Olivia.

One day he received a letter from Tom Derks. Inside was a photo of Tom, Grace and a chubby little black baby with a big grin. Benjamin Dippenjarra Derks was born on 19 February 1944 and must be almost nine months old, Norman calculated. It was a happy photo of a smiling Tom and a proud Grace. They looked remarkably content together, and Norman thought all his misgivings might have been off the mark.

Posted to Norman at Bradfield, the letter had taken a few weeks to get to him. Tom wrote that he'd been on a secret mission and had only seen his son months after he was born. He was proud of the little boy and his letter was full of good spirits. He'd bought a plot up near Rum Jungle, close to the Stapleton place, and had built a small house for himself and his family during a month's leave. Grace's brother George and some mates had helped build it. The picture had been taken on the porch.

Tucking the photo and letter into his wallet, Norman smiled at the thought of his friend adapting to life as a father. *He'll probably do all right*, Norman thought. He wondered how Freck would be doing, and Bob. He already missed their company.

———

Bob thought he'd seen it all at Batchelor, but Merauke was by far the most hellish place he'd ever come across. Mosquitoes were everywhere; it was hot, bug-infested and plagued by torrential rains, jungle fever and malaria. Getting through the day was like fighting a relentless enemy. Even the Japanese, who had conquered swampy corners of the Pacific without batting an eyelid, steered clear of Merauke—and who could blame them, Bob thought.

Due to the reduced Japanese presence in the region, his missions were limited to strafing attacks on Japanese positions, as well as attacks on small ships or aircraft off the coast of New Guinea. Most of the targets turned out to be 'friendlies', so he was often forced to return to his 'hell' with a planeload of idle bombs and a lot of dispirited thoughts.

By now MacArthur had been deploying his 'island hopping' strategy for almost a year and it was paying off. The idea was to secure island after island in the South Pacific, to bypass heavily fortified Japanese positions and instead concentrate the Allies' limited resources on strategically important islands. For the enemy these islands were of less significance and so defence was minimal. MacArthur, however, realised they would be vital in supporting the drive to conquer Japan. The plan was to enable US bombers to get within range of the Japanese mainland, making it possible for the Americans to eventually launch an invasion.

The Japanese were continually apprehensive because they had no idea which island would be targeted next. Attacks to the north as well as the southern areas of the Pacific enhanced the element of surprise. A force led by Admiral Chester Nimitz made its way north; after recapturing the Gilbert and Marshall Islands and the Marianas, they were advancing in the direction of the Bonin Islands. The southern advance, led by General MacArthur himself, targeted the Solomons, New Guinea and the Bismarck Archipelago, heading towards the Philippines.

Bob knew that MacArthur's main objective would be to recapture the Philippines. After being forced to flee them two years earlier, the general had promised he'd return. It had become a matter of self-respect to fulfil that promise, not only to himself but to the Philippine people. After recapturing the Solomon Islands and the southern part of New Britain, MacArthur's army made its way along the northern borders of Australian New Guinea. The newfound passageway made it possible to seize Hollandia. Making his base at Biak and intending to push through to the Philippines, MacArthur ignored the other areas of the East Indies. Bob would rather have seen the general concentrate more on the former Dutch areas, but Maurenbrecher told him to be patient and that everything would happen in good time. Patience was one virtue Bob did not possess, however, especially when the fate of so many, including his fiancée, still remained uncertain.

Bob filled free days by playing cards with the men from his unit or playing chess with Smokey Dawson, who'd come to Merauke as a liaison officer. Bob got along well with Dawson and liked his no-nonsense approach. Dawson also hated Merauke, and claimed that New Guinea was like a cancerous sore, oozing grief and misery. He openly questioned MacArthur's efforts to reclaim the island, thinking it was a waste in every respect. 'What did you Dutchies ever see in it?' he asked.

As they played chess, they'd philosophise about the war, debating whether the Japanese really believed they were liberating Asia from the Europeans as they claimed. The Europeans and their allies certainly believed they were fighting for the freedom of the Asians from Japanese imperialism. Both men questioned whether the islanders would profit from the ultimate outcome once the war was over.

'As soon as we recapture the islands, the native people will be answerable to the Dutch, Australians or the British again,' Dawson predicted.

Some islanders were already demanding autonomy when and if the war ended. A young Javanese man named Sukarno was collaborating with the Japanese. He'd studied at Bandung's prestigious university, becoming a representative for nationalists even before the war. The young engineer had hoped the Japanese would help his nationalists fight colonialism. Bob began to fear that chasing off the Japanese might not end the battle for the Dutch East Indies.

—◼—

Both Bob and Dawson's six-month tours were about to conclude. With the possibility of a couple of weeks' leave and getting out of the sweaty jungle, both men were in good spirits. A plane from Cairns was coming in the next day and would take them back to Australia. Its arrival was all very hush-hush, but Bob and Dawson didn't care as long as it took them away from this place for some much needed R and R. About twenty men and women were scheduled to board the plane for the return trip the next day.

Bob decided to saunter along the river one last time as the sun started dropping behind the trees. He was about to set out when he accidentally bumped into someone leaving the officers' mess. He looked up and it took him a moment to register who he was about to apologise to. A bird screeched in the nearby bamboo, and Bob went berserk.

Scattered about outside the mess, his men had just finished their dinner and were standing around drinking a lukewarm beer. Before anyone realised what was happening, their squadron leader had launched himself at the man in front of him. Bob Derks, the quiet, thoughtful lieutenant, always snuffing out a fight or a quarrel before it became nasty or venomous, had lost control, leaving his men baffled and confused.

Bob was half his opponent's width and height, but the difference in size did not stop his fist connecting with the man's chin. The impact cracked some of Bob's knuckles, but appeared to have otherwise done little damage, because the man stood unwavering in front of his assailant. It took four of his men to pull Bob away, and they had to use all the strength they could muster to contain him. They could think of no other explanation than that their squadron leader had gone troppo.

'You bastard!' Bob shouted, spraying saliva with his words. 'I thought they'd put you in a cell to rot!'

The big, burly man observed Bob with a condescending stare. Suddenly smiling, he asked, 'And how's your brother?' Then he turned and casually walked off while Bob shouted profanities at his back.

At the sound of the tumult, Maurenbrecher had come scuttling out of the mess, only to find a squirming and bellowing Bob Derks restrained by his own crew. His men had to hold onto him for quite a while before he calmed down a little. Bob was the most reliable leader Maurenbrecher had ever had. Never had the man displayed any behaviour like this before. Concern about his fiancée had sometimes left him depressed and gloomy, but the CO had never known him to become violent.

Once Bob's anger had subsided, he was escorted to the general's quarters, where Maurenbrecher served him a large shot of whisky. Bob drank, then told his CO the story of Ed Timmer and his brother.

'What the fuck is he doing here?' he spat at Maurenbrecher.

'He's from NEFIS.'

'Intelligence?'

The CO nodded.

'He almost killed my brother and then he was rewarded with a job at NEFIS?'

Maurenbrecher did not have any answers. He appeared to know as little as Bob about Timmer and why he was in Merauke. What he did know was that he'd be leaving the next day on the same flight as Bob.

'No way,' Bob said, 'I will *not* get on the same plane as that man!'

Maurenbrecher realised that putting Bob and Timmer in a confined space together would be courting disaster, and jeopardise both the plane and its passengers. Unless they were both in straitjackets, the two of them together would probably wreak havoc. Maurenbrecher would have to arrange something else.

The next day, 6 September 1944, a C-47 Dakota DT-941 with twenty people on board left Merauke. Among those on board were Timmer and Les 'Smokey' Dawson.

Maurenbrecher had given Bob orders to ferry a P-40 Kittyhawk to Australia. The plane had been standing idle under one of the camouflage nets for weeks. Some of its electronics had blown and it would need maintenance that couldn't be provided at Merauke. It could be flown to Australia but, without all the electronics, it would need a good pilot to fly it. The Dakota and the Kittyhawk left just fifteen minutes apart. One was headed for Cairns, the other for Archerfield in Brisbane.

On 7 September, Cairns Airport rang No. 3 Fighter Sector headquarters in Townsville, inquiring if they had any information regarding a Dakota due at Cairns at 1845 hours. The aircraft had radioed the Cairns duty pilot when it was ten to twenty minutes' flying time from Cairns and had not been heard of since. All Volunteer Air Observer Corps posts were instructed to keep a lookout, and two Avro Ansons set out from Cairns to search for the missing plane. Radar stations were alerted and asked to concentrate on any signals coming from the area north of Cairns.

Other search parties combed the area for the missing Dakota in the following days. Between 8 and 16 September 1944 they searched the coastline as well as the sea for any remains. They found no sign of the missing aircraft.

24 RETURN TO JAVA

During the last year of the war, Tom Derks turned into a happy man. It was strangely comforting to come home after a day or two flying over the Australian countryside to find his little boy and Grace waiting for him. Grace was quiet and content, and the baby looked healthy, his big eyes exploding with wonder as he explored his little world. Tom had built the house on stilts to keep out the snakes, crocs and anything else that might cause harm to his family. It didn't always help, though, and one morning Grace had come out onto the porch to find a big brown snake contentedly basking in the sun. Danger was a part of life there, and Tom accepted that he wouldn't always be there to safeguard his family from all its perils.

Just after Ben was born, Tom had contemplated proposing to Grace. She'd never shown any desire to make their bond official in any white man's way, and as long as Tom kept her brother George happy with tobacco and an occasional bottle of whisky, he also appeared to expect nothing else in the way of formalising their relationship. Still, Tom thought it would be the right thing to do. It was Winnie who explained the complications this might involve.

It wouldn't be easy, she'd told him. Mixed marriages weren't looked on favourably and at the very least, Tom would have to apply for a government permit to marry Grace because she was a ward of the state. Tom wasn't an Australian citizen and didn't even officially live in the country. If anything, he was in Australia on a temporary basis. That would make it difficult to be granted a permit. And where the child was concerned, well, he was of mixed descent and would most likely be taken away and put in an institution if the authorities discovered he was living with an unmarried mother. She might have to hide Ben from Welfare when Tom was away.

Tom decided the best place to keep or hide his family would be Rum Jungle. Mining had died down there, and a few shacks and dirt roads marked spots that had once appeared promising. The land was cheap and after the war he could make a living as a hunter, selling the meat and hides. He'd come to know the area well and had decided it would be the ideal spot to settle, with no one to judge them for the colour of their skin. It was familiar, and so were the very few people living there. So Tom pegged out a plot close to a creek and paid Grace's brother and a couple of station hands from Stapleton to help him build a house. His thoughts of Betty were becoming few and far between. Grace was modest and had nothing of Betty's coarse candour. She didn't smoke, didn't drink and approached motherhood with a serious delicacy that moved Tom. He could hardly take his eyes off her when she busied herself with their son. But sometimes he missed that slight crudeness of Betty, which had unleashed feelings within him that he hadn't experienced before. It had made him feel fantastically alive.

Being based with the 18th Squadron in Batchelor allowed him to visit his family on a regular basis, and serving with the transport unit pretty well kept him from any active combat duty. The Japanese hadn't been spotted on the mainland for weeks, so flying around Australia was now relatively safe.

Then in September, NEFIS called him in for another chat. The Japanese weren't conquered, not by a long shot, and the Dutch command wanted to boost morale in the POW camps on Java. Tom and Hagers received orders to fly over the camps and drop leaflets to let the prisoners know they hadn't been forgotten and that their liberation was imminent. The two men were to leave on separate B-25s, one flying over Batavia and the other over Bandung.

'Paint our red, white and blue flag under the wings. I want them big and clear,' Major General Van Oyen ordered.

As they left the building, both Tom and Hagers were in good spirits. The idea of flying back to Java, although quite hazardous, felt like a Christmas present to Hagers. He said he wanted to fly to Bandung right away, but he was going to take more than the official message with him. To help locate his wife, Lienke, he'd install loudspeakers at the rear of the plane and, while flying over the camps, he'd let the people below know he was looking for her. Tom immediately thought of Colette, and Hagers promised to send out a call for her as well. The job would be dangerous, but they were willing to take risks if there was even a remote chance of locating their loved ones.

Hagers was so overjoyed at being able to return to Java that he'd absentmindedly left his flight book on Van Oyen's desk. As he turned back to pick it up, Tom stopped on the footpath and lit a cigarette. A taxi pulled up, stopping almost in front of him.

A woman emerged from the back seat. Betty. She looked glamorous as ever with a scarf around her auburn hair, sunglasses shielding her eyes and her voluptuous red lips sucking on a cigarette, staining the tip with her lipstick. Suddenly he found it hard to breathe; memories of the nights he'd spent with her raced through his mind, making him uncomfortably hard. She'd been so hungry for him, so full of venom, that sometimes she'd bite him when they made love. At times she'd scared him. She'd always attracted him in a way that disturbed him. All that hungry viciousness had made her even more desirable. He'd never seen it in a woman before.

As she stepped away from the taxi and onto the footpath, she suddenly noticed him. They were so close, almost touching, but the sunglasses hid any emotion she may have felt. With unexpected gentleness, her hand made its way to his face.

'War scars.' It was what he told everyone, and her hand dropped as she turned her head.

'I'm sorry,' she said, knowing how it had happened and looking the other way, as if she was expecting someone.

He looked around, wondering if her husband might show up and what he'd do if he did.

Tom shrugged but she didn't notice. It didn't matter. The silence descending on them was as uncomfortable and awkward as his erection. He wanted her and would always want her. His happiness with Grace was a clear emotion but all too easily smudged, he realised. And it startled him. His tongue felt paralysed.

'They think he's dead,' Betty suddenly said, dragging on her cigarette. The smoke escaping from her lungs funnelled into the air. 'Ed,' she explained.

The questioning look on his face turned to surprise.

'His plane left from Merauke,' she went on casually, dropping her cigarette to the footpath and grinding it out with the tip of her high heel. 'It never arrived. They looked for weeks. They've stopped searching now.'

He'd seen Bob just a few weeks earlier, when he'd told him about his encounter with Ed in Merauke and his refusal to join the man on the plane back to Australia. Tom had been furious that Ed might not have been punished for what he'd done to him. But now here was Betty telling him that the authorities thought her husband was dead, and Smokey Dawson along with him.

Tom would have expected to experience some satisfaction on hearing this news, but he was strangely baffled and truly sorry for the death of Dawson. Bob's encounter with Ed and his refusal to board the same plane had saved his life. Tom stared at Betty, not knowing what to say.

Then Hagers came out of the building with his logbook in his hand. He did not seem to recognise Betty and only tipped his cap to her as he turned to Tom and asked: 'We good to go?'

'Yes.' Tom tore his eyes away from Betty.

'Bye,' she said, taking off her glasses as she pushed the door open. The doors swallowed her. She never looked back at Tom Derks.

—■—

In a remote location at Batchelor, a group of men worked in utmost secrecy to prepare two B-25 Mitchells for the almost impossible task ahead. Hagers and Tom set to work, painting Dutch flags under the wings and on the sides of the aircraft. Maintenance men polished, stripped and tuned the planes to improve their operational range.

The tail guns were removed, as were the top turrets. In the radio compartment, an extra 150-gallon tank was installed. The bomb racks were removed and that whole space turned into a large fuel-storage area. 'It's become a fuel tank with wings,' Tom said to Hagers as they stood admiring the B-25. 'At least we'll go out with a bang if any enemy fire hits us.'

On a test run, their speed reached 257 miles per hour, which meant they'd be able to outrun even a Spitfire. Each aircraft was loaded with 150,000 leaflets. Hagers initially thought their weight might prove too great, but taking weight and balance into account, both Tom and Hagers decided it was achievable.

They departed Australia from Potshot, which was closer to Java and had a longer runway than Batchelor. Close to midnight, Tom and his crew took off for Batavia and, just fifteen minutes later, Hagers took to the air, heading for Bandung. Both planes were fitted with emergency rations, fresh water, parachutes and a rubber dinghy.

A plan had been devised for dropping the leaflets. The planes would fly over the camps at mast height, which would ensure that the POWs below could read the leaflets before the enemy could take action. Their orders were not to fire at anything, so as to avoid hitting innocent bystanders. What no one officially knew was that both aircraft had been fitted with loudspeakers at the tail end. Tom and Hagers realised they probably wouldn't receive a message back, but it would at least mean that if Colette and Lienke were in the camps they'd know their men were alive and searching for them.

Tom reached the coast of Java after six hours. It was very misty when he arrived, and the coast was almost hidden from view, so he had to rely on his instruments to know when he made landfall. For his crew it was an unforgettable moment when they hit land; four of them had been born and raised on the island.

There was just enough visibility to manoeuvre carefully between the mountains. As Tom flew over Kalidjati Airfield— the airport he'd once tried to reach such a long time ago—he too felt a pang of emotion. They could almost smell the lovely herby odours coming from the kampongs as they flew deeper inland. The Bandung tableland was blanketed by heavy fog, but the observation towers of Lembang and the beautiful Villa Isolde stuck out like beacons.

The fog lifted and, as visibility improved, they were surprised to see that villages and towns appeared surprisingly normal. Cars and motorbikes drove along the dimly lit roads and people were waiting on platforms for early morning trains as if the war was a distant rumour. Even Batavia's trams still trundled down the streets as if nothing in the country had changed, except those who ran it.

When they spotted the camps, Tom descended as far as he deemed safe while one of his men threw out the leaflets. They ditched thousands of leaflets over Priok, Kramat and Batavia, and Tom turned on his speakers to ask about Colette and Lienke. Men, women and children below scrambled to pick up the message, raising their heads in wonder and joyful astonishment when they identified the Dutch flag on the wings. Some waved. In the camps, scrawny people cheered and Tom felt rage as he saw people dressed in rags being clubbed back into their barracks by Japanese guards.

They had been given orders not to fire a shot, but they'd see about that, Tom thought. Firing at the Japanese guards would be dangerous—the chance of hitting one of the prisoners was too likely—so he headed towards the governor-general's palace, where the Japanese flag fluttered in the wind. He steered his plane as close as he could to the flag, while his gunner blew holes in the big red sun in the middle of the white rectangle. As they flew past the palace, the tail gunner pumped a few rounds into the rear of it, hitting the palace balcony and shattering some windows. Frightened by the noise, the deer in the grounds dashed from one end of the compound to the other.

When the Batavian people started to gather and cheer, Tom knew it wouldn't be long before the Japanese sent their Zeros up to try to take them out. Surprised that the enemy had so far not even fired a shot at them, he decided not to stretch his luck. He circled the compound, then steered the B-25 towards the mountain range.

Nothing followed them as they made their way into the shelter of the misty giants. No gunfire; not a Zero to be seen. It was a strangely encouraging experience—flying over Java for almost an hour and a half, unloading thousands of leaflets, taking photos and firing at the governor-general's palace. Having survived it made them feel invincible. They threaded their way through the mountains and popped out to sea twenty minutes later, leaving Java behind. Rising to 10,000 feet, they headed for Potshot.

It was midday when they got back, almost thirteen and a half hours after they'd left. When Tom landed, he saw that Hagers' aircraft was already there and he let out an audible sigh of relief. Only then did he realise how dangerous the mission had been.

Hagers told him later that a Zero had come after him, but the pilot had aborted the pursuit when Hagers disappeared into the low clouds between the mountains. It was no secret that sometimes, when the Allies and the enemy encountered one another in the air, both would turn a blind eye and head in separate directions, neither of them particularly anxious to die that day. No one boasted about it.

Other leaflet drops soon followed. On 28 January 1945 they flew across the Java Sea again and once more used the speakers to ask about the whereabouts of Colette and Lienke. Flying over Tjideng camp near Batavia, Tom managed to discover where Hagers' wife was.

In Tjideng the Japanese had brought thousands of women and children together in an old Indonesian prison camp. Hundreds of women came out to catch the leaflets, and then something strange happened. After he'd dropped the leaflets, as well as the food parcels, the women waved at the plane, as if beckoning it. As Tom circled the camp, they grouped together, unmistakably forming a 'J' and an 'A'—*Ja* the Dutch word for 'yes'.

One woman distanced herself from the others and waved a white sheet. On it, Tom read the name 'Lienke' in big black letters. He circled once more and said through the speakers, 'I'll let Guus Hagers know where you are.' He waved to her, took his plane up and headed back.

Hagers would be ecstatic, but he'd have to tell Bob he'd been unable to find Colette. When he pointed to Colette's name on the side of his plane, the women grouped together to form an 'N'.

———————

At the beginning of 1945, the 120th Squadron was ordered to move to New Britain to support Australian Army operations there. The move would also involve the 18th Squadron. Bob was less than pleased—New Britain was the wrong way—and he marched into Maurenbrecher's office bristling with anger and frustration.

'Why aren't we heading for Java?' he demanded. 'My brother's been flying over the island dropping leaflets and food. They haven't even fired a shot at him yet. The Japs are disappearing, and I'm sure we could save the people in the camps.'

Maurenbrecher understood Bob's frustration and guessed that many of his men shared his feelings. He also knew that it would take a while for them to move to New Britain. The airfield at Jacquinot Bay would need months of work before it could accommodate the new squadrons, so it would be March or April before they moved.

'Bob, this war is proceeding rapidly. Changing from day to day,' he said, scratching his two-day beard. 'Who knows where we'll be, and what will be happening in April. Patience, man, patience.'

'I'm just letting you know that I will not move to New Britain. If the Australians and British want me to fight for them, then that's fine. But first things first.'

On 30 January 1945, Tom set out on another leaflet drop to Java. When he returned, he phoned his brother to let him know there was still no news of Colette. By now, horrifying stories were beginning to find their way to Australia about the terrible treatment Dutch nationals had received in the Japanese camps. Men who'd escaped brought these stories with them. For Bob the wait was becoming unbearable.

MacArthur's island hopping had liberated Hollandia, nearly all of Dutch New Guinea, Biak and Morotai. Before the war this had all been Dutch territory, but now the Brits and the Australians wanted something in return. They wanted the Dutch to join in the fight to liberate former British and Australian parts of the Pacific. Bob knew the request wasn't unreasonable, but every fibre of his being was leaning the other way. New Britain was east and Colette was to the west.

By March, Jacquinot Bay airfield was still not ready. Rain and terrible conditions made work there difficult and sometimes almost impossible. In February, the Americans had managed to recapture Manila; just two months later, in April, the good old 18th Squadron helped sink the light cruiser the *Isuzu*. The attack units had flown over in close formation and damaged her with two direct hits. She hadn't sunk immediately, but had been forced to seek refuge in Sumbawa Bay, where American submarines sunk her the next day.

At the beginning of May, Bob and his squadron received orders to proceed to Batchelor, where they'd again serve under the No. 79 Wing, before moving to Jacquinot when it was ready. That was expected to be in just a few weeks' time, but on 5 May the Germans declared the unconditional surrender of their troops in the Netherlands, Denmark and north-western Germany, and two days later they surrendered all forces unconditionally.

Bob wanted to kiss the ground MacArthur walked on when the general sent a telegram explaining that plans had now changed and the 120th would be expected to move to Biak. The 18th Squadron were to proceed to Morotai, but Bob would be going to Biak, which was Dutch territory.

25 LOST AND FOUND

When the 120th moved to Biak, life changed considerably for the squadron members. Merauke had made the men lethargic. They'd hardly seen any Japanese in the months they'd been stationed there. When they were sent out, the 'enemy' often turned out to be one of their own. Moving to Biak meant missions to be flown and targets to be attacked, and Bob jumped at the task with greedy eagerness.

On 12 June, just days after they'd settled on the island, Bob and ten other Kittyhawk pilots received orders to proceed to Geelvink Bay. They were to strafe and bomb Japanese targets in Moemi on DNG. In the following days they attacked Japanese positions along the Waranai River, destroyed huts along the Prafi River and later went back to Geelvink Bay to target the fuel tanks there, turning them into awesome torches as the precious oil blazed itself into extinction. Bob watched from above, his face gleaming with satisfaction.

Although he'd never enjoyed destroying things, this daily

targeting of enemy positions gave him a strange sense of fulfil-
ment. He went about it with determined tenacity, flying over
the targets and dropping his bombs, then returning to Biak and
leaving the next day to drop more bombs. To Bob it was all
about Colette. Defeating the Japanese had become synonymous
with being reunited with her, and he was determined to keep at
it until they were driven out. Constantly running on adrenaline,
like most of his squadron, his highs were very high and his lows,
when he returned to Biak, were very low.

The place was crawling with former internees, islanders for
the most part. The Japanese had treated them abominably;
when the Americans found them, they were half starved and
half dead. But their Japanese guards weren't in much better
shape. They too had almost starved on the island, fighting the
Allies almost to annihilation: 6100 Japanese had lost their lives
fighting against British and American troops; 450 had eventually
surrendered and been shipped to Australia.

The islanders stayed. To see these starved and apathetic
former prisoners on Biak as they tried to regain some dignity
filled the men with horror. They realised that if the islanders had
been treated this badly, surely the Japanese would have made
the whites suffer even more. It was difficult to be confronted by
this reality on a day-to-day basis; Bob tried to push away the
image of Colette suffering in one of those camps, but he couldn't.

The day Bob strafed the power station at Manokwari, he
was heading back across the sea to Biak when he noticed that
his engine was spewing blue smoke. There'd been anti-aircraft
fire around the power station and although the Kittyhawk had

only one engine, he hadn't realised he'd been hit until he was well out over the sea. It wouldn't be easy to ditch the plane, but Bob knew his options were limited and that he'd be unable to make it to land. The engine had gone from sounding slightly distressed to sputtering and coughing, as if it was about to die. He pulled on his lifejacket and inflated it, preparing to get wet.

The sea was calm. A Kittyhawk flown by Piet Hollander stayed, circling above him, protecting him, knowing Bob's plane would never make it back to Biak. Before he bailed out, Bob requested a nearby PT boat to pick him up at the coordinates he gave them. Opening the hatch, he got ready for impact.

Because he was relatively short for a pilot, Bob always sat on a kapok cushion; he now pulled this from under him and put it in front of his face, to cushion it as it smashed into the window. As a last protective measure, he shoved his seat as far back as possible and braced himself with his arms.

When the engine stopped altogether, about ten feet above sea level, Bob let the plane drop and held tight as it crashed. On impact, water immediately gushed into the cockpit and, when he undid his safety belt, he was lifted to the surface by the surge, which pushed him through the hatch and spat him out into the sea.

Hollander was still circling above him. Bob gave him the thumbs up to let them know he was all right. In the distance, a boat was speeding towards him. His aircraft had already started to sink.

Floating in the sea, Bob could feel his ankle had been hurt; his knees felt bruised. He didn't know the severity of these injuries, but on impact he'd felt his legs smash into the control panel and, as he braced his feet and the plane hit the waves, his right ankle was crunched.

The PT boat was there within minutes. Hollander waved to him as the boat came alongside; once Bob had been hoisted safely aboard, he left the scene.

As soon as he was out of the water, Bob's legs refused to hold him and he collapsed on the deck. When they got back to the army hospital in Biak, it was discovered that he'd broken his ankle and a few bones in his foot. They'd mend, the doctor said, but he wouldn't be seeing any active duty for a while.

Because the island hospital was poorly equipped, Bob was flown back to Brisbane for further treatment. Tom paid him a surprise visit there, in the midst of transporting Dutch personnel. Tom told Bob he was welcome to stay at his house until he'd mended.

'Grace will take care of you,' he said, 'and Ben will get you up and around a lot quicker than you will if you lie around here.'

The doctors saw no reason why Bob wouldn't be able to heal at the house at Rum Jungle. If there was any sign of infection or swelling of his foot or leg, he was to visit the hospital in Darwin immediately. Tom had to fly back down to Canberra first, but he promised to pick up Bob on his way back.

Before Tom could return to Brisbane to pick up his brother, however, on 6 August 1945 America dropped a bomb named 'Little Boy' on a Japanese port called Hiroshima. The bomb produced a flash of light and a rush of air that just about blew the city out of existence. Within the first second almost 80,000 people perished, leaving 10,000 wounded and badly burnt.

The Japanese were stunned. They had not even fathomed what had happened before another bomb exploded above Nagasaki just three days later. Such a brutal display of power had never been seen before. It took the Japanese leadership two days to think things over before they capitulated. The Pacific war was over.

On the morning of 16 August, the news of Japan's surrender was printed in block capitals on the front pages of every newspaper in Australia. Bob almost leapt out of his hospital bed. A doctor rushed in to keep him from getting to his feet while the whole ward, patients and nurses alike, cheered, kissed and went mad with joy.

Bob immediately wanted to fly to Java to find Colette. When Tom came to pick him up, he didn't want to go to Batchelor and urged his brother to head straight for Java instead. Tom understood his brother's need, but he told him that the Imperial Japanese Army on Malacca and some of the islands in the Netherlands East Indies had not yet surrendered. It would probably be a matter of days but, in the meantime, MacArthur warned that all troops must refrain from entering occupied areas until peace had been officially signed. The signing would take place on the American battleship USS *Missouri* in Tokyo Bay. Bob, forced to wait, reluctantly flew to northern Australia.

Hobbling around on his crutches, Bob actually enjoyed staying in his brother's little house. Grace was sweet and looked after him with concentrated devotion. Little Ben walked around, sucking up life and all its wonders. It made Bob aware of how numb the war had made him. He'd blocked out so much that it had become hard to feel anything at all. To the child everything

that crawled, every flower and every blade of grass was mysti-
fying and enchanting. Ben laughed, giggled and stood stupefied
as he watched a centipede wriggle by on its many legs. The little
boy's moods swung from crying pitifully one moment, as if his
world had just shattered, to uncontrollable fits of laughter in
the next moment. *Just like his father*, Bob thought.

Bob had forgotten that life could be like this. He hoped
Colette would one day have his children. Witnessing all the
destruction of the last few years, he'd come to realise that nothing
was more precious than new life.

When Tom returned to stay with his family for a few days,
Bob noticed how much his brother loved this remote country.
But Bob was very different: he missed the order and neatness of
the country of his birth—those green square fields bordered by
narrow channels, the well-organised cities and, if one did dare
to travel into the laughably tiny piece of forest in the country,
signs at every crossroad to prevent anyone ever getting lost.

To Bob, Australia was wild and unpredictable; it made him
jumpy and ill at ease. Here roads stopped in the middle of
nowhere, or were blown away by dust storms; the native animals
gave the impression that they'd been created in a test lab on
another planet and dropped there by accident. He simply didn't
feel at home in this strange land.

His brother, on the other hand, moved through his adopted
country with ease and confidence. Tom had been an unhappy
teenager in the Netherlands, concealing his anger with indiffer-
ence and bravado. Bob understood that being motherless coupled
with Tom's poor relationship with their father had had a lot to

do with this resentment. But as soon as he left the Netherlands, it was as if a load had been lifted from Tom's shoulders. On Java, the blond, tall, good-looking and cheeky Tom had come to realise that women liked him. Java had given his confidence a boost, but it was here in Australia that Tom had finally settled.

While Bob waited for his foot and ankle to heal, he listened to the radio. The nationalist leader Sukarno held a speech in his backyard on Java, declaring the independence of a new republic called Indonesia. This would change things drastically, and Bob became painfully aware that it would take more than a simple flight to Java to retrieve his fiancée. He almost went crazy with despair as his hope disintegrated and the Dutch in Australia got ready to wage another war. This time the enemy they were facing was an unforeseen one; the thought of having to fight the islanders themselves was something most of them had not countenanced and could barely grasp.

Tom came home from Melbourne with news that the Dutch were getting ready to take up arms again, but in Melbourne, Australians were beginning to regard the Dutch as colonists and oppressors. The friendliness of the Australians towards their former allies was slowly turning into antagonism. Waterside workers were refusing to supply Dutch ships in port in Melbourne. Some of the Australian RAAF 18th Squadron crews volunteered to join the Dutch in their effort to regain control of the islands but Australia's prime minister, Frank Forde, refused to let them go. It had become a tricky matter and public opinion was turning. Forde did not want to get involved in the dispute.

Having no fight to pick with the Indonesian nationalists, and certainly reluctant to take up arms to drive them out, Tom considered leaving the service. He didn't much care who ruled Java or Borneo, or DNG for that matter, and he didn't want to fight the Javanese. Like his brother, Bob didn't feel the need to go back to war, but he would if it meant getting Colette back.

To assess the situation, Major General Van Oyen flew to Batavia to speak to Sukarno. Hagers flew the aircraft but after the general had finished his business, Hagers asked to be allowed to take his wife back to Australia. The general refused permission so Hagers refused to fly him back. When Van Oyen pointed out that it was forbidden to take back internees, Hagers told Van Oyen that he wouldn't leave Lienke behind and to find himself another pilot. The general knew the agitated pilot might just leave him stranded, so he sent a taxi to pick up Lienke.

When Bob Derks visited a Darwin hospital to have the cast removed from his foot, he heard that Colette had been found. Apparently, a farmer had picked her up as she wandered around the outskirts of the jungle near Batavia. She appeared confused and was unable tell anyone who she was and where she'd been. She was taken back to the camp at Tjideng. Hagers had heard all this from Lienke.

Bob was still limping and on crutches, but now that he knew Colette was alive, he sought ways to get her to Australia. He was told by the authorities that, like so many others, she'd have to wait at Tjideng for the outcome of the negotiations with the nationalists. General Mountbatten had made it crystal clear that no Dutch troops would be allowed to land on Java, or the rest of the Dutch East Indies, until things were sorted out. The Dutch were stupefied. They were all waiting to go back and claim back the land they thought was rightfully theirs, and they were prepared to fight for it if necessary. Tom understood Bob's anger at Mountbatten's decision, but he also knew that Bob didn't care who ruled the former Netherlands East Indies—he just wanted Colette.

When Tom was selected to go to Java on 17 September, as part of a recovery team to pick up Allied prisoners of war and internees, Bob realised this might be the chance he'd been waiting for. Tom was chosen for this particular mission because of the knowledge he'd acquired when dropping leaflets: he knew exactly where most of the camps around Batavia were positioned. Tom promised Bob he wouldn't return without Colette.

After they landed on Java some of the pilots and crews in Tom's team became overwhelmed with emotion, kissing the ground they'd loved and cherished most of their lives. They were back and it felt unreal; they sniffed the air and savoured the smell of 'home'. Just a handful of Japanese came to meet them; although they did not appear overly happy about the arrival of the Dutch, they seemed to have accepted the fact that the war was over and they could do nothing about it. The islanders, however, grouped together in sullen silence, gave the men cause for concern. A number of B-25s were still to land and they circled above, just in case anyone turned hostile. Although none of the islanders applauded, they showed no outward signs of disapproval either.

The stand-off ended when Tom took the lead and boldly claimed a Japanese staff vehicle standing on the airstrip. None of the Japanese objected. They stood motionless as Tom, three soldiers, a doctor and a nurse got into the car and drove out of the airport. Tjideng was one of the larger camps, and Tom had especially requested to be sent there. The doctor and nurse were to assess the medical condition of the prisoners. After that, they'd start registering everyone.

The roads on the island, once perfectly sealed and well maintained, were now dotted with potholes. Moving through the city, Tom noticed many red-and-white nationalist flags adorning the kampong huts. None of the islanders seemed to be welcoming them. Everyone in the car felt something brewing close to the surface. The atmosphere became threatening when they asked for directions; men draped in red-and-white flags suddenly stormed towards their vehicle and menacingly waved their sharp *goloks*, big machete-like knives used for clearing scrub.

Tom stepped on the accelerator and tore down the road, leaving the enraged group spitting and shouting curses at them. They hadn't been briefed about this, and Tom could only hope things would get no worse. Although he was armed, he'd been ordered to exercise the utmost restraint; no one wanted an incident that might endanger the brittle truce with the nationalists.

When their Japanese vehicle finally stopped in front of the camp, the internees must have thought their Nippon guards had returned. They retreated into their huts and watched from a distance. It was only when Tom and the doctor stepped out of the car that the internees grasped who they were and started shuffling slowly towards the gate.

The sight of those wretched souls winded Tom like a punch to the guts; for a moment he could only stare. It took an effort to keep the horror from his face, and he looked away as he tried to regain some form of composure. They reminded him of a photo he'd seen in the papers of the shrivelled prisoners in the German concentration camps.

The women shuffling towards him were clothed in rags. Their sunken eyes locked onto him as if he were something precious. Tom dared not think about what those hollow eyes had witnessed. Scrawny arms reached through the bamboo palisades, trying to touch him as toothless mouths begged for information about loved ones. They craved word about husbands, children, fathers or mothers. Tom had nothing to give them but his own tears.

The doctor and nurses worked all day, writing down names, dates and birthplaces, and checking each person for diseases. All the internees suffered from malnutrition; some had dysentery or tuberculosis. There were no beds and many slept on the stone floors. There was no running water and outside, near the small shacks, a filthy open sewer ran next to the camp gate.

Unbelievably, amidst all this chaos, Tom actually managed to find Colette. When he asked around, a small child had taken his hand and led him to her. She was sitting in a shack, wearing a lovely but dirty pink dress that clung to her body like a second skin. Even dirty, she still looked like something from a fairy tale among all these raggedy people. Children who'd never seen such a beautiful dress crowded around her, carefully touching the cloth as if they were caressing the gown of a princess. Tom didn't recognise her at first and thought the child had mistakenly brought him to someone who only resembled her.

The girl sitting there looked like Colette, but her eyes and her whole demeanour were distinctly different. When she looked up, Tom almost drew back. The eyes, always her best asset, had lost their life, their brilliance. Her manner was detached and aloof. It was Colette, but not the Colette Tom had known. She showed signs of recognition, but her face had changed and her brows furrowed when he said her name. 'I'm taking you back to Bob,' he said and then she smiled at him. He took her hand carefully and led her out into the sunlight.

In fact, Colette did not appear to be in as bad a shape as most of the other women in the camp; to Tom's surprise, she looked 'healthier'. For this reason, it took all of his most resolute insistence to persuade the doctor to draw up a document that would allow him take Colette away.

'Tom, I know you are doing this for your brother,' the doctor said, 'but there are people in much worse condition than she is, and we're going to have to leave them behind.'

After a lot of debate, the doctor finally handed him a document that stated Colette la Grande was physically and mentally exhausted and that her condition qualified her to be evacuated as soon as possible.

Tom appreciated what the doctor had done. He knew that if the authorities ever found out, there'd certainly be consequences. 'I owe you,' Tom said, but the doctor waved him away.

When they were ready to leave, women and children clung to them and begged to be taken with them out of the country. The nurse and doctor tried to explain that this wasn't possible right now, but that they'd be back.

Tom swallowed hard as they drove out through the gate. He doubted if the Dutch would manage to come back for them any time soon. Already rebellious young men were running around waving their machetes. What would happen if their wrath turned on the whites in the camps?

On the plane back to Australia, Colette sang children's songs all the way. The songs were like some mantra—Dutch kids' songs, happy rhymes—and Tom couldn't shake the idea that Colette was trying to flee from something. To Tom it was obvious she'd suffered some kind of mental breakdown, but she was at least physically strong. He hoped that, as soon as they got some food into her and she was reunited with Bob, she'd slowly become her old self again.

The woman Tom Derks brought back to his brother that day was Colette la Grande. But she was not the Colette his brother had been forced to leave when the war began. The woman who came back had not fully returned from Java; a part of her would stay lost forever.

26 MESSAGE FROM A DON R

At the end of the war, it became evident that a majority of the indigenous population of the Dutch East Indies wanted autonomy. The younger generation had welcomed the Japanese as liberators. The new occupiers had interned all Dutch citizens and passed leadership and administrative positions on to the islanders. They'd also trained and armed the young Indonesian men and women.

In October 1945, the British were in charge and they fought a bitter battle with Sukarno's loyalists for the town of Surabaya. The nationalists were driven out of the city, but they were by no means defeated. It wasn't until March 1946 that Dutch troops started taking over control from the British. But what the Dutch saw as an annoying rebellious movement was a smouldering bushfire about to flare. Newspapers in Australia, Britain and America supported the nationalists, portraying the Dutch as oppressors.

After Tom returned with Colette, the four adults and little Ben lived for a while in the tiny Rum Jungle house. Tom and

Grace would sleep outside on the verandah, leaving Bob and Colette to sleep in the only bedroom. For Bob and Colette the lack of privacy soon became uncomfortable.

Colette was still aloof and silent. The war had scarred her in ways none of them could comprehend. During those first weeks, she told them that her father had died when they sought sanctuary in Bandung's mountain range after the Japanese landed. Betrayed by the Javanese, the Japanese came to arrest them. Her father had tried to reason with them, begging them to let his wife and daughter go. The uniformed men stood in silence as he talked to them and took aim when he put his hand into his breast pocket, but he held up his left hand to assure them he had no ill intentions, while producing money and a chequebook with his right hand. They smiled at him and la Grande smiled back, and for a moment, it looked as if the family would be free to go. As a businessman, her father had learnt that one could buy almost anything if one had enough money, but in this case he was wrong. Still smiling, they simply shot him and took his money and chequebook. Her story ended there and, although they asked many questions, she did not answer any of them.

Bob had hoped that telling this story would help Colette open up or heal slightly, but it appeared to have the opposite effect. She closed down completely and Bob was truly afraid she might go insane. He thought she might fare better if she had a place of her own but taking her to the Netherlands did not seem like a good idea. Born and raised on Java, she had never travelled to the Netherlands, and in any case had no family there. Bob decided to make a home for her in Australia for the time being, relatively close to his brother, Grace and Ben. His savings from the air force had been substantial, because he never spent much—he didn't bet and he wasn't a heavy drinker. So he bought a block of land at Adelaide River and drew up a plan to build a two-storey house.

Bob missed a lot of things from home—snow, seasons, Gouda cheese. And also stairs, because Australian homes didn't seem to have any. It took him and a crew of men two months to build the house; the day he carried Colette over the threshold, he felt proud and content for the first time in years. It was also the day Bob married her. Expecting Colette would be unable to cope with an elaborate ceremony, he decided to let the local magistrate draw up a certificate they could sign, with Tom as their witness. It took no more than fifteen minutes.

Bob and Colette's two-storey became a novelty in Adelaide River. Locally known as the 'White House', it even attracted visitors from out of town. It was, of course, way too big for the two of them, but Bob hoped to fill it with children in time.

Hope was all they both had left and Bob realised that, without hope, they'd have no future, nothing to look forward to. Sitting in that empty house at night, he came to realise that it was the only thing that kept him going. It was his fuel. Colette would go to Cowley's store to buy groceries, but she'd never really look the storekeeper in the eye. She felt uncomfortable because her English wasn't up to scratch and her Dutch accent was thick and her words clumsy.

Unlike the residents of Adelaide River, Grace did not take much notice of Colette's oddness; in fact, she appeared oblivious to it. Tom and his family would visit regularly, and Colette felt very comfortable with her sister-in-law; she'd comb Grace's hair, oiling and braiding it until every unruly curl on Grace's head was beaten into submission. Grace loved the attention and Colette loved giving it. Little talk was needed to accompany the things they did together, and both women felt at ease with one another. In each other's presence they could simply be who they were.

It was May 1947 when Norman Harris sent invitations to his wedding to Tom and Grace, Bob and Colette, and Winnie and Harry Sargent. His bride-to-be was Olivia Perry. Grace and Colette did not want to go, both feeling uncomfortable for different reasons.

Tom and Bob debated how they'd travel to Melbourne— by plane, train or car? It became a bit of an issue until Tom drove his brother to Batchelor one day. The airstrip, abandoned and quiet, looked a little forlorn, Bob thought, remembering the hustle and bustle of the old days. He'd never been back to the place and wondered why his brother had brought him there. Driving onto the Batchelor airstrip, Tom stopped in front of what looked like a hill sitting at the edge of the strip.

'Funny,' Bob said, 'I can't remember that being there.'

'It wasn't,' Tom replied.

Getting out of the truck, he began to remove some rubble and Bob saw levers appear from under it. Tom pushed part of the 'hill' aside and a small generator emerged. When Tom started it up, Bob's mouth opened as the 'hill' slowly began to move.

Well, not move exactly—it levitated. The 'hill' had been created from old army camouflage netting, adorned with all kinds of plants and mud to make it look exactly like its surroundings.

Tom stood there with a smug smile on his face as he watched his basically simple contraption come to life. There were ropes tied to the netting and they in turn were slung over the higher tree branches; using a simple block and tackle, and powered by the generator, the 'hill' ascended to reveal what was hidden beneath it: a Lodestar.

'How? What?' was all Bob could stutter.

'I stole it,' Tom said, walking up to the Lodestar. 'It was standing here when I drove by at the very end of the war, and they were supposed to pick it up. But I think they forgot about it. Later I hid it.'

Walking around the plane, Bob couldn't believe this was one of the old Lodestars. The thing shone and looked brand new. Tom told him he'd spent many a free hour or day working to spruce up the Lodestar. It was the most reliable plane he'd ever flown. He'd even taken Ben up in it a couple of times. The boy had loved being up in the air, and had marvelled at what he saw as he looked down on his country. From up high, the country became an abstraction.

'Looks like we have our wheels to Melbourne,' Bob said.

And so early on 16 May, Tom, Bob, Harry and Winnie boarded a Lockheed Lodestar at Batchelor and flew to Melbourne to attend the wedding.

Norman and Olivia were married in the town of Lara. They'd bought the only general store there months earlier. The small town was an up-and-coming community, Norman said, conveniently located between Geelong and Melbourne, with an established railway station. The wedding service was held in Norman and Olivia's backyard; as a backdrop, the low ridges of the You Yangs poked up from the otherwise flat scrub, as if dropped there by mistake. The ceremony was beautiful, with magpies carolling in the paperbarks and the mothers of the bride and groom wringing out wet hankies when it was over.

Freck came in a tad late, but everyone was surprised that he showed up at all. Just before the end of the war he'd passed his pilot exams and got a job with MacRobertson Miller Airlines in Western Australia. He'd managed to get a flight to Melbourne by telling his boss, Horrie Miller, that Norman was his brother. It was a blatant lie, but close enough to the truth for Freck not to feel too remorseful.

Afterwards they all gathered under a large oak, the women around the bride and the men around the lucky groom. With his hair sticking up and his ears sticking out, Freck looked self-conscious in his light blue suit and tie. Tom and Harry stood itching and squirming in their ties and stiff garb, and poor Harry's neck had turned an angry crimson from chafing against the collar of his suit. The only man who felt comfortable in his suit was Bob.

They thumped Norman on the back, telling him his freedom had just ceased to exist and to start getting used to shackles. Beer was passed around and, when all the clichés about married life had been aired, they fell silent, staring into their glasses and wondering what to say.

Harry got them started, reminiscing about the day Norman and Tom fell from the skies, how they had emerged from that Lodestar window 'like bloody fish spilling from a broken tank'. Freck retold the tale of a tin of spaghetti masquerading as Norman's splattered brains and the Dutch boys emptying their guts, not realising Norm's head was a hard nut to crack.

The beer helped their memories surface, and when the mood turned melancholy, it also brought back the dead. There was Keesmaat, the soft-natured mechanic who'd been unable to get to his parachute and died because of a silly accident. And old Smokey Dawson's disappearance. Deep down, they knew the bad memories outweighed the good.

The terrible sequence of war had changed everything—not only the landscape but the people in it—but life went on regardless. People got married and others rebuilt Darwin, while the Dutch settled into a futile colonial war. In a small country town in Victoria, a group of men and women chatted and laughed under the paperbarks as the sun sank and the first stars blinked. They would always be bound together by what they had shared. That night they talked about what they'd seen and what they'd experienced, and tried to make some sense of it all.

EPILOGUE

GUS WINCKEL

Gus Winckel married his second wife, Yvonne, on Java in 1949 and moved to New Zealand in 1950. In 2013, almost 101 years old and still happily married to Yvonne, he died. A street in Broome is named after him and a statue was erected in 2009 in his honour at Moruya to commemorate the sinking of a Japanese submarine on 5 June 1942.

GUUS HAGERS

Guus Hagers and his wife Lienke moved to the United States in 1950. Hagers had been offered a job as a spray pilot in east Oregon. According to Lienke, Hagers was 'tickled pink with the prospect of flying again but it soon became evident that the planes were not maintained properly by the company he was flying for'. Lienke suggested he should give up his job but he did not feel right about breaking the contract. On 19 June 1952, Hagers was killed when his plane crashed along the ravines of Wallowa, Oregon. Lienke later remarried and still lives in America.

ATTACK ON BROOME

On the morning of 3 March 1942, many Dutch refugees lost their lives on Roebuck Bay in Broome. Most of them are buried in the Perth War Cemetery Dutch Annex in the Karrakatta Cemetery. Only a small portion of the diamonds carried on Captain Iwan Smirnoff's DC-3 were ever recovered. Beachcomber Jack Palmer was accused of stealing the diamonds when he stumbled on them after scouring the DC-3 wreckage at Carnot Bay (now re-named Smirnoff Bay). A trial was held at Perth but Palmer was acquitted due to lack of evidence.

BURCK, DE LYON AND KELDER

Wil Burck, Eric de Lyon and Harry Kelder, the three men accused of treason, were tried in Colombo on a Dutch ship, M/V *Plancius*, in 1943. Burck was sentenced to life in prison while Kelder and De Lyon were both sentenced to twenty years. Many people, including Guus Hagers, made an effort to have the three exonerated after the war. In 1950, after serving seven years in jail, the three men were released, pardoned by the Dutch Queen, Juliana, on her birthday. Burck died in 1981, a bitter and lonely man. De Lyon died in 1976 and Kelder in 1997. They were never rehabilitated.

SIMON SPOOR

Simon Spoor, who had caught Burck, De Lyon and Kelder, passed away on Java in 1949 after lunching in a restaurant. At first his family thought he had died of a heart attack but they later came to believe he was deliberately poisoned. To this day some still support a conspiracy theory concerning the mysterious death of General Simon Spoor.

MISSING AIRCRAFT WITH SMOKEY DAWSON ABOARD

Royal Netherlands East Indies Air Force C-47 Dakota DT-941 (VH-RDK), with 'Smokey' Leslie Dawson and nineteen other people on board, disappeared near Mossman in Far North Queensland on Thursday, 7 September 1944, on a flight from Merauke to Cairns. In 1989 *The Canberra Times* ran an article about the discovery of the missing aircraft. Apparently, seven members of the Australian New Zealand Scientific Exploration Society stumbled upon the wreckage while collecting plant specimens on jungle peaks, west of Mossman. Civil registration markings, VH-RDK, on the tail quickly identified the plane as the missing Dutch Dakota. Rumours about a shipment of 'valuables' transported on the plane began to circulate just after it went missing but this was never officially confirmed and no valuables were found on board.

MAURENBRECHER

Hans Anton Maurenbrecher, commander of the No. 120 Squadron on Merauke, went back to the Netherlands after the war. He built a ship that he christened *Oranjebloesem* (*Orangeblossom*) and sailed from the Netherlands to Australia. In 1965 Maurenbrecher set off from Cairns in an attempt to become the first man to sail around the world solo. He first headed for Thursday Island but never arrived at his destination. Two months later the remains of his boat were found floating around in the sea near the Torres Strait Islands. There was no sign of Maurenbrecher.

JESSURUN

Lieutenant Colonel Reinier Jessurun died in a plane crash during a storm on Borneo in May 1949.

SCHWENKE'S GOLD

On 26 April 1946 *The West Australian* published an article about a former RAAF major who had staked out an area near Batchelor, claiming he had found a rich gold lode there. His name was E. Schwenke. While stationed in the area in 1943, Schwenke had come across an extremely rich gold lode. After being discharged from the army, he had returned to make applications for goldmining leases. The Clutha Development Co. also showed interest in the find and applied for leases. Schwenke was very reluctant to disclose exactly where he had found the lode but people suspected it was near Rum Jungle.

Newspaper reporters questioned Harry Sargent about the find but he said Schwenke never actually disclosed to him where the lode was located. Asked about the possibility of the lode being located at Rum Jungle, Harry only shrugged.

GHOST PLANE

In 1948 and 1950 *The West Australian* published a series of articles about ghost planes landing and taking off from the former RAAF airstrip at Batchelor.

Taken from *The West Australian*, 19 January 1948, page 10:

Widespread police enquiries are continuing in the Batchelor District, and it is believed that evidence of recent aircraft landings on the former R.A.A.F. air strip at Batchelor, has been found. Fettlers living two miles from Batchelor, told the police that they have heard aircraft at night circling, without navigation lights, over the Batchelor Strip on several occasions during the last few months. Prospectors engaged in gold mining, are believed to have heard planes at night in the same area.

The police also believed that the plane might have been used for smuggling arms, gold or immigrants. After track marks were found on the runway, a trap was set by the police. They waited for three days but there was no sign of the plane.

BIBLIOGRAPHY

ARCHIVAL MATERIAL

Hagers, A., 1942–45, Museum Militaire Traditie, 't Schilderhuis,
    Driebergen, the Netherlands
Hagers, A. Netherlands Institute of Military History, The Hague, the
    Netherlands, collection no. 700, inventory no. 1748
Letter, Fiedeldij, National Archives of Australia, Canberra, NAA:
    A705, 151/2/324
Letter, Air Vice Marshal A.T. Cole, National Archives of Australia,
    Canberra, NAA: A11093, 320/96N

DIARY AND LETTERS

Coleman, Brian A.D., wartime diary, RAAF 31880, 1942–46, courtesy
    of Brian Coleman
Wallace, Gordon, letters home, 1942–1944, *Up in Darwin with the
    Dutch*, Melbourne: Gordon Wallace, 1984

INTERVIEWS

Camerus, Pieter, interviewed by Tom Poederbach, 2010
Giezen, Jan (John), taped recording by the author, 2003

Heikoop, Willem, notes by the author, 2003
Marks, John, notes by the author, 2003
Porter, Roy, notes by the author, 2003
Stellema, Dirk, taped recording by the author, 2003
Van Vliet, Albert, taped recording by the author, 2003
Winckel, Willem Frederick August (Gus), taped recording by the
    author, 2003

NEWSPAPER ARTICLES

'Adelaide River races', *Northern Standard* (Darwin), 20 June 1939,
    page 3
'Darwin gold find', *Kalgoorlie Miner*, 26 April 1946, page 4
'Derailment of train: "Spirit of Protest" off line', *The West Australian*,
    27 January 1950, page 23
Dexter, Frank, 'They don't forget Rotterdam', *The Australasian*
    (Melbourne), 16 October 1943, page 12
'Dutch pilot relates end of submarine', *The Canberra Times*, 6 June
    1942, page 1
'The Dutch troops still fighting', *The Mercury* (Hobart), 13 March
    1942, page 1
'Jungle gives up its secret', *The Canberra Times*, 15 February 1989,
    page 21
Moorehead, A., 'Alan Moorehead writes of Rum Jungle', *The
    Advertiser* (Adelaide), 5 July 1952, page 2
'N.T. airstrip tyre marks clue to gold racket?', *Sunday Times* (Perth),
    18 January 1948, page 2
'Plane's wheel marks show on airstrip', *Sunday Mail* (Brisbane),
    18 January 1948, page 1
'Rum Jungle gold', *The West Australian*, 11 May 1946, page 4
'Skeleton found: Believed to be missing airman', *Warwick Daily News*,
    4 December 1946, page 3
'Sky escort: RAAF on convoy duty', *Albany Advertiser*, 26 June 1941,
    page 5
'The story of Batchelor', *Kalgoorlie Miner*, 5 April 1948, page 2
Watt, S.D., 'The Dutch used Batchelor', *The West Australian*,
    31 January 1948, page 17

BOOKS IN DUTCH

Bijkerk, J.C., *The Colombo Tragedie*, Franeker: Uitgeverij Van Wijnen, 1991

Boer, P.C., *De Luchtstrijd om Indie: operaties van de Militaire Luchtvaart KNIL 1942–1942*, Houten: Van Holkema & Warendorf, 1990

Hagens, G.J., *De KNILM Vloog Door: Java's evacuatie 1942*, Haarlem: Uitgeverij Bakens, 1972

Quispel, H.V., *Nederlandsch-Indie in den Tweeden Wereldoorlog*, London: Netherland Publishing Company, 1945

Smirnoff, Iwan W., *De Toekomst heeft Vleugels*, Amsterdam: Elsevier, 1947

Ward, O.J., *De Militaire Luchtvaart van het KNIL 1942–1945*, Weesp: Romen Luchtvaart, 1985

Wittert, Rene, *Het Vergeten Squadron*, Bussum: Van Holkema & Warendorf, 1976

BOOKS IN ENGLISH

Ford, Jack M., *Allies in a Bind: Australia and the Netherlands East Indies in the Second World War*, Brisbane: Australian Netherlands Ex-Servicemen and Women's Association, 1996

Hurst, Doug, *The Fourth Ally: The Dutch forces in Australia in World War II*, Canberra: Doug Hurst Publications, 2001

Marks, Roger R., *Queensland Airfields WW2: 50 Years On*, Brisbane: R. & J. Marks, 1994

Steijlen, Fridus (ed.), *Memories of 'the East': Abstracts of the Dutch interviews about the Netherlands East Indies, Indonesia and New Guinea (1930–1962) in the Oral History Project Collection*, Leiden: KITLV Press, 2002

Wallace, Gordon, *Up in Darwin with the Dutch*, Melbourne: Gordon Wallace, 1984

——, *Those Airforce Days*, Melbourne: Gordon Wallace, 1986

WEBSITES

Central Australia the War Years 1939–45, <http://www.thewaryears.alicespringsrsl.com.au/>

'Merauke', *Andere Tijden*, NTR, <http://anderetijden.nl/aflevering/603/Merauke>

'Netherlands East Indies Army—RAAF flying units', Monuments Australia, <http://monumentaustralia.org.au/themes/conflict/ww2/display/105407-netherlands-east-indies-army-raaf-flying-units>

'The track: 1000 miles to war: Adelaide River', Northern Territory Library, http://www.ntlexhibit.nt.gov.au/exhibits/show/track/adelaide

ACKNOWLEDGEMENTS

Special thanks to:

Richard Walsh for his wise editorial comments and guidance and for believing in the story.

Everyone at Allen & Unwin who played a part in making the book come true.

Tom, my brother, my friend, who has been with me since the dawn of my personal stories.

Marty Sprong for giving me the scrapbook, and Saskia and Bryn for pointing it out to me.

John Giezen, who introduced me to the members of the No. 18 Squadron RAAF/NEI back in 2003.

Brian Coleman, former No. 18 Squadron RAAF, who helped where he could and sent me his diary.

Tom Poederbach for interviewing Peter Camerus in Denver and for all his helpful information.

Astrid and Paul for their eternal friendship.